G000151339

ARGUMENTS FOR THE SAKE OF HEAVEN

ARGUMENTS FOR THE SAKE OF HEAVEN

EMERGING TRENDS IN TRADITIONAL JUDAISM

JONATHAN SACKS

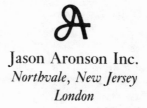

Jason Aronson Inc.
Northvale, New Jersey
London

Library of Congress Cataloging-in-Publication Data

Sacks, Jonathan, Rabbi.
    Arguments for the sake of heaven : emerging trends in traditional
Judaism / Jonathan Sacks.
        p.   cm.
    Originated in an international symposium held at Jews' College,
London, May 1989.
    Includes bibliographical references and index.
    ISBN 0-87668-783-4
    1. Orthodox Judaism.   2. Judaism—20th century.   I. Title.
  BM565.S2   1991
296.8'32—dc20   90-807

Manufactured in the United States of America. Jason Aronson Inc. offers books and cassettes. For information and catalog write to Jason Aronson Inc., 230 Livingston Street, Northvale, New Jersey 07647.

For Elaine

CONTENTS

PREFACE

In *Pirkei Avot*, that classic tractate of rabbinic ethics, Akavya ben Mehalalel advises Jews to reflect constantly on three questions: Where have you come from? Where are you going? And before Whom will you eventually be accountable? The present book tries to do this from the vantage point of the Jewish people as a whole over the past two centuries.

The idea for the book had its origin in an international symposium convened by Jews' College, London, in May 1989. The title of the gathering was *Traditional Alternatives: Orthodoxy and the Future of the Jewish People*. What lay behind it was an accumulating sense of rift and conflict throughout the Jewish world. I felt then, and still do, that Orthodoxy faces a considerable challenge of leadership in this situation. Our aim in the symposium was to bring into dialogue a whole series of Orthodox voices. For when there is no immediate solution to problems confronting the Jewish people, the most important religious imperative is to engage in what the sages called "argument for the sake of Heaven." One of the themes of the present study is a plea for recovery of what I call "tradition as argument."

As I reflected on the controversies we were to confront, it

became increasingly clear that they could not be understood without first setting them in context. I decided therefore to sketch the broad historical and sociological background against which they had arisen. What emerged was a study of modern Jewish identities, the conflicts among them, and the way these might be minimized if not immediately overcome.

The book was published in England prior to the symposium under the title *Traditional Alternatives*, and I was delighted when Arthur Kurzweil of Jason Aronson Inc. suggested the possibility of an American edition. The themes of the book are as much American as British, and I welcomed the chance of a wider discussion of its ideas. I have made some minor changes, and I hope that American readers will recognize some of the dilemmas faced by the fictional Anglo-Jewish family with which the book begins and ends.

Several debts of gratitude must be recorded: to Lord Jakobovits, the British Chief Rabbi, for his advice in planning the original symposium; to Mr. Stanley Kalms, then chairman of Jews' College, for the restless questioning that was the impetus of this and many other initiatives; to the staff of Jews' College for their support and stimulus; to Ezra Kahn and Marilyn Redstone for help in obtaining the books needed for the research; and to my secretary Adele Lew for deflecting the distractions while the book was being written.

Special thanks are due to Arthur Kurzweil for suggesting this edition and for his help and encouragement throughout. Above all I owe an incalculable debt to my wife Elaine, and our children, Joshua, Dina, and Gila. Without their patience and encouragement, neither this nor any other of my activities would have been possible.

The book touches on sensitive and controversial topics. I therefore end with the prayer of R. Nechuniah ben ha-Kaneh, one that was very much in mind as I was writing: "May it be Your will that I do not err in a matter of halakhah, declaring pure that which is impure, or impure that which is pure."

Jonathan Sacks
London
24 Shevat 5750
19 February 1990

INTRODUCTION

Since the early 1980s a series of tensions has been evident throughout the Jewish world.

One the growing rift between Orthodoxy and Reform, particularly in America. Reuven Bulka, for example, has warned that "if present trends remain unchecked, the policies which prevail within Reform Judaism and the commensurate reactions which they will surely evoke within the Orthodox camp" may well "result in a cataclysmic split within the North American Jewish community." This could eventuate in "the total renunciation of a significant number within the Jewish community by another group." America's Jews might become two distinct and noncommunicating peoples, differing on the most fundamental issues of who and what is a Jew. To some extent this has already occurred.

A second has been the parallel conflict between religious and secular groups in Israel. Some years ago President Chaim Herzog warned that the greatest danger facing the State of Israel was not external but internal, the clash of cultures between secularist Israelis and two kinds of religious Jews, the non- or anti-Zionist *charedim* and the "national religious" Gush Emunim. Tensions reached a height in the summer of 1986, when bus shelters carrying swimwear advertisements were burned by groups of *charedim*, and in retaliation a synagogue was set on fire, a yeshiva vandalized, and vehicles attacked by groups of militant secularists. Concern has been voiced on both sides of the divide, by secular analysts like A.B. Yehoshua, Amos Oz, Amnon Rubinstein, and Yehoshafat Harkabi, and by a range of religious thinkers, among them David Hartman, Shlomo Riskin, Yehudah Amital, and Nachum Rabinovitch.

The third has been the increasingly tense relationship between Israel and the diaspora since the 1982 Lebanon War. Prior to that, especially in the wake of the 1967 Six Day War, Israel had been a primary focus of diaspora Jewish identity. Jews in the *golah* were internally divided between secular, ethnic, denominational, and Orthodox expressions of identity. They were united by their concern and support for and vicarious pride in the State of Israel. Recently, though, Israel's international isolation and the wide-spread criticism of her policies in Western media has made at least some sections of diaspora Jewry increasingly uncomfortable, some-times publicly critical. Attitudes toward Israel—the government, if not the state—have become among the most contentious and divisive issues facing diaspora Jewry.

This too took on a religious dimension when, in the immediate aftermath of Israel's 1988 general election, greatly increased sup-port for religious parties made it seem likely that the Law of Return would be amended to recognize only halakhic conversions to Judaism. Orthodox opinion was divided on the tactical wisdom of insisting on the amendment, which in any case would have had only a marginal impact on Israeli society. Its immediate effect would have been on the diaspora, for it would have implied a formal delegitimation by the Israeli government of the Reform and Conservative rabbinate. The protests, especially in America where these movements constitute a majority of synagogue affiliations, were instant and vociferous.

None of these tensions has as yet proved fatally divisive. They flare sporadically and then die down in a subsiding murmur of diplomacy and reassurance. But for none is a substantive resolution in sight. And there is a disturbing sense of impending crisis, as if they were mere preludes to a volcanic eruption that will shake the Jewish world and irretrievably change its contours.

Orthodoxy Resurgent

At the heart of all of them has been the revival of Orthodoxy. As late as the 1960s, Orthodoxy had been seen by some observers to be on the brink of eclipse. In 1967, the French sociologist Georges Friedmann published a book entitled *The End of the Jewish People?* in which he diagnosed world Jewry as poised between an assimilating diaspora and a secular Israel. The prediction began to prove itself false almost as soon as it had been uttered. Since then, the renaissance of traditional Judaism has been astonishing, evident in the proliferation of Jewish day schools and yeshivot, their success in resisting the forces of secularization and acculturation, and the high birthrates of Orthodox families.

This, though, has taken place against the backdrop of a still deepening secularization of Jewry as a whole, in both Israel and the diaspora. In the diaspora this is relatively easy to monitor. It takes the form of an overall continuing decline in religious observance and synagogue affiliation and an increase in the number of those who receive no Jewish education. It can be measured in terms of low birthrates and high rates of intermarriage.

In Israel the markers are less clear-cut. In several respects the religious factor has become more prominent in Israeli society in recent years. The *charedi* community has grown through its own birthrates. There have been highly publicized cases of *chozrim bi-teshuvah*, alienated Jews returning to their religious heritage. In the political arena, religious groups have adopted a higher profile. In terms of national culture, religious motifs have been increasingly prominent, as against the aggressive secularism of the early years of the state. Nonetheless, as Daniel Elazar has observed, "The rise of a generation of nontraditional Jews whose links with Judaism are tenuous in the extreme has increased the gap between the religious quarter of the population and the other three-quarters."

So the paradox of an Orthodox revival on the one hand and the progressive secularization of Jewry on the other has brought confrontation and conflict. But not only between Orthodoxy and others. The same high levels of tension are palpable within Orthodoxy itself. There have been fierce antagonisms and a growing sense of distance between *charedi* and *dati*, the so-called traditionalist and moderate or centrist Orthodox. The two major forms of the latter—Modern Orthodoxy in America and Religious Zionism in Israel—have been undergoing a period of demoralization and decline. A cluster of associated attitudes has been in eclipse: the "synthesis" between Judaism and secular culture; a degree of tolerance and pragmatic cooperation between Orthodox and non-Orthodox groups; a positive religious attitude toward the State of Israel; and a tendency toward political moderation and a concern for world opinion. In their place has come an identification of religious authenticity with extremist positions.

Nor is the *charedi* world itself unitary and united. There have been angry, even violent, confrontations between different groups of *chasidim*, divided in their attitudes toward the State of Israel. There has even been a revival of the eighteenth-century hostility between the *chasidim* and their opponents, the *mitnagdim*. This led, in the last Israeli general election and before, to division within the ranks of the major *charedi* political organization, Agudah. One past president of the Rabbinical Council of America, Rabbi Louis Bernstein, has argued that Orthodoxy's greatest contemporary weakness is its fragmentation. "Minute differences metastasize into insurmountable obstacles. These differences, viewed in retrospect, are almost comical, but they open wide and painful wounds in their contemporary context."

The Underlying Questions

These conflicts, painful in themselves, may nonetheless be a sign of the intense vitality of the contemporary debate about the Jewish identity and destiny. As such, though, they call for serious and sustained reflection rather than sloganizing, confrontation, and mutual delegitimation.

And they point beyond their immediate causes to deeper questions about Jewish continuity and responsibility. Does the growth of the *charedi* community and the relative decline of other groups point to a need for all Jews to reconsider their survival strategies? Is the diaspora destined to self-destruct through assimilation, inter-marriage, and a failure to create its own future generations? Does Jewish survival in an open society require a self-imposed segregation from non-Jewish associations and culture? "Modern" Ortho-doxy, since the days of Samson Raphael Hirsch, has assumed that a secular-Jewish synthesis is possible. In the late twentieth century, is this intellectually plausible? Is it pragmatically wise? Does not all secularization threaten the disintegration of Jewish loyalties and the stability of Jewish families? These questions have implications for the future development of Orthodoxy.

Are the social processes at work in Israel and the diaspora likely to generate a general return to tradition or an increasing polarization between a secularizing majority and an intensely religious minority? Can there be dialogue across the divide? Does Ortho-doxy carry the responsibility for the religious fate of all Jews, or must it focus on its own survival? These questions have implica-tions for the relationship between Orthodoxy and non-Orthodox Jews.

What is or should be the relationship between Judaism and the development of Israeli society? Should religious groups be represented by parties in the political process? Should they be involved, apolitically, in shaping education, collective sentiment, and national culture? Are the key religious issues "religious"—safe-guarding Shabbat, standards of modesty, and the dignity of the dead—or are they social and economic too? Is Israel a place in which Jews can live among Jews or is it the context of a Torah society with specific approaches to social justice, compassion, and minority rights? What is the relationship between the State of Israel and the messianic process? These questions concern the relation-ship between Orthodoxy and Zionism.

What, too, is the relationship between the Jewish people and humanity as a whole in the wake of the Holocaust and the rising international tide of anti-Zionism? Jewish concerns have turned markedly inward in the last two decades, from universalism to particularism, from "example" to survival. Is concern for world opinion part of Israel's ethical imperative, or is it instead a failure of moral courage? How far should Jews in the diaspora be involved in the moral and social issues of their wider society? Is this a religious duty or a form of assimilation? What are the contemporary implications of the command of *kiddush ha-Shem*, to "sanctify God's name" through conduct that inspires admiration? These questions concern the relationship between Judaism and its wider environment.

The Covenantal Conversation

Currently there is no available consensus on these dilemmas for which different groups and individuals offer different answers. This fact is not significant in itself. Of greater importance is how we approach the conflict of judgment and evaluation.

The classic Jewish response was to seek guidance from the sources, from the canonical texts of revelation and interpretation, the biblical and rabbinic literature. Nor was this an individual and subjective process. It involved finding a teacher, one who was versed and immersed in the tradition and could give an authoritative judgment that carried the weight of many centuries of rabbinic deliberation.

But there was not always a definitive answer. Maimonides distinguished between *halakhah leMoshe miSinai* "a law transmitted [orally] from Moses at Sinai" and the wider ambit of the Oral Law. The former represented judgments and imperatives on which there was no recorded argument in the tradition. The rest of the Oral Law comprised matters on which there *was* argument. That is one of the great characteristics of the rabbinic tradition. The classic sources of rabbinic thought—Mishnah, Gemara, and Midrash—are essentially collections of arguments. Few religious literatures have so celebrated dialogue, debate, and dialectic. The very process of argument was a central feature of the religious life.

There is a reason for this, and it goes to the heart of Jewish spirituality. Judaism begins with and is constituted by a covenant. And a covenant is a binding relationship which, however unequal the parties, respects the integrity of each. Throughout the biblical period, the mode through which the Divine will was known was *revelation*. But throughout the rabbinic period, it was *interpretation*. Through interpretation the sages applied Torah to their time. And because the entire covenantal community—the congregation of Israel—was involved in this process, argument was of its essence.

In revelation, there is no room for argument. There are true prophets and there are false prophets, but there is neither dialogue nor consensus between them. But in interpretation, there is always room for argument. An application of the sources to the unfolding challenges of history is rarely unchallengeable. There are ways of reading the classic texts differently. There are ways of characterizing the present situation differently. In the covenantal situation, process may be more important than product. The fact that the entire community of sages is engaged in dialogue with Israel's destiny is itself the ongoing activity called Torah.

To be sure, there were large areas in which the sages insisted on normative rulings. Roughly speaking these make up the entire territory known as *halakhah*, Jewish law, and for the most part they were arrived at through consensus and the rule that "one must follow the majority." But there were equally large areas in which no consensus was sought and in which the argument was allowed to continue open–endedly. These were the domain of, in its broadest sense, *aggadah*: the literature in which the sages explored Jewish values, attitudes, and ideals.

By and large, the issues which have confronted Jews in modernity have been questions of *aggadah*. How shall a Jew live in an open society? How is Jewish identity to be combined with participation in a secular state and its culture? How, in this environment, is a Jew to be educated? Against the backdrop of nineteenth-century emancipation and nationalism, how was the Jewish destiny to be continued? If it meant Jewish nationalism and a return to the land of Israel, how was this to be reconciled with traditional Jewish quietism and a patient waiting for Providence? Where is the State of Israel to be located on the Jewish map of history between exile and redemption? What is the contemporary meaning of *galut*: exile or dispersion?

These are not questions to which a definitive answer can be reached through the classic sources of Jewish tradition. Nor are they the kinds of questions on which we would expect a normative consensus. Yet they fatefully shape the lives Jews lead and the relations that exist among them. Supremely, they are the covenantal questions of the last two centuries, for they raise in the most acute form the question of which route the covenantal people should take through history in response to the mandate of Sinai.

Yet the traditional response of interpretation and argument has broken down. So long as Jews were held together by halakhah, there could be disagreement on matters of *aggadah*. Jews were a people, said Saadia Gaon, by virtue of their laws. Those laws constituted Jews as a community, and on that foundation there could be individual differences on larger issues. But the most momentous fact of modernity is that Jews have ceased to be a people held together by *halakhah*. Today they are linked, if at all, by more tenuous bonds: a common vigilance toward anti-Semitism, a sense of shared history and ethnicity, concern for the State of Israel, and a feeling of collective responsibility for the safety and welfare of other Jews.

Whether Jewish peoplehood can survive on so slender a base is an open question. Certainly there is room to doubt whether Jews can chart a common future if they lack a shared language with which to discuss that future. In such a situation there is an overwhelming need to recover as far as possible the tradition of interpretation and argument, in which the covenantal community engages in dialogue on its historical vocation.

The sages called this process *machloket le-shem shamayim*, argument for the sake of heaven. The phrase roughly meant Torah is truth. But at times we must uncover that truth through serious exploration of the Torah's words. This is a collective rather than an individual process, and it calls for a critical listening to a multiplicity of voices. In this way argument, rather than being confrontational and divisive, becomes part of the texture of community and its ongoing covenantal conversation.

Argument for the Sake of Heaven

In illustrating what they meant by an "argument for the sake of heaven," the sages contrasted the arguments between Hillel and

Shammai, which exemplified it, with the arguments of Korach and his followers, which did not. The difference between them is worth restating in an age in which Jewish argument has often degenerated into controversy and from there to mutual hostility and delegitimation.

R. Menachem Meiri explains the distinction thus. There is a difference between argument for the sake of truth and argument for the sake of victory. Hillel and Shammai argued out of a desire to discover the truth. Korach argued with Moses out of a desire to win a personal victory. Whoever argues for the sake of truth wins a kind of immortality: his words are destined to endure. Whoever argues for the sake of victory merits a kind of oblivion: his words are not destined to endure.

The two kinds of argument are readily distinguishable. The one focuses firmly on the subject itself and avails itself of reason, inference, and the resources of tradition. The participants know themselves to be engaged—even as they disagree—in a collaborative rather than confrontational enterprise. To lose the argument is as enlightening as to win it, for truth is the outcome, and truth transcends the person who first uttered it. It is said of R. Nachum ha-Amsoni that when he found a counterexample to his theory of biblical interpretation, he retracted his life's work with the words: "Just as I received a reward for the exposition, so I will receive a reward for the retraction." There can be no more inspiring example of the primacy of truth over subjectivity. To be defeated by the truth is to experience the one defeat that is also a victory. This is argument for the sake of heaven.

The other kind of argument fails to focus on the subject, for the subject of the controversy is not, so to speak, its agenda. It is marked by rhetoric and abuse. It frequently becomes *ad hominem*. Its aim is to defeat the opponent. Therefore its ends are served as well by attacking the person holding the contrary position as by attacking the position itself. The Korach rebellion—the rabbinic paradigm of argument not for the sake of heaven—is, from one point of view, an obscure narrative. Read the text carefully, and one finds not one but several different and incompatible positions being advanced. From another point of view, though, the rebellion is all too lucid. It aimed not at truth but at victory. Crucial to its strategy was a delegitimation of Moses. In such an argument, victory for either side is defeat for both. Had Korach won, the religion of revelation would have been defeated by the politics of power. Moses won, but only at the cost, uniquely, of invoking a miracle and his opponents were destroyed, and of provoking the subsequent reaction of the people: "You have killed the people of the Lord." In this kind of confrontation there is no benign outcome. One can only aim at minimizing the tragedy.

The History of Jewish Identity

My aim in the present study is therefore twofold: to explore the "arguments for the sake of heaven" that currently divide the Orthodox world, and to defend the endangered etiquette of "argument for the sake of heaven" itself. The concept does not imply a pluralism that sees all interpretations as legitimate and all truth as relative. The argument between Hillel and Shammai was in fact decided in favor of Hillel. But it does imply a willingness to engage in reasoned dialogue with views with which one disagrees. It stands alongside another monumental rabbinic conviction, that "scholars increase peace in the world." Through intellectual conflict comes resolution and, eventually, reconciliation. These are values that need restating in a fragmented Jewish world.

But that task cannot itself be done without also examining the wider issues that led to the collapse of halakhah as the unifying framework of Jewish existence as a whole, and the intractable conflicts to which this has led in the present. Orthodoxy itself needs to be understood in the context of Jewish peoplehood in its widest sense. And that too I have tried to do. The present volume, then, sets the background of current intra-Jewish debates while suggesting how these might be conducted less divisively in the future. It is offered as a personal perspective, from the vantage point of one who sees halakhah as the constitution of the Jewish people and the only viable framework for Jewish unity. It is, too, an informal presentation. I have tried to avoid loading the text with footnotes and academic digressions. Some of the issues touched on are explored in a more scholarly way in my forthcoming books,

Tradition in an Untraditional Age and *One People?—Tradition, Modernity and Jewish Unity.*

The central questions that currently divide the Jewish world flow from the clash of a series of very different perceptions of what it is to be a Jew. Those perceptions cannot be fully understood without a clear sense of their history. How did it come about that the relatively unified idea of Judaism and Jewish identity that existed prior to the eighteenth century, broke apart in modern times? That is the issue explored under the heading "Past." In "Present" I examine the current state of Jewish identity and the several unexpected developments that have taken place in Jewish consciousness since the 1960s. In "Future" I consider how the currently tense relationship between Orthodoxy and the rest of the Jewish world *might* develop, and how I believe it *should*. The sections headed "Prologue" and "Epilogue" bring the argument from a global perspective to its impact on a single imaginary Anglo-Jewish family.

This then is my attempt to set the scene for the tense and intense drama of Judaism's contemporary dialogue between its commanding past and its as yet uncharted future.

PART I
PROLOGUE

1

A Family Portrait: Jews Today

Pesach is a time for families, a time for answering children's questions and handing on the story of the Exodus across the generations. It was so in biblical times; it is so tonight in David and Miriam Cohen's house in a Northwest London suburb.

The *haggadah* speaks of four children, one wise, one wicked, one simple, and one unable to ask questions. There are four children this evening ranged around the Cohens' table. They are not precisely the children of the *haggadah*. For one thing, they are older. For another, words like wise, wicked, and simple sound strange and out of place in our nonjudgmental culture.

But the Vilna Gaon suggested that the four children represent two pairs of contrasts. The "wise" and the "one unable to ask" are cognitive opposites. Perhaps we would call them, today, the intellectual and the nonacademic. The *rasha* and *tam* are spiritual opposites, one a rebel against, the other faithful to Jewish tradition. Today we would not call a rebel "wicked." He is more likely simply to be the product of a secular culture profoundly at odds with the assumptions of Judaism. Still less would we translate *tam* as simple. The patriarch Jacob is called an *ish tam*, which Samson Raphael Hirsch translates as "a single-minded man." Single-mindedness is a

3

religious virtue equally at odds with the complex roles and relativities of a pluralistic culture. Thus understood, the terms could well describe David and Miriam's children.

The Intellectual

Ruth is 23, dark-haired, attractive, and articulate. An eldest child, she has always carried with her an air of seriousness, perhaps even to excess. She went to Jewish schools and then to a seminary in Israel before returning to take a degree in psychology and a teaching qualification. She teaches at a Jewish secondary school. In August she is getting married. Her husband-to-be is a mathematics lecturer at a London college, an alumnus of an Israeli yeshivah who wears a *kippah serugah* and twice a week attends a *shiur*.

David and Miriam, Ruth's parents, have always been Orthodox but in the relaxed style of many of the Anglo-Jews of their generation. Most *Shabbatot* they went to the local synagogue, more often when the children were young, less often now. On Friday nights they lit candles, made *Kiddush*, and ate a traditional *Shabbat* meal. But they had also been known to switch on a light or watch television. Their home is kosher, but on holiday they allow themselves a fish and salad meal in a non-Jewish restaurant. Neither of them keeps their hair covered except in the synagogue. They know vaguely about the laws of family purity and the *mikveh*, but neither they nor their friends ever seriously considered observing them. They are in their way typical of their local congregation.

Ruth, from an early age, was uneasy with what she saw as their equivocations and compromises. A self-contained child, she did not argue the point. She simply took as her reference group her Jewish studies teachers at school and the friends she made in her youth group and later at the seminary. Her own home, she has decided, will be strictly observant. She tells her friends that she is going, *b'ezrat ha-Shem*, to have five children and that, of course, she will give up her career in teaching to look after them.

The prospect of *mikveh* and the family purity laws do not raise in Ruth any inner conflict. She can see the logic of a discipline of sexual tact and restraint. Nor is she worried by the decision she and her fiancé have taken, that she will wear a *sheitel*. Wigs, these days, are attractive. And besides, she has a strong feeling for that value she has never tried to explain to her non-Jewish friends—she knows they would laugh—namely *tzeni'ut*, modesty.

Ruth has a clearly ordered set of values. But it would be wrong to think that in arriving at them she has experienced no tensions. Her decision to go to a university after the seminary was frowned on by her teachers and many of her friends. In retrospect she can see their cause for concern, though she does not regret her choice. She found the college environment disturbingly at odds with the protective, monolithic atmosphere of her school and seminary. Its intellectual detachment, skepticism, and, at times, cynicism toward positions she herself held was at first unnerving and led to disturbed nights of conflict and doubt.

It was the first time, too, that she had had non-Jewish friends. What worried her most was that she liked them. Her education until now had led her to take for granted that there were deep distinctions and dichotomies between the Jewish and non-Jewish world. But at college, over coffee, getting to know her fellow students, she found them refreshing and congenial company. She could hardly approve of their life-styles, but they had an easygoing good humor and a camaraderie that she found relaxing. One or two of them were formidably intelligent, which she admired. Their world seemed free of the nervous intensity and inner constraints that formed an almost tangible atmosphere in her Jewish environment. She was studying in London and living at home. It occurred to her one night that if she had gone to a university in another town, meeting, falling in love with, and perhaps marrying a non-Jewish boy would not have been an impossibility. That frightened her and strengthened her decision to leave no gaps in the protective wall she would create for her own children.

Past that crisis now, her occasional qualms are less serious. She has long since stopped going to her parents' synagogue. Its vast architectural pretensions seemed to her to be an embarrassing imitation of the Gentiles, a Jewish church, a *chukkat hagoi*. On *Shabbat* as a child she used to see one of her parents' friends arrive at the synagogue by car, which he would furtively park round the corner. This, too, made her smile. It was the women's gallery, though, that finally drove her to distraction. The show of clothes and the ceaseless gossip seemed to her more appropriate to a coffee klatch than to a religious occasion.

Since then she has transferred he allegiance to a local *shtibl*, a *shul* that is no more than a house with ad hoc extensions. Here, at least, there is no clerically robed minister, no cantor, no choir, no show of grandeur, no social agenda. The members, as she puts it, come to *davven* and learn, not to talk and be entertained. But not everything about it is quite what she hoped for. Behind the thick curtain that screens the women's section she is conscious that, in synagogue terms, she, a woman, is something of an irrelevance. It occasionally bothers her that she will not be able to attend a *shiur* with her future husband. Once in a while, though not for long, she sighs for the career she will have to abandon. She has read about the apron some American Jewish wives have taken to wearing, with its slogan: "For this I went to college?"

She is concerned, too, with some of the values of the world she and her husband are going to join. She knows of the fur-coat-and-Jaguar syndrome among sections of the very Orthodox. She has seen some of the one-upmanship and conspicuous consumption at their bar mitzvahs and weddings and wonders whether religious devotion can really be combined with aggressive materialism. She dislikes the factionalism of the highly Orthodox world: there are sixteen different *minyanim* within a mile of where she plans to live, and she does not expect to have close friends from any of them except her own.

She senses, too, that she and her husband will have to be discreet about certain aspects of their lives: their university background, and their love for Israel. She knows that they will be closely observed, with initial suspicion and reserve, and that the social controls of the group are real and powerful. It is a little frightening, but it is a price she knows has to be paid if she is to be confident of bringing up children who will be as Jewishly committed as she is. Doors have to be closed against an open society.

Ruth keeps her questions to herself. She has made her choice with open eyes, and if her world is not perfect she will live with it. She is used to sacrifice, to closing options. Her whole life-style is built on it. She is, all appearances to the contrary, very much of her time. Her deep Jewish commitment is grounded less in theology, which she sees as a typically male abstraction, than in a vivid sense that she does not want the alternatives. She does not want to be pressured into a physical relationship with a boy on her third date. She does not want a marriage to be only as secure as the partners' compatibility. She does not want to be haunted by the fear that her children will drop out or marry out. She feels the sheer power of the Jewish family tradition and knows—all the more so after college—that modern secular life offers no equivalent. She knows, too, just how vigilantly it must be guarded these days.

Her parents sometimes criticize her for, as they put it, "going back to the ghetto." That is precisely what she has chosen to do and for compelling reasons. She knows the alternatives, and sees no other way of protecting her values, her marriage, or her future children.

The Rebel

Richard, younger than Ruth by a year, is just finishing college. His *yarmulka* sits uneasily on his unkempt hair. He is wearing it, under protest, to please his parents. He refused, though, to wear a suit at the table. His clothes—jeans, a T-shirt, and a denim jacket—are a calculated act of aggression. So, too, was his peremptory reading of the *Haggadah*. His Hebrew, remembered from primary school and bar mitzvah training, is still better than his father's.

David and Miriam never quite knew what to do with Richard. When he was 4, they knew he was going to be bright. At 7 he was quick-witted and already impatient with his teachers. At 10 he was frankly facetious about the religious instruction at his Jewish school. It was, he complained, boring, juvenile, and irrelevant. He would lie awake, even then, reading science and history books. At 11, by common consent, he went to an English public school. At 18 he won a place at Oxford. He delayed it for a year to go hitch-hiking round the world.

Now in his final year at Oxford, he is contemplating a career in investigative journalism. This Pesach evening, with its déjà-vu rituals, he regards as a penance. It is, he tells himself, the price of having parents. Richard spends much of his time being angry: with the Conservative government, cuts in social services, growing inequalities, economic individualism, South Africa, the bomb, ecological exploitation, and the policies of Israel over the last decade. Anger, for Richard, is not so much an emotion as a life-style. This evening he has turned its full force onto the *Haggadah* and its assumptions.

Partly to provoke his parents, partly out of conviction, he has called the story of the Exodus paranoid and racist. "Listen to this tiny people," he says, "having the *chutzpah* to believe that the history of the universe revolves around it. Plagues strike, the sea divides, all so that the Israelites can achieve their nationalist goals, no matter what the cost to an innocent Egyptian civilian population. No wonder that Jews find themselves the object of animosity in every generation." Who, he asks, would not resent a minority who claimed to be the elect, the chosen people? Wouldn't you, he asks his parents, if you were on the other side of the conversation? "Could you honestly invite a non-Jew to the *seder* and carefully translate every word—from Rabbi Akiva's multiplication of the plagues to 'Pour out Thy wrath on the nations'—and *not feel embarrassed?*"

David and Miriam often ask themselves where they went wrong with Richard. They have not yet found an easy answer. From his mid-teens he out-argued the rabbis they invited to have a word with him. They have tried the tactic of the *Haggadah* for the rebellious son: confrontation. They said: "If you had lived in Germany in the 1930s, for all your rejection of Judaism, you would have been condemned as a Jew, transported as a Jew, murdered as a Jew. If you had grown up in the Soviet Union you would have had your rights curtailed as a Jew. Even in Oxford or London, if you succeed too well and too fast you will still feel, behind the politeness of your intellectual friends, a suspicion of you as a Jew. You can't reinvent yourself. In the eyes of the world an un-Jewish Jew is still a Jew."

Part of Richard's anger is undoubtedly due to the fact that subliminally he knows this to be true. He rages against it. Everything else that he is, he has chosen to be. His school, his university, his opinions, his future career: at every stage he has felt his life to be a matter of exploring the alternatives and making a choice. He was intoxicated by the intellectual and social variety of Oxford. His sense of personal power is built on the feeling that, with enough intelligence and willpower, he can turn himself into whatever he chooses to be.

Except for this one fact. He was born a Jew. Why, he asks, does he have to take on himself the sufferings, the history, the hopes, the guilts, the inhibitions, the unbearable self-consciousness of this tormented people just because of an accident of birth? What does it have to do with him? Yes, he sympathizes with the plight of Jews in Russia. But he feels the same involvement with the blacks of South Africa and the people who live in slums in the inner cities and those others he has seen sleeping in the streets at night.

There was a time when he felt a strong attachment to Israel. He even thought he might try living there one day. That feeling began to disintegrate in 1982 during the Lebanon War and has been declining ever since. He has shocked his parents tonight by saying that if the *seder* story were being written now, the roles would be reversed: Israel would be cast in the role of the Egyptians, and it would be the Palestinians who would see themselves as the Israelites of the Bible. The remark was meant to offend, but it expresses for Richard a profound disillusionment. The one aspect of being a Jew to which he could respond was the passion for justice that came from being part of a powerless minority. To be a Jew was to be an outsider, a social critic, a religious revolutionary. Nowadays he sees his parents and their friends as politically conservative, economically established, and remorselessly middle-class. He sees in the State of Israel the compromise of power, necessary for its survival, perhaps, but not something that compels his ethical admiration.

He has broken away from his parents' set of contentments: their Anglican-Judaism, their annual trips to Netanya, their narrow gossip, their ethnic pride. It is all, he thinks, not offensive or objectionable but simply *small*. Judaism was once greater than this, but if this is all it currently has to offer, it does not speak to him. It may be years before he comes to terms with his identity. Ruth, his elder sister, is dismissive of his *Sturm und Drang*. It is, she tells her parents, a typical second-child syndrome. How Richard will turn out, no one knows. For the moment he hates the impositions and presumed attachments of being a Jew and wants to forget them as soon as possible.

The Single-Minded Child

To the rest of the family, the child sitting between Richard and David has always been known as Paul. For the past two years, though, he has insisted on being called Pinchas. Paul/Pinchas went to the same school as Richard. But while Richard was extrovert and aggressive, Paul was quiet, inward and solitary, and much given to poetry which he wrote as well as read. It was never easy to tell what Paul was thinking, but no one in the family paid much attention to him. He kept himself to himself.

He was scheduled to go to a university. He decided to spend the months between the end of school and the beginning of his college term in Israel. Wandering abstractedly round Jerusalem one Friday, he was invited by a young rabbi to spend *Shabbat* at a yeshivah in the old city. Having nothing better to do, Paul agreed.

He has been there ever since. He is not enjoying this trip home, and wants to be back as soon as Pesach is over. He knows it is a *mitzvah* to honor his parents. But they no longer speak the same language; he has had to supervise the kitchen himself to make sure it meets his newly exacting kashrut standards; and he feels that every day in the prosaic atmosphere of home diffuses his religious energies. Paul is a *baal teshuvah*, a religious returnee, one of many in Jerusalem today. His yeshivah and several others in the vicinity are full of young men with a similar story to tell. By now they are an identifiable group with their own distinctive subculture.

As Pinchas he is only too happy to speak about what has happened to him, about why this ex-public-school boy now wears a beard, a dark bedraggled suit, and only occasionally a tie. It was, he explains, Divine providence, *hashgachah*, that brought him to that particular spot in Jerusalem at that particular hour. His whole previous life, he now realizes, was a case of mistaken identity. His unhappiness at school was symptomatic of a Jewish soul—a *nitzotz*

Eloki, a Divine spark—struggling with cultural clothes, *levushim*, that did not fit because they were never made for *him*.

No, he is not going to a university, despite the constant pressure from his parents. What will he do for a living? "I leave that," he smiles, "to *ha-Shem*." Does he read secular books any more? No, he says, they are full of *kefirah*, denial. They mistake the world of the senses for reality, pleasure for happiness, reason for truth, subjective choice for the Divine command. When provoked, he says with sudden intensity: "Look at the world out there. Look what a secular society has made of itself. Wars, drugs, casual sex, AIDS, violence, materialism, consumerism, nuclear weapons, doubt, loneliness, and the meaningless pursuit of profit and success: hollow, all of it, and most of it confusion. Is that what you want me to want? When I can live a life of *kedushah*, holiness?"

Pinchas has told his parents, in response to Richard's outburst about the Exodus and politics, that the going out of Egypt was not just a historical event with political repercussions. The word *Mitzrayim*, Egypt, means boundaries or limitations. The Exodus, he explains, is something each of us must undergo. We must move beyond our limitations, beyond the roles society assigns to the role *ha-Shem* has cast us in. "You think," he tells his parents, "that there is something important about living in this neighborhood, going to a university, having a professional career. That is the Egypt I am escaping from. The Torah is above space and time. A *mitzvah* links us to infinity. When I eat this matzah I am affecting invisible universes. Torah, *Yiddishkeit*, is bigger than this room, this suburb, the nice-Jewish-boy scenario you have mapped out for me."

Pinchas sees his parents' Judaism as simply superficial and uninformed. Ruth's way of life, despite its greater consistency and depth, does not appeal to him either. It is too cold, intellectual, and measured. Prayer, he believes, is not a matter of saying the right words at the right time. It is a mystical experience, a fire, a sacrifice of self. Life as a Jew is more than a sequence of *mitzvot*: it is constant *teshuvah*, an endless process of self-transformation. Through the soul, a Jew can reach out to something greater than the world, to the mysterious infinity that surrounds and penetrates it. The political, communal, and institutional dimensions of Juda- ism matter less to Pinchas than this personal drama of self-transcendence. Israel, where he is studying, is less a place or a nation than a state of mind. The imperfections of society, he argues, are mended not through the political process but in the hearts of individuals.

David and Miriam have gone through successive phases of reaction to Paul's metamorphosis. At first they were delighted when he wrote home to say that he was spending time at a yeshivah. As it dawned on them that he was not going to return, they became anxious. When they went out to visit him for the first time they were shocked at the change in his appearance. Gaunt, ascetic, bearded, his facial expressions subtly changed, he reminded David more of his grandfather than his son. Who was this smiling stranger?

They fear, sometimes, for his health, more often for his future career. Also, though they do not admit it, he makes them feel a little guilty about their own religious standards, which they defend in his presence with an overcompensating vigor. "You have to live in the world," they say. "From faith you don't make a living. Don't *smile* when we're angry." To their friends they say, "It could have been worse. It could have been drugs or the Moonies." To themselves, Paul remains a mystery.

The Child without Questions

To David and Miriam, Susan, their youngest, is the one normal child in the family. Still at school—Jewish but not religious—she wears jeans, dates boys, likes Michael Jackson, watches *Neighbours* and wishes she were Kylie Minogue. She looks attractive, has a sense of humor, and finds heavy talk about Judaism a bore.

Of all the four children, she alone is prepared once in a while to accompany her parents to synagogue. She likes looking down at the boys from the women's gallery and thinks they are altogether smarter and more appealing than the non-Jewish boys she sometimes meets at discos, with their rough clothes, their single earrings, and their passion for beer and football.

She wants to marry a Jewish boy, a real estate agent perhaps, or someone in merchant banking. She has decided that they will live in one of the spacious outer suburbs, have two children (Gavin and Caroline, she has already decided), drive a Honda, and belong to the *shul* but not go there too often.

If asked, Susan would say that she is not religious but that she feels completely Jewish. She supports Israel and would not mind if her future children decided to live there. She belongs to a young Jewish fund-raising group and once in a while demonstrates with her classmates on behalf of Soviet Jewry.

But her interests in life lie elsewhere. Between her local rabbi and George Michael, between a religious youth group and an evening out with friends, between summer at a seminary and a fortnight in the Mediterranean, there is no contest. Susan is not Ruth. She finds her eldest sister cold and funless. Judaism is fine: she wants to get married in a synagogue and see her son celebrate his bar mitzvah. So long as it does not ask too much of her, she will not ask much of it, except to be there when it is needed.

David and Miriam can't help liking Susan. She is what they were thirty years ago. But thirty years ago is not today, as their other children testify. They wonder, sometimes, whether Ruth might not be right: that Jewish identity now needs stronger defenses. Will Susan meet the right Jewish boy or is there a danger that she or her children will marry out? How strong will her marriage be? How safe, humanly and Jewishly, is her free-floating life-style? There is, they have decided, no point in speculating. They will wait and see.

The Fifth Child

There is a fifth child in the Cohen family, but he is not present at the *seder* table to share in the story of the Exodus. He has made his exodus already and is living in Israel. Alan, 21, and known to his friends as Avi, was married last summer to an American girl. Together they live and work in a small, isolated, and highly defended settlement in the West Bank territories of Judea and Samaria.

Avi has no doubts about the meaning of Pesach. It means a willingness to leave exile, the *golah*, and take on the challenge of building a new society in Israel. One year, the last he spent at home, he delivered an impassioned speech at the *seder* table. "What's wrong with us? The story of the Jewish people begins with Avraham leaving home and traveling to the land. The book of *Bereishit* is about the promise of the land. The other four books of the Torah are about leaving Egypt and traveling toward the land. And yet, when it comes to the land, our nerve seems to fail us.

"Why this obsession with *galut*? We received the Torah in exile, in the wilderness. In exile Jews invented the synagogue, wrote the Babylonian Talmud, produced the commentaries of Rashi, the poetry of Judah Halevi, and the philosophy of Maimonides. We have flourished spiritually everywhere on the face of the earth, except as a people in our own land under our own rule.

"Abraham, Isaac, and Jacob went into exile. Jacob's children went into exile for more than two hundred years. When Moses came to take the Israelites out, at first they did not want to leave. They told him not to make trouble. On the brink of entry, the spies lost courage. Moses himself never set foot across the Jordan. When Cyrus allowed the Babylonian exiles to return, only a part of them did. The rest were comfortable and stayed where they were. For eighteen hundred years, between the Roman destruction and the nineteenth century, Jews settled in the most distant, improbable lands, from South America to Siberia, the West Indies to China. The one place they made no serious attempt to settle was Eretz Yisrael.

"And yet everything in Judaism points to Israel, our prayers, our festivals, above all the *seder* service. How long can we go on saying 'Next year in Jerusalem' without meaning it or doing anything about it? During this century Jews suffered a worse catastrophe than the slavery in Egypt: six million corpses in the concentration camps. During this century we experienced a greater miracle than in the days of Moses: our own land, a state, Jerusalem rebuilt. How can those be mere accidents of history? They were the hand of Providence, forcing us out of the *golah* into Eretz Yisrael.

"This time our nerve must not fail. For thousands of years we have been saying 'Next year.' 'Next year we will be free.' 'Next year we will be in Israel.' 'Next year the *mashiach* will come.' And now it is as if God had performed all the signs and wonders and yet the Israelites were still saying, 'Leave Egypt? Moses, what's the hurry? Next year.' To be a believing Jew in London when there is a *medinat Yisrael* is a contradiction in terms. We worship God and yet we turn our backs when He reveals Himself in history. I cannot live in that kind of lie. Next year I *will* be in Israel." And he was.

It is a difficult life for Avi. The settlement is windy and exposed. Ringed around it are Arab villages. The land is inhospitable, the buildings rudimentary; there are no luxuries here. Avi must carry an automatic weapon wherever he goes. Six months ago there was a tragedy at a neighboring settlement. Arab infiltrators broke into the *bet ha midrash* and killed two students. Despite this, he has had no second thoughts. His ideals, formed in his youth group, Bnei Akiva, and inspired by the writings of father and son, R. Avraham and R. Zvi Yehudah Kook, are clear. He is engaged in the highest of all *mitzvot*, *yishuv haaretz*, settling the land. He has no doubt that the historical events of the last half century, its unprecedented tragedies and triumphs, are part of a turbulent Providential process, the birth pangs of a new and messianic age.

The penultimate chapter of the Jewish destiny is, he feels, being written here in these desolate hills. It needs courage and faith and a steadfast refusal to be influenced by local or world opinion, which Avi and his friends in Gush Emunim know are against them. Of one thing he is sure on this Pesach night as he thinks fleetingly of his family thousands of miles away. They are telling the story of a journey from exile to a new and holy land. He is living it.

Avi used to think of the *seder* service in patterns of four: four cups of wine, four expressions of deliverance, four children. This year, studying the commentaries to the tractate of *Pesachim*, he has discovered a reference to a fifth cup of wine. Asking about it, he has found that there are not four but five expressions of deliverance. The fifth? "And I will bring you to the land." Four cups for leaving Egypt. A fifth cup for entering Israel. Five cups, five redemptions, and after all, thinks Avi, five children. Who is the fifth child? Avi has his answer. The child who does not ask questions about Jewish history, but instead chooses to make it.

Multiple Identities

Five children, fictions all, but each a different answer to the question of what it is to be a Jew in the late twentieth century. There are many others. Our imagined family is Orthodox. Even Richard's rebellion was formed in his rejection of Orthodoxy of a particular kind. But around the world this Pesach evening are Jews whose Jewishness is expressed in quite other ways. Many of them are telling the same *seder* story, conscious of being part of that unique, shared history that stretches from Abraham across almost four thousand years and an unparalleled series of wanderings to the present. But for each, it holds quite different implications for what it is to be a Jew today.

There are those who see Judaism as a religion but who are nonetheless not Orthodox in practice or affiliation. They are Liberal or Reconstructionist or Reform or Conservative Jews. Then there are those who see Jewishness in terms of ethnicity. Being Jewish, for them, may be a matter of having Jewish parents, friends, memories, and customs without investing these with any religious interpretation. There are others who see Jewishness in terms of nationality, a matter of living in Israel, or wishing to. Yet others see their Jewishness in political, or cultural, or ethical terms. Some, if asked, would simply say that being a Jew is being an outsider, or that Jewishness is an awareness of anti-Semitism. Many would not know how to answer the question. They are Jews; they feel Jewish; but they could not, and would not wish to, define what that means.

This, then, is our starting point. Jewish identity—rarely before the subject of questioning and doubt—has become intensely problematic in the past two hundred years. Ruth and Richard, Pinchas, Susan, and Avi and their many alternative archetypes are contemporary figures. But behind each lies a history and a philosophy: a specific past as well as a distinctive present.

The issues that divide Jews today, as they divide the children of our imagined family, have a background. What led to the splinter-ing of the common coherent idea of Jewish existence—an idea that lasted until relatively recent times—into these different and incom-patible options? How did a once unified idea of the content and shape of a Jewish life come to be fragmented into these several and multiplying options?

PART II
PAST

2

A Religion or a Nation?

Moreover than two hundred years ago, in 1789, the Count of Clermont-Tonnerre rose to make a speech in the French National Assembly. It was a fateful moment in the history of Western Europe and it was to have repercussions for Jewish identity that have lasted to this day.

The French Revolution had ushered in, earlier that summer, the modern democratic state. The National Assembly had made its momentous declaration of the rights of man: "All men are born, and remain, free, and equal in rights. . . . No person shall be molested for his opinions, even such as are religious, provided that the manifestations of these opinions does not disturb the public order established by the law."

The question was: did these rights apply to Jews? In theory, yes. But theory was at variance with public sentiment. There was powerful antagonism to Jews, particularly in Alsace where the local peasantry, in a wave of revolutionary fervor, rioted against the Jewish population. Jews were seen, and to some extent saw themselves, as outsiders: not so much Frenchmen as a section of the Jewish nation in temporary exile.

It was in response to the reports of the riots that the count rose

21

to make his speech. He defended the idea of the separation of church and state. The law, he reaffirmed, has no concern with a person's beliefs. It is interested only in his actions. Jews therefore were entitled to equal rights within the state. But he made one proviso: if Jews were to be part of the French nation, they could not at the same time be members of the Jewish nation. "The Jews should be denied everything as a nation, but granted everything as individuals. . . . It is intolerable that the Jews should become a separate political formation or class in the country. Every one of them must individually become a citizen; if they do not want this, they must inform us and we shall then be compelled to expel them."

Were Jews adherents of a religion or were they members of a people with its own distinctive laws, governance, and homeland? This was the choice the count called on Jews to make, and it was to determine the course of emancipation for Jews throughout Europe during the course of the nineteenth century. The question demanded, in effect, a revolutionary transformation of Jewish identity. It led, as we shall see, to radical and divergent ideas of what it was to be a Jew. Ultimately, it was to divide Jews to such an extent that Martin Buber was to say later that emancipation had led to the end of *knesset Yisrael*, the idea of the Jewish people as a single entity standing before God.

A People Apart

The choice was, of course, impossible. Judaism is a *religion* with its distinctive beliefs and practices. But it is the religion of a *people*. To be sure, there are conversions and apostasies, entrances and exits, but for the most part Jewishness is a matter of birth. The concept of an unbelieving Christian is self-contradictory; that of an unbelieving Jew is not. And it is a religion tied to a particular *land*, the land of Israel. During their long dispersal, Jews saw themselves in but not of their geographical and cultural environment. They were not merely scattered, they were in *galut*, exile. They had a homeland, which they had left not voluntarily but "because of our sins" and to which they believed they would eventually return. It was toward Jerusalem that they prayed; Jerusalem that they remembered at the heights of religious emotion; nowhere outside Israel was ultimately home.

In a real sense, then, prior to modernity, Jews constituted a single if scattered nation. They were divided by country, language, culture, and custom. But they were united by a common history, beliefs and hopes, and above all, by the shared discipline of conduct spelled out in *halakhah* or Jewish law. They were a people apart. To a certain extent, this was a matter of belief. Jews were a singular and chosen people, the children of the covenant. They were linked together as the family of Jacob, bound by the sense that "All Israel are responsible for one another."

In part, too, it was a matter of conduct. Jewish law maintained a code of difference. In the book of Esther, Haman describes Jews as "a certain people, dispersed and scattered among the peoples . . . whose laws are different from those of all other peoples," and this distinctiveness was not accidental. It had been one of the dominant motifs of biblical law that Jews and Judaism should be kept apart from the pagan practices of surrounding nations. Intermarriage with idolaters was forbidden, and Ezra and Nehemiah waged a successful campaign against it. Rabbinic law extended some of the biblical fences against intermarriage and too close a social interaction between Jews and non-Jews.

These internal safeguards were reinforced by the external reality of the Middle Ages in which Jews were usually minorities in an Islamic or Christian culture. Their participation in society, in terms of the occupations they could engage in and the areas they could live in, was limited. For the most part they had little access to the main avenues of political power. There were times in which they were made to wear distinctive clothing; others in which they were confined to specific and enclosed locations, the ghettos. They were subjected to suspicion, sporadic attacks, and arbitrary and restrictive decrees. They suffered periodic expulsions. The biblical concept of exile precisely matched the historic reality.

Their apartness from the central institutions of the majority culture had another consequence. Throughout the Middle Ages, Jewish communities exercised a degree of autonomy, governing their own educational, welfare, and judicial functions. The *kehillah*, or self-governing community, imposed both Jewish law and local legislation and had at its disposal the coercive sanction of fines and excommunication. Since, for the most part, a Jew could only leave the Jewish community at the cost of conversion to another faith— something to which Judaism embodies a profound aversion—the power of the community to impose its will on individuals was considerable.

A New Identity

The premodern Jewish world, then, was one in which much else was problematic but Jewish identity was not. To be a Jew was to be born into a society, history, destiny, and way of life whose content was coherent and shared by other Jews across space and time. But that identity did not fit into the abstract conception of the modern state as embodied in the French Revolution. Jews were no longer to be members of the Jewish nation who were temporarily located in France. They were to be French citizens first, and only secondarily Jews.

The Count of Clermont-Tonnerre did not spell out specifically what this might mean. But it became clear in the questions directed by Napoleon a generation later to the assembly of Jewish notables and to the specially convened group of rabbis, the Napoleonic "Sanhedrin." Did Jews, Napoleon wished to know, practice their own laws of divorce, distinct from those enforced by civil courts? What judicial powers did rabbinic courts possess and what sanctions were available in enforcing their decisions? Were Jews allowed to marry non-Jews? Did they consider non-Jewish Frenchmen as "brothers" or as "strangers"? Did French-born Jews consider France their country?

These questions, untroubling now, went to the heart of the new situation. A social order that had dominated Jewish existence since the destruction of the Second Temple was coming to an end. Jews were to be fully integrated in the secular state. They were no longer to be outsiders. This meant opportunity but also sacrifice. The conditions were unstated but implied. Jewish self-government would have to cease. Jews would no longer have the power to fine or excommunicate individuals who disobeyed community ordinances. In addition, Jews would have to demonstrate that in their language, dress, and etiquette they were fully part of the majority culture.

The implications for Jewish identity were profound in two respects. Firstly, Judaism was henceforth to be a voluntary commitment. To be sure, Jewish law was not directly affected. One who was born a Jew was still bound by the commandments and prohibitions. But existentially, there were choices available to a Jew in the new situation that had not existed before. If he chose to ignore Jewish law, the community could not compel him to do otherwise. Moreover, the secularization of the state meant that one could cease to be a Jew without becoming a Christian. When Benjamin Disraeli was asked what his religion was, he took an English Bible and pointed to the blank page between the Old Testament and the New. "I," he said, "am that blank page." That "neutral space" had not existed before.

Secondly, to be a Jew was now only one aspect of personal identity, not its totality. Emancipated Jews were expected to work and mix socially with non-Jews and to become fully conversant with European culture. Their Jewishness, it was tacitly agreed, should not be too obtrusive. Jews had to pass through what one writer has called "the ordeal of civility." This meant a new double identity, one that the poet Judah Leib Gordon described as being "a Jew at home and a person in the street." Sigmund Freud, for example, spoke of the "dissimulation [which] I practice every day." The art was to be Jewish without seeming to be. This was sharply at odds with the integrated identity of traditional Jewish societies. How far was the new order compatible with Jewish tradition itself?

Moses Mendelssohn

Moses Mendelssohn (1729–1786), the first Jewish philosopher of emancipation, argued that it was. In 1783 he published *Jerusalem*, his plea for freedom of religious conscience. The laws of the state and the commands of religion are, he insisted, two entirely separate realms. Religion uses education and persuasion, not power, to secure the loyalty of its followers. Excommunication is "diametrically opposed to the spirit of religion." What then of the fact that the Bible prescribes punishments for sins? That, he argues, was only as long as Jews were a nation in their own land, when an offense against the law of God was also a crime against the state. Since then, Judaism "knows of no punishment, no other penalty than the one which the remorseful sinner *voluntarily* imposes on himself."

Already, then, we see in Mendelssohn an argument for the voluntariness of Judaism and an attempt to persuade the Jewish community to renounce its self-regulating powers and embrace the new terms of emancipation. What is more, he suggests, Judaism is a model of rationality and tolerance. "It boasts of *no exclusive* revelation of eternal truths that are indispensable to salvation." What was revealed at Sinai were not truths like the Divine creation of the world. These are arrived at by reason, and are thus available to any rational human being. They constitute the "universal religion of mankind." The revelation at Sinai disclosed only "revealed legislation," the commands that are peculiar to Jews. Here, in philosophical terms, is the distinction crucial to the Jewish response to emancipation, between the "Jew at home" practicing his particular religious heritage, and the "man in the street" engaged in the pursuit of universal truth and the general welfare.

Mendelssohn was a traditional Jew, who proposed no halakhic or intellectual reforms. But already we sense the strain to which Judaism would be put in this new environment. Why, we ask ourselves reading *Jerusalem*, should Jews continue to practice their ancestral faith when a new and glittering secular culture was beckoning? To this question Mendelssohn can give only the most negative of answers. "Adapt yourself to the morals and constitution of the land to which you have been removed; but hold fast to the religion of your fathers, too. Bear both burdens as well as you can! It is true that on the one hand, the burden of civil life is made heavier for you on account of the religion to which you remain faithful, and on the other hand, the climate and the times make the observance of your religious laws in some respects more irksome than they are. Nevertheless, persevere; remain unflinchingly at the post which Providence has assigned you. . . ." This is not an argument calculated to inspire.

Nonetheless, it provided the basis on which Jews in England, France, and Italy came to terms with their new situation. Jews could indeed be both loyal and active citizens and remain within the classic terms of the Jewish tradition. To be sure, they prayed for a return to Zion. But that was in the messianic future, not the immediate present. Within their countries of birth they heeded Jeremiah's words to "seek the peace and welfare of the city to which I have carried you in exile; pray to the Lord for it, because in its prosperity you shall prosper." In France, a semblance of the old *kehillah* was recreated, the *Consistoire*, under state supervision. In England, it took the form of voluntary but governmentally recognized institutions: the Board of Deputies, the Chief Rabbinate, and the United Synagogue.

In England, in particular, the course of political equality ran slowly but smoothly. There were no preconditions asked, no religious reforms or declarations. Victorian society was both liberal and traditional, and Jews of all social classes acculturated without seeking religious legitimation for their new behavior patterns. The institutions of Judaism, for their part, adapted to the new environment through merely cosmetic changes: grand synagogues, ministers who wore canonicals with more than a passing resemblance to those of the church, sermons in the vernacular, choirs, and an insistence on decorum during services. The style was eminently English; the substance remained within the boundaries of Judaism.

But it was in Germany that Jews encountered the greatest hostility to emancipation. It seemed that as Jews they remained suspect and unacceptable. There was, in the last decades of the eighteenth century, a wave of conversions to Christianity, especially among the most affluent and cultured. They counted among their number several of Moses Mendelssohn's own children. Heinrich Heine famously described Judaism as not a religion but a misfortune, and called the baptismal certificate "the ticket of admission to Western culture."

One of Mendelssohn's disciples, David Friedländer, proposed a form of general conversion to Christianity that he believed might

find favor among Jews and Christians alike. Mendelssohn had, after
all, described a universal religion of reason. What was distinctively
Jewish about Judaism was its rituals, and these could be abandoned
in favor of their Christian equivalents. The church should invite
Jews into its ranks without insisting that they believe in Christian
dogma. Jews then would merely be exchanging one set of practices
for another. Within sixteen years of Mendelssohn's defense of
Judaism, therefore, his own arguments were being employed to
argue for its total dissolution.

The Legacy of Spinoza

Friedländer's proposal outraged both sides, but it is a measure of
the traumatic impact of the new situation in which Jews found
themselves, especially when the equality they sought was being
actively and politically resisted. The nineteenth century saw a
retreat from this conversionary brink. But it was in Germany that
two radical Jewish proposals emerged. Their inspiration came, not
from Mendelssohn but from an earlier and more disturbing figure,
Baruch Spinoza (1632–1677), who in his early twenties had been
excommunicated by the Amsterdam Jewish community for prop-
agating heretical views.

Spinoza was the first of a series of intellectuals of Jewish
origins—Marx, Freud, and Durkheim were others—who not
merely rejected Judaism and religion generally but sought to
explain and thus exorcise it. For Spinoza, God was not supernatural but was nature itself under a different aspect. It followed that
there were no supernatural events and therefore no revelation. The
Torah was the work of human beings (Spinoza was a forerunner of
"biblical criticism") and the commandments were a system of
national legislation. It followed that, with the destruction of the
Second Temple and the loss of national autonomy, the commandments no longer applied and Jews themselves had ceased to be the
chosen people. They had continued to exist as a separate people
only because anti-Semitism blocked the way to assimilation. Where
tolerance reigned, Jews would and should merely abandon Judaism, though, in an aside, Spinoza conjectured that "if the founda-

tions of religion have not emasculated their minds" they might yet rebuild their nation in Israel and "God may a second time elect them."

These views are, by any standard, radically destructive of Judaism but they were to exercise a powerful influence over Jews grappling with the phenomenon of German anti-Semitism, and they were to lead eventually in two diametrically opposed directions.

The first was Reform. To understand the development of the Reform movement in Germany, it is necessary to remember two things. The first was that enlightened defenders of Jewish emancipation like Clermont-Tonnerre did not demand that Jews renounce their Jewishness completely. But they did assume that Judaism was, or could be turned into, a religion in the "Protestant" sense of a private faith of individuals. The second is that opponents of Jewish emancipation seized on just those aspects of Judaism that did not conform to this definition, but instead seemed to mark Jews as a people apart, a group who were incapable of being fully integrated into society.

Some of these features had little to do with Judaism as such. Jews spoke a distinctive language, Yiddish, and were concentrated in trading and financial services. These facts, their critics argued, showed that Jews kept themselves apart and were naturally exploitative. But there were other objections that had everything to do with Judaism. Jews believed that they would one day leave Europe and return to Zion. Johann David Michaelis, in 1782, accordingly argued that "The Jews will always see the state as a temporary home, which they will leave in the hour of their greatest happiness to return to Palestine." Their dietary laws kept them from fully mixing in Gentile society. Michaelis drew the conclusion that "As long as they observe the laws about kosher and nonkosher food it will be almost impossible to integrate them into our ranks." The laws of *Shabbat*, too, Michaelis argued, prevented Jews from accepting the full responsibilities of citizenship. The "Jews will not fight on the Sabbath, for they are forbidden to do so if not attacked." They would not provide reliable soldiers for the German army and would not therefore contribute fully to the state.

Nineteenth-Century Reform

Was it possible to construct a Judaism that met these objections? In 1817 a Reform "Temple" was opened in Hamburg. Its major innovation was the elimination from the prayer book of all references of the ingathering of exiles and the return to Zion. The name Temple itself signaled its founders' intentions. They no longer yearned for Jerusalem. A temple could be built in Hamburg as well. It was, its constitution declared, a "church," a purely religious institution without the political–national motifs hitherto associated with Judaism. Many of the prayers would be said not in Hebrew but German. The *Shabbat* services would be accompanied by an order and choir. It was a significant breach with Jewish tradition, and was denounced, a little over a year later, by a group of distinguished rabbis. The breach between Reform and the classic terms of rabbinic Judaism—or Orthodoxy as its opponents now named it—had begun.

It was to widen. Opposition to Jewish emancipation, often couched in brutally hostile terms, continued. German Jews were making their own compromises with a non-Jewish world and were rapidly abandoning religious observance. The early efforts at the "Germanization" of Judaism, represented by the Hamburg Temple, were seen by some to be inadequate. A fresh wave of radical reform took place in the 1840s. There were those who advocated an abandonment of the laws of *kashrut;* others who promised a curtailment of the laws of *Shabbat;* there were even those who proposed the transfer of *Shabbat* to Sunday. Some argued for the abolition of circumcision; others for the abandonment of the Jewish laws of divorce in favor of recognition of civil divorce as an adequate termination of Jewish marriage. These became the hallmarks of radical reform as it developed in Germany and America.

These were violent assaults on the substance and spirit of Jewish life as hitherto conceived, and they produced strong reactions. In 1845 a previous sympathizer, Zechariah Frankel, broke with the Reform movement and proposed in its place a more traditional, evolutionary form of Judaism. This he called "positive historical," and it eventually became known in America as Conservative Judaism. A Galician rabbinic authority, R. Zvi Hirsch Chajes, who was deeply impressed with the Enlightenment and contemporary secular culture, nonetheless proposed, in his 1849 pamphlet *Minchat Kena'ot*, a formal ban declaring Reform leaders total Gentiles in Jewish law. The most modern of Orthodox leaders in Germany, R. Samson Raphael Hirsch, devoted a significant part of his energies to a ceaseless campaign against Reform. The discontinuities between Reform and tradition were obvious. What were the continuities? By what logic did the radical reformers defend their innovations as lying within the parameters of Judaism?

There were two dominant schools of thought. One, advocated by Abraham Geiger (1810–1874), argued for a historical understanding of Judaism that would see both its biblical and rabbinic forms as not a fixed orthodoxy but a process of constant development and adaptation. In Geiger we see the influence of Spinoza's "biblical criticism" allied to a Hegelian idea of history as evolution. What was fundamental to Judaism was its monotheism and morality. Ritual could and should change as Judaism developed from its early particularism to a more universal mission to humanity. Judaism was not fixed for all time at Sinai. Instead, it was an expression of "Progressive Revelation."

More radical still was his contemporary, Samuel Holdheim (1806–1860). Holdheim argued that there were two elements in biblical Judaism: religious and ceremonial. The religious element— with Geiger, he saw this as monotheism and morality—was eternally valid, but the ceremonial law applied only as part of the constitution of a Jewish state. Since the state had ceased to exist with the Roman destruction in 70 C.E., it was now null and void. "Now that Jews have become integral elements of other peoples and states . . . all laws and institutions of Judaism which were based on the election of a particular Jewish people—yes, of a particular Jewish state—and hence by their very nature implied exclusiveness and particularism . . . have lost all religious significance and obligation and have given way to the national laws and institutions of such lands and peoples to which the Jews belong by birth and civic relationship."

This was a restatement of Spinoza's argument in the *Tractatus Theologico-Politicus*. Emancipation heralded a new messianic age of universal brotherhood, and all laws which tended to keep Jews as a separate people were irrelevant at best; at worst, they impeded the progress of civilization. Holdheim's revolutionary stance was adopted as the ideology of the American Reform movement in its Pittsburgh Platform of 1885. Thus, Spinoza had inspired radical reform.

The Birth of Secular Zionism

But German Reform showed how extreme were the implications of Clermont-Tonnerre's either/or. Was Judaism a religion of individuals or was it the national expression of a people? Holdheim's Reform carried to its logical conclusion a positive answer to the first alternative and a rejection of the second. Judaism, to be turned into a religion in a sense acceptable to German opinion, had to be stripped of its most fundamental laws, those of *Shabbat, kashrut,* circumcision, and divorce. They represented a dimension of nationhood in Judaism that Holdheim and others felt was inappropriate to the new age. Emancipation proposed to recognize Jews as individuals, not as members of a collective people. German Reform was a Jewish response to this unprecedented dichotomy.

But, as was already evident in the France of 1789, theory was one thing, public emotion another. Throughout the Middle Ages, Jews had suffered from a Christian anti-Judaism that at times—during the Crusades, fifteenth-century Spain, and the periodic blood libels—exploded into persecution and violence. The Enlightenment promised an era of rationality, religious freedom, and tolerance. It did not happen. Already in the writings of Voltaire (1694–1778), one of the most powerful advocates of Enlightenment, we sense that Jews were to be the exception to the rule of universal toleration. We find in Jews, he wrote, "only an ignorant and barbarous people, who have long united the most sordid avarice with the most detestable superstition and the most invincible hatred for every people by whom they are tolerated and enriched." He made one concession. "Still," he added, "we ought not to burn them."

A new phenomenon was making its appearance: hostility to Jews without a theological framework to justify it. An emotion that had

had a specific place within an ordered religious world view was in the process of being secularized. Christian anti-Judaism was being transformed into racial anti-Semitism. Anti-Semitism as such—the hatred of Jews not for what they believe and do but for what they are, because of their supposedly indelible racial characteristics—is, properly speaking, a phenomenon of the nineteenth century. And it led one perceptive Jewish thinker to conclude that the entire project of European emancipation would fail. Jews would never be accepted within German society, however they adapted their dress, language, mores, and religion. For they were now experiencing a hatred that was directed not at externals of behavior but at their very birth and being. Clermont-Tonnerre's choice still stood before them. But Jews must see that their future lay in the opposite direction to that taken by Reform. They were a nation, not a religion. And they must seek their future not in Europe, where anti-Semitism was ineradicable, but in a rebuilt land of Israel. Individual emancipation in the diaspora would fail. The only alternative was collective emancipation in a land of their own. It was in this series of perceptions that secular Zionism was born.

Moses Hess

The author of these ideas was Moses Hess (1812–1875). Hess had been deeply influenced in his youth by the work of Spinoza. His first book had been entitled *The Holy History of Mankind, by a Young Spinozist*. From there he moved on to the cause of international socialism, in which role he became a friend and collaborator of Karl Marx. In this vision Judaism had no place. To the contrary, he believed, as Isaiah Berlin put it, that "The people chosen by God must disappear forever, that out of its death might spring a new, more precious life."

Three phenomena, however, influenced Hess in a new direction. The first was the rise of European nationalist movements in the 1840s. Nationalism rather than internationalism was the order of the day. The second was the profound shock he and other European Jews experienced at the revival of the medieval blood libel in the Damascus Affair of 1840. This shook Hess's assumption of a new era of tolerance in which Jews would benignly assimilate, much as the Dreyfus Affair a half century later was to radicalize another alienated Jew, Theodor Herzl. The third was the escalating anti-Semitism Hess detected in Germany. Nothing Jews could do to reform their religion would have the slightest effect on this animosity since, he wrote, the Germans, "hate the peculiar faith of the Jews less than their peculiar noses."

These slowly maturing observations came to expression in Hess's brief but powerful book *Rome and Jerusalem*, published in 1862. It was prefaced by a personal declaration of *teshuvah*, spiritual home-coming: "Here I stand once more, after twenty years of estrange-ment, in the midst of my people. . . . A thought which I had stifled forever in my heart is again vividly present with me; the thought of my nationality, inseparable, from the inheritance of my ancestors, the Holy Land and the eternal city." Hess's argument was simple. "That which Jews were not able to obtain as individ-uals, the people can secure as a nation." Instead of emancipation, Jews should seek self-emancipation as a people in their own right. Jewish nationalism was, after all, far more ancient than European nationalism, and if the French could establish and create their own revolutionary state, so could the Jews. With the French Revolution began the rebirth of the nations who owe their national historic religion to Judaism.

Reform Judaism, he argued, was utterly misconceived. "Danger threatens Jewry only from those reformers of its religion who, with their newly invented ceremonies and stale rhetoric, have sucked the last marrow out of Judaism and have allowed nothing to remain of this sublime phenomenon of history but the shadow of a skeleton." The reformers believed that anti-Semitism could be deflected by a change of conduct on the part of Jews. But it cannot be done. Firstly, "even baptism itself" does not protect the Jew from "the nightmare of German Jew-hatred." Second, Jews are a primary race whose distinguishing features cannot be disguised. Third, the denial of the national components of Judaism is ethically unaccept-able. The Jew who argues that Judaism is a religion only is "a traitor to his people and to his family."

The Jewish tradition had always seen religion, peoplehood, and nationalism as inseparable. The biblical and rabbinic literature sprang from a "deep national fountain of life." Jews felt bound to one another as members of a single family: "All Israel are responsible for one another." Jewish identity went deeper than religious identity: "The Jew who sins remains a Jew." Judaism, through its holy deeds and days, preserved the memory of its national past. On the ninth of Av, Jews sat in mourning for the ruins of Jerusalem. In their messianic hope they longed for the reconstruction of the nation in its own and promised land.

Never, prior to the nineteenth century, had it been thought possible to separate Jewish religion from nationalism. Enlightened European Jews felt a sense of inferiority to Christians, but they were wrong. Christianity was purely a religion; therefore it was threatened by the decline of religion in a secular age. Judaism was more than a religion; therefore it would be lifted on the rising tide of nationalism. "Only from the national rebirth will the religious genius of the Jews draw new powers, like that giant who touched the mother earth, and be again animated by the sacred spirit of the prophets."

Spinoza and the Secularization of Zionism

Hess was not the first Zionist. In one sense he was only a precursor. It was to take another generation before the Russian pogroms of the 1880s and the Dreyfus Affair of the 1890s energized Pinsker and Herzl to set the movement into motion. In another sense he was only a follower. It had been two Orthodox rabbis, Zvi Hirsch Kalischer (1795–1874) and Yehudah Alkalai (1798–1878) who first argued for a new program to settle the land of Israel, set up agricultural colonies, revitalize the Hebrew language, and create a land-purchasing scheme under the leadership of Jews of international stature like Sir Moses Montefiore and the Rothschilds. Hess acknowledged Kalischer as an influence and inspiration.

But Hess's seminal significance is that he was the first secular Zionist. Alkalai and Kalischer spoke within the classic religious vocabulary. The return to Zion was part of the Divine process of redemption, even though, they argued, the first steps must be taken by man. Hess, by contrast, spoke in terms of national spirit and the processes of history in which "race struggle is primary, class struggle is secondary." His work is punctuated by a secular messianism that owes more to Marx than to Moses. His greatest mentor, whom he constantly acknowledges, was Spinoza. Reading *Rome and Jerusalem* for the first time, in 1901, Theodor Herzl remarked, "Since Spinoza, Jewry has brought forth no greater spirit than this forgotten Moses Hess."

To be sure, Jews had always longed for the return to Zion. At the twin peaks of the religious year, on Pesach and Yom Kippur, they had said with deep feeling, "Next year in Jerusalem." But, as Yehoshafat Harkabi has pointed out, "Zionism is not an idea; it is the realization of an intention, a political program." A certain secularization is implicit in the translation of the longing for Zion into a practical and political movement. Throughout the Middle Ages, Jews like Judah Halevi, Maimonides, and Nachmanides had traveled to Israel. At the threshold of modernity, figures like the Vilna Gaon, R. Moses Sofer, and a number of chasidic leaders, had encouraged settlement there as an antidote to the corrosive forces of a secularizing Europe; perhaps even as a mystical means of hastening the messianic age.

The first *yishuv*, the settlement of Jews who had arrived in the land between 1840 and 1880, was composed primarily of deeply religious Ashkenazi Jews who sought to create a religious community on Eastern European lines. But their vision did not extend to creating the infrastructures of an economy, a defense force, and a government, nor did it envisage political action to generate international support for the Zionist cause. To the contrary, such action would have seemed heretical, "forcing the end" by seeking redemption through secular channels.

In Jewish mystical thought, the idea of Israel had become deeply spiritualized. R. Nachman of Bratslav (1772–1811), chasidic leader and great-grandson of the Baal Shem Tov, shortly before his own visit to the land, reported on a conversation he had had with some other *chasidim* who had just returned. Before they had gone, they told him, they could not visualize the land of Israel as actually existing in this world. They had imagined that the holy land was located outside time and space.

Nor was this the primary obstacle to religious Zionism. Since the failure of the Bar Kochba rebellion in the early second century, Judaism had encouraged a stance of quietism and political passivity. In 1770 a German nobleman suggested the idea of a Jewish state in Palestine to Moses Mendelssohn. Mendelssohn replied that the idea was quite implausible. The Jewish people, he lamented, was "not adequately equipped to undertake anything great." The long exile had sapped its spirit. "It is not our fault; but we cannot deny that the natural urge to freedom has completely ceased to be active in us. It has transformed itself into a monkish virtue and expresses itself in prayer and patience, not in action."

It was here that Hess found Spinoza liberating. For it was Spinoza who had "demythologized" the land of Israel, describing it not as a land possessed of intrinsic holiness but as a "certain strip of territory" on which Jews "could live peaceably and at ease." It was Spinoza who had reconceived Jewish history in naturalistic terms, without Divine intervention. It was Spinoza who had stressed the national component of biblical Judaism. And it was Spinoza who, as Hess wrote, "believed that the restoration of the Jewish state depended merely on the courage of the Jewish people." All these effectively secularized the ideas of the Jewish people, Israel, and the connection between them. They allowed them to be translated into the emerging European vocabulary of nationalism. They turned the return to Zion from a religious hope into a political program.

Discontinuities

Spinoza, a thinker who had actually argued the dissolution of Judaism, thus ironically became the inspiration of two radically opposed conceptions of Jewish identity, each of them a revolutionary break with the past: German Reform Judaism and secular Zionism. The Enlightenment, and its political expression in the French Revolution, embodied a sharp dichotomy between religion and state. The state itself was neutral and secular. Religion was to be the private persuasion of individuals.

For a Christian Europe this was a gradual and internal development. For Jews it came as a sharp external demand, stated with unavoidable clarity by Clermont-Tonnerre at the very threshold of emancipation. Was Judaism a religion or the framework of a nation? It could not be both. Holdheim's Reform took the first alternative to its limits, Hess's Zionism took the second. The former denationalized Judaism, the latter secularized it. Each involved a fundamental rewriting of Jewish history and tradition. Thus were born the two major alternatives to Orthodoxy that have persisted into the late twentieth century.

There were other revolutionary Jewish identities, particularly in Eastern Europe: Jewish socialism, culturalism, and a movement for diaspora Jewish autonomy. None proved durable. We will, in a later chapter, encounter a peculiarly twentieth-century alternative, neither religious nor national though mixing elements of both: the phenomenon of Jewish ethnicity. But this chapter has shown how the French Revolution set in motion a questioning and redefinition of Jewish identity that had no precedent in the previous seventeen centuries of exile. It led—in two opposite directions—to a dramatic break with tradition. Was this inevitable, or were there ways of preserving Jewish continuity within the classic terms of faith and practice? What were the traditional responses to the challenges of modernity?

3

Traditional
Alternatives

During the deliberations of the Napoleonic Sanhedrin in 1807, the secretary of the gathering, Abraham Furtado (1756–1817), a communal leader of progressive views, grew restless with the conservative positions of the traditionalist rabbis. He sought for a word to describe what he saw as their obduracy in the face of change. He called them in one of the first recorded uses of the phrase—"Orthodox Jews."

The birth of the adjective "Orthodox" marks a significant turn in Jewish history. Hitherto there had been Ashkenazi and Sefardi Jews, rationalists and mystics, saints and scholars. There had been, during the previous century, sharp antagonisms between *chasidim* and their opponents, the *mitnagdim*. Jews had been by no means a monolithic people. There were, among them, geographical, cultural, and intellectual differences. But these distinctions were set within an encompassing and unifying framework of belief and action.

To be a Jew was to be subject to halakhah, the vastly ramified provisions of Jewish law. That law, in turn, was derived either directly or indirectly from the Torah, the written record of the Divine revelation at Sinai. Rabbinic Judaism, as the ongoing application of the Oral Law, gave Torah its authoritative interpretation and safeguarded its observance through protective enactments and decrees. "Israel is only a people in virtue of its laws," Saadia Gaon had written in the early tenth century, and the description remained accurate until modern times.

Lacking a common land, language, and culture, Jews remained identifiably a single people for they represented a community of action. They ate and refrained from eating the same foods. They celebrated *Shabbat* and the festivals in the same ways on the same days. They prayed using, by and large, the same words. They institutionalized the rabbinic passion for study in their schools and houses of study. They explored the shared canon of texts: *Tenakh*, the Hebrew Bible, the Mishnah and Babylonian Talmud, the commentaries of Rashi and the codes of Maimonides and Joseph Karo. They could claim to be, indeed they were, linear descendants of the fathers of the rabbinic tradition: Hillel, Akiva, R. Judah ha-Nasi. The tradition itself traced its provenance back through the Great Assembly to the prophets, to the elders, and to Moses.

Since the destruction of the Second Temple by the Romans in 70 C.E., nothing significant had changed in the terms of Jewish life. There were exiles and expulsions, inquisitions and pogroms, libels and disputations; but these were variations on a theme already set forth in the great Mosaic visions of national catastrophe in the books of Leviticus and Deuteronomy. The Jewish people was in exile because of its sins. One day its sufferings would be ended, its punishment fulfilled, and though they were scattered to the farthest corners of heaven, Jews would be carried back to their land on Providence's wings.

They remembered Jerusalem with sadness in the midst of their celebrations and they prayed toward it. But for the most part, though speculation was unending, they were hesitant about predicting the exact date of the messianic moment or doing anything to hasten its arrival. The centuries of exile had witnessed a succession of self-styled messiahs. Each had ended in disillusionment. The latest and most disruptive had been Shabbatai Zevi (1626–1676), a contemporary of Spinoza, whose promise of redemption had gripped the Jewish world from Italy to Yemen, from Turkey to Amsterdam. It ended in his forced conversion to Islam. From the

Bar Kochba rebellion to Shabbateanism, anticipations of a new era had proved uniformly disastrous. Redemption would not be brought by revolution, but by piety, scholarship, and mystical devotions. The studied rabbinic indifference to history, between the end of the biblical period and the nineteenth century, was born of the bitter experience of premature utopias.

Challenges to Tradition

This tradition was threatened by modernity in a series of ways. Intellectually, the Enlightenment was hostile to tradition in general, seeing it as a vehicle of irrationality and superstition. A chain of thinkers of unquestionable eminence—Voltaire, as we have seen, was one; Kant, Hegel, Schopenhauer, and Nietzsche were others—reserved their particular scorn for Judaism. It was faulted either for having failed to evolve into Christianity, or, in the case of Nietzsche, for having given birth to Christianity. It represented, said Hegel, a slave morality; it was, argued Nietzsche, antinature and hence antilife. So deep was the German hostility to the Jews of the ghetto that proponents and opponents of emancipation alike agreed that Jews were uncivilized. The only question was whether this was due to their environment or their nature. Their friends believed that Jews could be turned into responsible citizens by education and assimilation. Their critics held that they could not. That Jews were presently below the threshold of social acceptability, none disputed.

Specifically, the nineteenth century was one that was dominated by the idea of history as evolution. This favored a historical and naturalistic approach to sacred scriptures and led to a massive development of Spinoza's early secularization of the biblical text. This now became the academic discipline of "biblical criticism" and it took as axiomatic, as Spinoza had done, that the text was to be understood not as unmediated Divine revelation directed at a particular historical community, but as the composite work of that community itself. How a given age reads the Bible tells us more about the age than about the Bible. The Enlightenment was an age of unlimited confidence in man and the progress of civilization. It took an unprecedentedly low view of the wisdom of the past. The Jewish idea of revelation—the power of the past to command all future generations—was almost impossible to translate into its terms of reference, as was the Jewish idea of covenant—the idea of a code of conduct binding only on a singular people. Any rule of behavior that was not universal, argued Kant, was ipso facto not ethical.

These ideas threatened Jewish belief at its roots. Of more immediate consequence, however, was the changing social environment. As we noted in the previous chapter, throughout the Middle Ages Jewish and non-Jewish perceptions coincided in keeping Jews a people apart. Now immense pressures, internalized by Jews, were directed at their social integration. The immediate result was a decline in the observance of laws that symbolized and enhanced this apartness: *kashrut* and *Shabbat* in particular. Reform legitimated this break with traditional behavior, but the break preceded the legitimation. The Jewish barriers against assimilation and intermarriage were collapsing.

Jews, too, were under pressure to give their children an education that would make them fully a part of the majority culture. The result was a collapse in the traditional system of *Talmud Torah*. Acculturation carried with it the price of a rapid decline in Jewish knowledge. A friend of Moses Mendelssohn, Naftali Herz Wessely (1725–1805) responded to the Austrian Emperor Joseph II's Edict of Tolerance which called on Jews either to send their children to Christian schools or to open schools of their own in which secular subjects would be taught. Wessely believed that the suggestion would enhance the position of Jews and he argued for compliance with it. There were, he argued, two sources of wisdom, the Torah of God and *Torat ha-Adam*, secular knowledge. They were compatible. Each enriched the other. But secular knowledge was universal. The Torah, on the other hand, was directed at Jews alone. Therefore, secular studies should precede Jewish studies so that the latter would be built on the firm foundations of the former.

Wessely's proposal was sharply criticized by, among others, the Vilna Gaon and R. Ezekiel Landau. But within a generation it had become the norm for a large section of the aspiring German-Jewish middle class. The extraordinary rabbinic culture of learning, in which personal standing within the community was to a large extent a function of knowledge and scholarship in the talmudic literature, was being replaced by the pursuit of secular literacy. By the mid-nineteenth century, a university education had come to be regarded as an essential qualification for the German Orthodox rabbinate.

Above all, the tradition could no longer be enforced. Mendelssohn's proposal for the abandonment of the community powers of fines and excommunications, controversial in its day, quickly became the norm. Judaism became a voluntary faith and code of practice. To be sure, as Mendelssohn was at pains to point out, in a sense Judaism had been voluntary since the beginning of its long exile. Judah Halevi in the twelfth century had spoken with wonder at how few Jews had defected when "by a word spoken lightly" they could have "escaped this degradation" and converted to the dominant faith. But now there were alternatives that fell short of conversion. One could be a secular, or a nonobservant, or a Reform Jew. The scope of choice had widened significantly. Tradition had ceased to be the given and self-evident context of social life and had become, instead, one among many competing affiliations in the free market of ideas.

It was in this context that the word "Orthodoxy" was born. It was initially a term of criticism. Samson Raphael Hirsch later complained that "It was not the so-called Orthodox Jews who introduced the name 'orthodoxy' into the Jewish sphere." It was first used by reformers as a pejorative description of the *Altgläubigen* or "old believers." Judaism, Hirsch insisted, "does not recognize any variants. It knows of no Mosaic, prophetic or rabbinic, and of no orthodox or progressive Judaism. It is either Judaism or it is not." But the word remained, for it designated a new reality. Orthodoxy represented the determination to continue Jewish existence in its classic forms in the conscious presence of alternatives. It was Jewish faith and practice in an environment that naturally supported neither. It was tradition in an untraditional age.

Western European Models of Modernity

The shock of modernity was not experienced in the same way or at the same time by the various Jewish communities of Europe. In England and France, as we have noted, emancipation proceeded without the formation of a significant Reform presence on the one hand or a revolutionary secularism on the other. Religious legitimation was not sought for social change, and the central Jewish institutions—the United Synagogue and Chief Rabbi in England, the *Consistoire and Grand Rabbin* in France—were able to adapt to the manners of a new age without substantive modifications of tradition. As Robert Liberles has described it, until the end of the nineteenth century "the religious institutions of England and France represented neither neo-Orthodoxy nor old Orthodoxy, but simply Jews and Judaism."

The same was true of Italy, where the Jewish community had a long tradition of exposure to secular culture and could draw on the expansive traditions of medieval Sefardi Jewry. In 1769 Isaac Euchel could describe the Jews of Leghorn in images of harmonious interaction with their Gentile neighbors. They live, he wrote, "in fine homes amidst the nobles of the land, and their homes are stone-built and most of its people are merchants and notables. . . . They speak the language of the people correctly and eloquently like one of their orators. . . . My heart gladdens and I am proud to see my brothers living securely amidst the Gentiles without foe or troublemaker." It was to the rabbis and scholars of Italy that Wessely turned when his program for a mixed secular Jewish education came under attack in Germany. Alone among the Jews of Europe they came to his defense. Strongly traditional and without desire for reform, Italian Jews nonetheless took it for granted that Torah was to be combined with an acquaintance and appreciation of non-Jewish culture.

In a quite different way, the *chasidim* of Eastern Europe avoided a direct and divisive encounter with modernity. Chasidism had emerged in the eighteenth century under the inspiration of the Baal Shem Tov (R. Israel b. Eliezer, *c.* 1700–1760) as a popular and pietist movement stressing mysticism, religious devotion, and enthusiasm. It was sharply opposed by traditional leaders like R.

Elijah, the Vilna Gaon, for its emphasis on prayer and religious experience over talmudic study, its liturgical and halakhic innovations, and its focus on charismatic leadership—the personality of the *Tzaddik* or *Rebbe*. Nonetheless, as the nineteenth century took its toll of other traditional groups, it became clear that Chasidism was a powerful antidote to assimilation. Its communities were strong. Its leaders exercised a hitherto unprecedented degree of authority over their followers. Its embracing view of life constituted a kind of total and alternative culture that was relatively immune to secularization. Born as it was when the first tremors of a new age were just beginning to be felt, the chasidic movement created what might be called the first voluntary ghettos. They were communities sheltered behind a spiritual, not a physical, wall. But the barrier they erected against modernity was effective nonetheless.

In none of these environments did Orthodoxy experience the need to define and defend itself against internal conflicts. That crisis took place above all in Germany, where Reform had been born and where it had its greatest strongholds. Throughout the nineteenth century, a series of outstanding Orthodox scholars and religious leaders rose to the defense of tradition. They represented a new model of rabbinic leadership, formidably intellectual and unbending in their commitment to halakhah and the principles of Jewish faith. They embodied a synthesis new to German Jewry. Most were recognized talmudic authorities. But most, too, had acquired a university education. How innovative this was may be judged by the fact that in 1840 R. Solomon Tiktin of Breslau maintained that anyone who had studied at university was unfit to serve as a rabbi. They included Isaac Bernays, Jacob Ettlinger, Seligmann Baer Bamberger, Azriel Hildesheimer, David Zvi Hoffman, Marcus Horovitz, and Nehemiah Nobel. The figure, though, who captured the public attention and most effectively presented the philosophy behind this "articulate and self-conscious Orthodoxy" was Samson Raphael Hirsch (1808–1888).

Samson Raphael Hirsch

Hirsch knew secular culture at first hand. Despite the fact that his grandfather, Mendel Frankfurter, had organized a Jewish school in Hamburg, Hirsch himself was sent to the local German grammar school. His Jewish studies were influenced by the Rabbi of Hamburg, Isaac Bernays, one of the first rabbis of the new type. At the age of twenty he studied for a year under another model, Jacob Ettlinger. He went on to the University of Bonn, where he developed a friendship with the future Reform leader, Abraham Geiger. In 1830 he accepted a position as the Rabbi of Oldenburg, a post previously held by Nathan Marcus Adler, later to become Chief Rabbi of England. It was there, during his eleven years in office, that Hirsch wrote the works that were to make him famous: *Horeb*, a systematic interpretation of Jewish law, and the *Nineteen Letters on Judaism*, published in 1836.

Hirsch confronted Reform on its own terms. Its premises could be granted, but the conclusions it drew were mistaken. Emancipation was to be welcomed for it offered Jews the chance more fully to live out their mission, which was to be an exemplary people set in the midst of other nations. It was to be a living witness to an existence determined not by the pursuit of power or pleasure but devoted instead to God. This imposed on Jews the "duty of separation, of ethical and spiritual separateness" while at the same time involving themselves in the welfare of their host nation as active and constructive citizens. "Picture every son of Israel a respected and influential priest of righteousness and love, disseminating among the nations not specific Judaism . . . but pure humanity."

This vision countered the claims of both the more defensive traditionalists, who saw participation in secular society as threatening, and the reformers, who argued that it meant giving up Jewish disciplines of "separation." A major part of Hirsch's work was devoted to showing that the commandments, far from being ritual to be accepted or rejected as "tradition," were in fact symbolic enactments of profound ethical truths. Particularly original was his understanding of the *chukkim*, "the nonrational" laws, as ways of living out "justice toward the earth, plants, and animals." Reform claimed to emphasize ethics over ritual. But it was, Hirsch argued, precisely in its ritual that Jewish ethics was concretely expressed. He pilloried Reform as an attempt to ease the burden of Jewish law, seeking to scale down Judaism to the level of man instead of raising man to the level of Torah.

Hirsch's Judaism was breathtakingly free of any nostalgia for the past, for the ghetto and its enclosed culture. "I bless emancipation," he wrote, "when I see how the excess of oppression drove Israel away from a normal life, limited the free development of its noble character, and compelled many individuals to enter . . . upon paths which they were too weak to refuse to enter." The secularization of culture also meant the liberation of Jewish thought from its dependence on non-Jewish systems of philosophy. Hirsch criticized Maimonides for entering "Judaism from without" and presenting it in neo-Aristotelian terms. The spiritual challenge of Jewry's newfound freedom was "to know Judaism out of itself" without apologetics or foreign borrowings.

The challenge could be met by a new form of Jewish education, one in which secular studies would be pursued from a specifically Jewish vantage point. "Nature should be contemplated with the spirit of David; history should be perceived with the ear of an Isaiah." Hirsch called this synthesis, using a mishnaic phrase that had been earlier revived by Wessely, *Torah im derekh eretz*, "Torah combined with the way of the world." He was critical of the schools of his day. The more traditional *chadarim* taught Judaism as "a mechanical habit." The Reform schools saw Judaism as "something which should be interred in the grave of a past long since dead and buried." A new kind of Jewish school would train young Jews to "be as familiar with the language of the Bible as they are with the language of the country in which they live. . . . Their eye should be open to recognize the world around them as God's world and themselves in God's world as His servants."

The Nineteen Letters still, a century and a half after their publication, have the power to surprise by their extraordinary exhilaration at the breakdown of the old structures of Jewish life. To be sure, Hirsch admits, religious authority has been undermined. Reform abounds. The medieval *kehillah* has been dismantled. There are grave dangers that Jews will prefer economic and social advance to religious duty. But in the new freedom no authority can compromise the pursuit of truth and the power of example. Hirsch is absolutely confident that authentic Judaism will thrive by the competition of ideas in an open society. "Let the scales swing! The freer they hang and the more violently they now swing up and down, the truer and purer will be the estimate of the right principle of faith and life which they will determine in the end."

Modern Orthodoxy

Hirsch was uncompromisingly Orthodox. Though he welcomed modernity, he made it clear that if there was a conflict between Judaism and the ethos of the age, it was the latter that would have to give way. "Instead of complaining that [Torah] is no longer suitable to the times, our only complaint must be that the times are no longer suitable to it."

He was bitterly critical of Reform's reduction of Judaism's demands to the social aspirations of the bourgeoisie. It had, he said, "distilled the ancient world-ranging spirit of the Torah into a single aromatic drop of perfume so fragrant that . . . they could carry it round with them in their waistcoat pockets without being ashamed." He was no less critical of the more conservative Zechariah Frankel for suggesting that the Oral Law was subject to historical development. He reserved some of his sharpest remarks for the movement for the academic study of Judaism, "Jewish Science." To treat Judaism as a subject of detached historical analysis was, he argued, to rob it of all vitality. "What they have produced is not a physiology of living Judaism, but a pathological anatomy of a Judaism which according to their idea is already dead." It was a criticism to be echoed a century later, in almost the same language, by the secularist Gershom Scholem.

But, though he himself did not use the term, Hirsch's Orthodoxy was distinctively modern. There was no going back to the ghetto, which he saw as artificially limiting Judaism's intellectual horizons. Hirsch made a clear distinction between custom and law. The particular forms in which Judaism had been expressed in the past were not sacrosanct except when expressly stipulated in the form of halakhah.

On the surface, this expressed itself in a number of cosmetic changes in synagogue style. In Oldenburg Hirsch adopted many of the aesthetic modifications that were associated with the early reformers. In the synagogue he wore clerical robes, preached in high literary German, introduced a choir, and insisted on decorum. He deleted the *Kol Nidre* prayer on Yom Kippur on the grounds that the renunciation of vows was being cited by critics as evidence of Jewish untrustworthiness. In Moravia he performed weddings inside the synagogue, then a new and suspect practice. In the fraught atmosphere of German Jewry these innovations seemed subversive. But Hirsch made a sharp differentiation between style and substance. Judaism could take on modern forms so long as its beliefs and laws were unchanged.

But the perception went deeper. Hirsch was the first to recognize that Jewish identity in the modern state was quite different from what it had been in the enclosed, autonomous community of the Middle Ages. There Judaism embraced the totality of life: language, dress, culture, cuisine. To be sure, it was not hermetically sealed against outside influences. Jews were inveterate borrowers from their surrounding cultures. But within the community such borrowings were quickly naturalized and became part of the organic texture of Jewish life.

Now, under emancipation, Judaism would embrace only part of life: the home, the school, and the synagogue. Vast areas of the Jews' experience—at work, in social life, as a citizen, and as a participant in the arts and sciences—would be conducted in a secular context. Hirsch saw that being secular rather than Christian, these experiences were halakhically neutral and thus permitted. But Jewish identity would not be split, rather than integrated, between Jewish and secular involvements—Torah and an increasingly significant *derekh eretz*. Hirsch called this dual personality *Mensch-Jissroel*, "man-Israel."

Hirsch did not see this as an inner conflict. But it is precisely here that his thought had most in common with nineteenth-century Reform. The synthesis between the two identities is created by Hirsch's emphasis on the Jewish "missions" to humanity, and his marked downplaying of Judaism's national motifs. The land and State of Israel were, he argued, not significant in themselves. They were merely one context of Judaism's religious role. Exile and dispersion were not a disaster. Instead they "opened a new, great and widespread field for the fulfillment of its mission." Jews prayed for a return to Zion, but that lay in the messianic future and "actively to accelerate its coming is prohibited to us." Hirsch was neutral or negative toward the developing Zionist movement, unlike his contemporary, Hildesheimer, and his Italian counterpart, Samuel David Luzzatto. His successors took this further and led the campaign for Orthodox dissociation from the Zionist movements, which resulted in the creation of *Agudat Yisrael*.

Hirsch, in other words, created an Orthodoxy for a post-emancipation diaspora. It proved remarkably effective, though not quite in the way he intended. European society was in no mood to regard Jews as models of "pure humanity." Nor did the academic study of science and history lend themselves, as Hirsch had hoped, to religious interpretation. To the contrary, Darwinian biology and Hegelian history challenged, if they did not refute, religious belief. What emerged instead was a *compartmentalized* identity, and what Hirsch's model community in Frankfurt showed was that such an identity—nurtured and supported by a strong school and synagogue framework—was viable and could be passed on across the generations.

One could be part of the modern world without religious compromise. But there was a price to be paid in divided selfhood. The traditional harmony of the religious personality was gone. That lack of integration between the Jew as Jew and as secular citizen has haunted modern Orthodoxy to the present day. A much later thinker, R. Joseph Soloveitchik, was to come to the conclusion, in the sharpest possible contrast to medieval Jewish thought, that the essence of religious experience lay in ceaseless conflict.

Rav Avraham Kook

Not surprisingly, there were others who dissented strongly from this conception of Jewish life. Traditionally, Judaism had embraced both private and public life. One could not confine it within the space allocated by modern society to religion—the family and the local congregation—without robbing it of its breadth, richness, and

diversity. The dichotomy, essential to diaspora modern Orthodoxy, between religious and secular, ran counter to the whole
thrust of Judaism which sought the sanctification of all aspects of
existence. The Torah had envisaged this taking place through the
building of an ideal society in the land of Israel. In exile, in their
autonomous communities, Jews had created a kind of surrogate
Israel with its own clear borders and its self-sufficient culture. But
the ghetto and *shtetl* were disintegrating. Emancipation now made
the terms of exile intolerable. Judaism would survive only among
the few, and even then in artificial and constricted forms. There
was no alternative but to rise to the challenge of messianic destiny
and once again attempt to build a Torah-centric society on the soil
of the promised land.

No one presented this view more forcibly than R. Avraham
ha-Cohen Kook (1865–1935), an Eastern European mystic who
became the first Chief Rabbi of Palestine. R. Kook came from
a world different from that of Samson Raphael Hirsch. The Jews
of Eastern Europe, unlike those of Germany, developed no
Reform movement. Enlightenment and the breakdown of tradition
came instead in the form of an often militant secularism. And
whereas Western European culture encouraged an emphasis on
the individual, the East was more collectivist in its thought. From
these influences came Jewish socialism and communism, movements for a Jewish cultural identity expressed in Yiddish and
Hebrew literature, and the main body of support for political
Zionism.

R. Kook could not interpret these expressions of secular Jewish
identity as negatively as Hirsch had seen Reform. Firstly, they
were strong affirmations of Jewishness, without the assimilationism
that haunted German Jewry. Secondly, some of the secularists had
deep roots in the tradition. Volozhyn Yeshivah, where R. Kook had
studied, included among its alumni the poet Chaim Nachman
Bialik (1873–1934), the writer Mischa Berdyczewski (1865–1921),
and the historian and literary critic Joseph Klausner (1874–1958),
all approximate contemporaries of Kook. Volozhyn, despite its
rigid policy of excluding secular study, became a center of heated
debate among its students about Zionism and modern thought. It
was here that R. Kook discovered the religious roots of Jewish

secularism. Thirdly, he was intellectually and temperamentally a mystic, convinced of the inner holiness of the Jewish soul, however rebellious its outer manifestations. These perceptions combined to produce the most positive evaluation ever given by an Orthodox thinker of non- and antireligious Jews. How, then, was the breakdown of Judaism to be explained and overcome?

The explanation lay in the face of exile, *galut*. The solution lay in the end of exile by the return of Jews to Eretz Yisrael. No Jewish thinker since the prophets had expressed himself in such visionary terms about the renewal of Jewish life in its land. "Eretz Yisrael," he wrote, "is part of the very essence of our nationhood; it is bound organically to its very life and inner being." Biblical, rabbinic, philosophical, and mystical motifs fuse in Kook's remarkable rhapsody to the power of the land to overcome the doubts and conflicts of exile. "It is the air of the land of Israel that makes one wise, that illuminates the soul to enlighten that element which is derived from the world of unity. In the land of Israel one draws upon the light of Jewish wisdom, upon that quality of spiritual life which is unique to the people of Israel, upon the Jewish world view and way of life which are essentially derived from the dominance of the world of unity over the divided world."

Exile leads to the slow death of the soul. In the diaspora "the pristine well of the Jewish spirit stops running." Judaism survives, but in attenuated forms, as the study of texts and the fulfillment of the commands. It is no longer coextensive with the whole of life. It cannot live in the present, for it is sustained only by the past and the future "by the power of a vision and by the memory of our glory." Naturally, then, some larger spirits—Kook called them "souls of chaos"—grow restless with conceptualized and institutionalized Judaism, and rebel. These are the "pangs of cleansing" that precede the messianic age. Exile has reached its natural and Providential end. "The diaspora is disintegrating at an alarming rate, and there is no hope for it unless it replants itself by the wellspring of real life . . . which can be found only in Eretz Yisrael."

The heart of the religious consciousness, for R. Kook, is the sense of the unity of all creation. Evil is only apparent. All falsehood comes from seeing objects, events, and ideas as things in themselves. Once their place in the order of creation becomes clear, so too does their goodness and essential sanctity. Thus socialism, considered in itself, is evil. It leads to materialism and oppression. But it has a holy core. It is a protest against injustice. Secular Zionism is an evil when it takes nationalism as an end in itself. It too, though, is essentially holy for it embodies a self-transcending love for the Jewish people. In R. Kook's kabbalistic terminology, exile is the "world of division" and tends naturally to make Jews think in segmented and divisive ways. Israel is the "world of unity" which will harmonize, and therefore sanctify, the various Jewish secularisms.

As well as unity, R. Kook's thought turns constantly on the idea of *teshuvah* or return, understood in its full range of biblical and rabbinic resonances: the religious return to tradition, the ethnic return to peoplehood, and the geographical return to the land. The three are inseparable. *Teshuvah* had been understood in rabbinic thought primarily as repentance for sin. But for R. Kook, sin means separation and *teshuvah* means reunification. Even secular Zionism was therefore part of this process, for it had reunited Jews with their people and land, and the third component—reunification of Jews with Judaism—was bound to follow. All this is seen, in R. Kook's writings, as part of the Divine flow of time, an evolutionary current that was bearing Jews, with or against their will, toward a spiritual rebirth.

R. Kook's conception of Judaism is almost a polar opposite of that of Hirsch. Far from seeing *derekh eretz* as neutral, R. Kook believed that the religious task was to sanctify the secular: agricultural labor, the arts and sciences, and the political process. He saw positive significance in the founding of the Bezalel Academy of Arts and the Hebrew University in Jerusalem. General culture, he wrote, was like a garment. Specifically religious acts were like the fringes on the garment, which revealed it to be a holy object. But Jews could only sanctify a culture that was in essence a Jewish culture. This was now impossible in the diaspora. Emancipation, far from heralding a new mission for Jews in exile, in fact signaled the end of that long chapter of Jewish history. A revival beckoned, but it would take place elsewhere.

The Strategy of Resistance

Hirsch and Kook represent the working out, within the parameters of tradition, of the tensions that produced the two great breaks with tradition—Reform Judaism and secular Zionism, respectively. Hirsch showed that the rich premodern life of Torah could be translated into the narrower ambit of a "religion" without any halakhic or ideological concessions to modernity. Kook showed that the idea of Judaism as the spirit of a "nation" could be articulated without secularizing the ideas of land, state, or people. Alongside Hirsch was a range of thinkers who, while subscribing to his idea of *Torah im derekh eretz*, interpreted it somewhat differently; most notably, R. Soloveitchik. Alongside R. Kook, too, were those who saw the relationship between Judaism and Zionism in less messianic, more pragmatic terms, most notably, R. Isaac Reines. Hirsch and Kook, then, do not between them exhaust the range of Orthodox responses to modernity, but they do define two broad directions, what one might loosely call modern Orthodoxy on the one hand and religious Zionism on the other.

But there was a third alternative. This was to reject the terms of Clermont-Tonnerre's choice altogether, and decline the offer of emancipation. Sociologists call this strategy neotraditionalism. In the contemporary Jewish vocabulary it is sometimes described as ultra- or right-wing or *charedi* Orthodoxy. What is important for our analysis is that—in common with Hirsch and R. Kook, and unlike chasidism and nineteenth-century English and French Jewries—it arises from a conscious confrontation with modernity. It is not tradition as such, but Orthodoxy in the presence of alternatives. Though it negates modern culture, it is dialectically related to it. Its architect was the great leader of Hungarian Jewry in the early nineteenth century, R. Moses Sofer (the *Chatam Sofer*, 1762–1839).

Born and educated in Frankfurt, R. Sofer had seen at first hand the early impact of the Enlightenment. Convinced that secularization carried greater dangers for Jewish continuity than the religious persecutions that had preceded it, he set about organizing an active defense of the old order. In strict halakhic terms, for example, Moses Mendelssohn had not advocated any religious reforms. But he had begun the process of German-Jewish acculturation. His translation of the Bible into German was, for many, the gateway into a new language and from there into its new and disruptive ideas. R. Sofer sharply opposed the translation, as he did the schools that had been created along the lines recommended by Wessely. They were attempts to rationalize tradition and render it acceptable to the intellectual assumptions of the age. As a result they would expose it to an environment in which it could not survive. What Hirsch was later to see as neutral, permissible changes of custom and style, R. Sofer saw as the first breaches in the fence around Jewish identity. Adapting a talmudic maxim, he declared *chadash assur min ha-Torah,* "the new is biblically forbidden."

His successors were to view the kind of adaptations undertaken by German Orthodoxy as a danger to Jewish survival, a kind of incipient reform. They opposed aesthetic changes in the synagogue—vernacular sermons, choirs, ministerial robes, and moving the *bimah* or reader's platform from the center to the front of the synagogue. Though R. Sofer was not opposed to all forms of secular education, he was certainly averse to giving it the independent legitimacy later to be implied in Hirsch's ideal of synthesis. His followers were also deeply suspicious of the professionalization of the rabbinate. Azriel Hildesheimer, who was ultimately to found a successful rabbinical seminary in Berlin, encountered massive opposition when he first attempted the project in the Austro-Hungarian community of Eisenstadt.

Underlying these attitudes was a judgment sharply at odds with that of Hirsch and Kook. Modernity is systematically destructive of Jewish faith, observance, and identity. There is no way of negotiating it successfully, either through diaspora synthesis or the dynamic of a Jewish state. The alternative is to resist it. This is not in itself a novel idea within the Jewish tradition. In a sense, Jewish life in biblical and rabbinic times had been built on separation and segregation. But the old barriers were collapsing. New ones had therefore to be erected in their place. This meant a conscious, deliberate, and voluntary withdrawal from secular society, and ultimately from those elements of the Jewish community that had accommodated themselves to it. The significance of R. Moses Sofer in the development of modern Jewry is that he saw the choice in these clear-cut terms and made his decision unerringly against the current of the age.

But this in itself would not have been successful had it not been for his further foresight. Only a minority could be expected to opt for an Orthodoxy thus defined. The problem was how to make that minority self-sustaining and turn it into an elite that would eventually, through its leadership, feed back into the wider community. The answer lay in the creation of a new institution, or rather the evolution of one of Judaism's oldest institutions: the yeshivah. The yeshivah had traditionally been simply a place of talmudic instruction and had been closely linked to the local community. The new yeshivah was to differ from the old in several important respects. It would be an independent establishment, financed by voluntary donations elicited by its emissaries. It would draw its students from a wide geographical catchment area. Its aim would not be merely educational. It would create within its walls an intense, enclosed, and total environment from which secular ideas would be excluded. Its students would be a peer group, a spiritual aristocracy. They would be encouraged to see themselves as the select guardians of tradition. They would be leaders in the defense of faith. The yeshivah would become, in other words, a fortress against a hostile world.

R. Sofer created his yeshivah shortly after his arrival in Pressburg in 1808. It quickly became the largest since Babylonian times. Others appeared throughout Eastern Europe: Mir, Slobodka, Telz, Lomza, and Ponevezh among them. Perhaps the most famous was the yeshivah of Volozhyn, founded in 1802 by R. Chaim Volozhiner and renowned for its outstanding teachers, R. Naftali Berlin (the *Netziv*, 1817–1893), and R. Joseph Baer Soloveitchik (the *Bet ha-Levi*, 1820–1892) and his son R. Chaim Soloveitchik (the *Brisker*, 1853–1918). Each had its own distinctive subculture and style of study, and they generated strong loyalties among their alumni.

During the second half of the eighteenth century, the confrontation that divided East European Jewry came between *Chasidim* and their opponents, the *Mitnagdim*. R. Sofer belonged to the antichasidic school. But it quickly became apparent that the two groups were on the same side in the battle against acculturation. Though they did not formally join forces until the founding of

Agudat Yisrael in 1912, they gradually developed strong structural similarities.

On the one hand, the yeshivah created an environment not unlike that of a chasidic community. Removed from home, segregated from the local community at a formative period of their lives, the students came to invest their yeshivah heads with the same kind of quasiparental authority with which *chasidim* regarded their Rebbes. Leadership dynasties began to appear, not least of which was represented by R. Sofer's own son and grandson. Many yeshivot, too, found it necessary to supplement talmudic study with devotional and ethical teaching. *Musar,* as this group of disciplines became known, was nonmystical, but it was a functional equivalent of Chasidism. In the opposite direction, as the nineteenth century progressed, the chasidic movement itself began to emphasize talmudic study and create its own yeshivot. Chasidic leadership became less charismatic and more organizational. Despite their profound differences, the two movements were converging sociologically and institutionally.

Covenantal Interactions

These, then, were the traditional alternatives. There were the Jewries of England, France, and Italy which adapted to modernity without the need for philosophical self-definition. There was German Orthodoxy, born out of the confrontation with Reform, epitomized in Samson Raphael Hirsch's articulate synthesis of Judaism and secular culture. There was R. Kook's religious Zionism, with its unique blend of mysticism and East European collectivism. And there was the movement, initiated in Hungary by R. Moses Sofer, to resist modernity by creating enclaves of Jewish learning.

They differed in their cultural styles and in their evaluation of and interactions with the wider society. Their emphases were different, as were their images of the ideal Jewish life. It should be clear though that these variations, pronounced though they were, were less due to the inner logic of Judaism than to the encounter between Judaism and several very different societies. In each case the Orthodox objective was the same: to preserve a community that embodies the values by which Jewish lives had been lived since biblical times. How this was best to be achieved depended on the social context. What was viable in Germany was judged counterproductive in Hungary. The challenges to Judaism differed between Berditchev and Birmingham.

What the various Orthodoxies held in common was the conviction that Jewish values and law were not human constructs, open to change, but a Divine revelation, commanding loyalty through the generations. They were nonnegotiable. Even radical social and intellectual upheaval could not change the terms of the covenant on which Jewish existence was based. If Jews had survived the destruction of the Second Temple and the loss of national autonomy, the Crusades and the blood libels, the Spanish Inquisition and Chmielnicki massacres, they would survive the blandishments and animosities of emancipation, and on the same terms: according to the laws of Moses and Israel. To the question, Which takes precedence, Sinai or the spirit of the age? an Orthodox Jew can give only one answer. Samson Raphael Hirsch spoke for all when he wrote: "We declare before heaven and earth that if our religion demanded that we should renounce what is called civilization and progress we would obey unquestioningly, because our religion is for us truly religion, the word of God before which every other consideration has to give way."

We have charted the diverging paths of Jewish modernity. The Count of Clermont-Tonnerre's speech to the French National Assembly in 1789 set in motion a fundamental questioning of Jewish identity that has lasted to the present. Some saw it as essentially religious, but were convinced that Judaism must make accommodations to its new environment. Thus were born a series of denominations, Reform, Liberal, Reconstructionist, and Conservative. Others saw it as essentially national. From them flowed a succession of Jewish secularisms, cultural, political, ethnic, and above all, secular Zionism, the project of rebuilding the Jewish people within the framework of its own modern state.

There were those, though, who believed as a matter of profound religious faith that the Jewish destiny must continue the path trodden by Abraham, Moses, Hillel, Akiva, Rashi, Maimonides, the Baal Shem Tov, and the Vilna Gaon. They were labeled by their opponents, "Orthodox." The existence of the adjective testified to the schisms already dividing European Jewry. Orthodoxy itself was united in seeing that the religious and national elements of Judaism could not be divorced from one another. But it was internally divided as to which should be emphasized as the imperative of the hour. Samson Raphael Hirsch stressed the religious, R. Kook, the national. Each agreed that modernity promised benefits as well as dangers to Jewish life. From this judgment, R. Sofer on the one hand, *chasidim* on the other, dissented. Judaism, they argued, should resist rather than go with the flow of the times.

Two hundred years later, how have these alternatives fared? Which evaluations proved accurate and which strategies successful? What is the state of Jewish identities in the late twentieth century?

PART III
PRESENT

4

Contemporary Affirmations

On the threshold of modernity Voltaire delivered a prediction. "When the society of man is perfected . . . the number of Jews will necessarily diminish. The rich among them are already beginning to detest their superstitions; theirs will be no more than the lot of people without arts and laws who, no longer able to enrich themselves through our negligence, will no longer be able to sustain a separate society, and who . . . ignorant even of their own books, will assimilate among the scum of other peoples."

One cannot evaluate the impact of modernity on Jewish life without coming to terms with the harsh implications of Voltaire's remark. Delivered in 1761, it was a secularized equivalent of an ancient Christian belief. Jews, in that theological perspective, would ultimately disappear as a separate people through their conversion to Christianity. Samuel Heilman has noted that emancipation was, in a sense, a "new version of the age-old Christian efforts to convert Jews." Now, instead of demanding a religious transformation, "Christians were demanding a Jewish conversion to secular citizenship." The effect would be the same. Through enlightenment, cultured Jews would be cured of their primitive religious beliefs. The others would lack leadership, knowledge, and, in the new commercial order, an economic base. They would simply disappear.

Visions of the End

It is impossible to read the literature of the nineteenth century without sensing how deeply this perception had, in one way or another, been internalized by Jews. Jews were in flight from Judaism. There were the systematic attempts of Spinoza, Marx, and Freud to exorcise Judaism by curing mankind of religion in general. Rational thought in the case of Spinoza, social and economic revolution in the case of Marx, and the cure of neuroses in the case of Freud would free humanity from the grip of religion and bring Judaism to an end.

There was the drive to assimilation, felt throughout Western Europe and the early Jewish settlement in America. Liberal Jews shared the conviction that anti-Semitism was, as Arthur Hertzberg has put it, a "chastisement for the sin of imperfect assimilation and the goad toward the messianic day when the Jews, by completely refashioning themselves in the image of proper Westerners, would have won the acceptance that they would then merit."

There was the alienation that Thorstein Veblen saw as the essence of the modern Jewish intellectual. "It is by loss of allegiance, or at best by force of a divided allegiance to the people of his origin, that he finds himself in the vanguard of modern enquiry." And there was the complex psychology of Jewish self-hatred from Ludwig Boerne and Heinrich Heine to Otto Weininger and Theodor Lessing.

Mordecai Kaplan began his analysis of twentieth-century Jewry with the sentence, "Before the beginning of the nineteenth century all Jews regarded Judaism as a privilege; since then most Jews have come to regard it as a burden." It was a burden they sought, where possible, to escape. The early Reform literature is pervaded by a sense of crisis. A generation of Jews was growing up with little knowledge of and still less sympathy for their religious heritage. Judaism was disintegrating, and there was a desperate need to salvage something, however reduced, of its essence.

The literature of nineteenth-century Orthodoxy is still more fraught. It has an overwhelming mood of pathos. The old structures were collapsing and religious leaders were powerless in the face of change. After the First World War, even the last refuge of tradition, the East European *shtetl*, was beginning to dissolve. In the year that the modernist Kaplan was diagnosing the fate of American Judaism, a traditionalist in Eastern Europe was lamenting, "At one time . . . the benches in the *Bet Midrash* in every town were full from corner to corner and the echo of the voice of Torah reached distant places. And now! The benches of the *Bet Midrash* are empty, the sound of Torah is stopped, a terrible stillness hangs over the *Bet Midrash*."

Even those who sought to create new forms of Jewish expression were haunted by the fear that their own work would prove quixotic and futile. One architect of the new "Science of Judaism," Leopold Zunz, declared that it was now possible to study rabbinic literature with academic detachment because the genre was at an end. The living tradition of Hebrew study had been carried "to its grave" and one could now examine it as a "sealed" historical phenomenon. Another member of the movement, Moritz Steinschneider, declared, "We have only one task left: to give the remains of Judaism a decent burial."

That was in Germany. In Eastern Europe secular Jews were creating a literary renewal. But here too there was a mood of fated failure. The poet Y.L. Gordon, wrote, "For whom do I labor? Who will tell me the future, will tell me that I am not the last poet of Zion and you my last readers?" As he was writing, a new poet was emerging, Chaim Nachman Bialik, who described himself, too, as "the last of the last."

The early Zionist theoreticians, for their part, were convinced that Jewish survival in the diaspora was at an end. Pinkser, Nordau, and Herzl saw the problem in terms of the dangerously high and rising current of anti-Semitism. Jacob Klatzkin believed that the Jewish people would disappear of its own accord even without persecution. "The hold of the forms of our religion, which have served as barriers between us and the world for about two thousand years, has weakened and there are no longer any strong ghetto walls to protect a national entity in the *Galut*." Even if some attenuated Judaism were to survive, it would not, he declared, be "worthy of survival." Jews would be condemned to a "rootless and restless wandering between two worlds" and would become "individuals diseased by ambivalence, consumed by contradictions, and spent by restless inner conflict."

If there is one leitmotif running through Jewish and non-Jewish responses to emancipation, it is that Jewish existence, especially in the diaspora, had reached its final chapter. Here and there Jews might remain. But Judaism, or some affirmative Jewish identity, was beyond recovery. These are not the stray perceptions of individuals afflicted with more than usual melancholy. They embody a mood that dominated several generations and ran across the entire ideological spectrum. One writer, Alan Miller, has described the nineteenth century as a collective Jewish nervous breakdown. Not since the Book of Lamentations had there been such bleak and unrelieved pessimism about the Jewish future.

The Persistence of Jewishness

The obituary was premature. Surveying the contemporary Jewish world two centuries after the French Revolution and the destructive and self-destructive forces it set in motion, a Jew surely feels moved—even as he remembers the ovens of Auschwitz—to recite the ancient words of the *she-hecheyanu* blessing, "Who has kept us alive, and helped us to survive, and brought us to this time." For the first time in almost two thousand years there is again a Jewish state in the land of Israel. Jews flourish in the diaspora. There is an unprecedented revival of Jewish learning. There are more Jews studying in yeshivot than at any time since the days of the Babylonian academies. In America, there are more than a thousand Jewish studies programs in universities. The literature of Jewish self-hatred is at an end. The fact of Jewish birth is no longer viewed as a burden, a stigma, a misfortune. All this seemed improbable in 1789, impossible in 1939. A half century after the Final Solution, young Jews sing in the streets of Jerusalem, *Am Yisrael chai*. The people Israel lives.

Why has it happened? Why did Jewish identity not simply

evaporate during the nineteenth and early twentieth centuries, as had been predicted by the most informed observers? There are no simple answers. But this at least is clear. The social processes that were generally believed to be moving in a single direction turned out to be more complex and multifaceted than was recognized at the time. Against the current of assimilation there were reactions and resistances. In part, these had to do with the unique Jewish experience of modernity. In part, they parallel more general trends in the secularization of society.

Assimilation is a two-way process. It implies a willingness on the part of a minority to be absorbed. But it also implies a willingness on the part of the majority to absorb. The liberal theorists who first propounded the social and political programs of emancipation had inordinate faith in the power of reason to dispel prejudice and superstition. They tacitly assumed that hostility to Jews in the majority society was a relic of Christian attitudes. Once culture became predominantly secular, tolerance would follow. The disappearance of anti-Jewish discrimination would open the way to the absorption of Jews into the social mainstream.

They reckoned without the persistence of prejudice. As Max Nordau was to say in his speech to the First Zionist Congress in 1897, "In order to produce its full effect, emancipation should first have been realized in sentiment before it was proclaimed by law." It was not. Suspicion of Jews remained. Law and theory were in advance of the public mood. The liberals were guilty, he said in retrospect, of trying to impose "creations of pure intellect [on] the world in reality." The result was a rebellion of popular sentiment and the mutation of Christian anti-Judaism into its secular equivalent: racial anti-Semitism.

Jews found themselves being excluded, as Jacob Katz has documented, from supposedly secular meeting grounds such as the Masonic lodges. Unless they converted and were baptized, they found avenues of professional advancement closed to them in the civil service, sciences and arts, and in the universities. There were many tragic cases of Jews who had made every effort to cast off their Jewish heritage and yet who found themselves rejected by the Gentile society of which they had tried so assiduously to become a part. Again, Nordau went to the heart of the problem. The emancipated Jew, he said, "flees from his Jewish fellows, because anti-Semitism has taught him too to be contemptuous of them, but his Gentile compatriots repulse him as he attempts to associate with them. He has lost his home in the ghetto, yet the land of his birth is denied to him as his home."

But if conversion was to be the only route to social acceptance, it was not a price most Jews were willing to pay. This was not an attitude of Orthodox Jews only. Across a wide range of commitments, the act of baptism seemed to Jews to be dishonorable, a form of betrayal. Even converted Jews, like Heine, were ambivalent about what they had done. Heine himself wrote a friend in 1826, "I am now hated by Christian and Jew alike. I am truly sorry that I permitted myself to be baptized. I do not see that my lot has improved; rather, since then, I have had nothing but ill-luck."

The Paradox of Assimilation

The combination of anti-Semitism and persisting Jewish loyalties led to a paradoxical development. It was precisely those who had been most inclined to assimilation who were most affected by, and sensitized to, anti-Jewish attitudes in the host society. Within the traditional community, an increasingly tolerant approach to Christianity had developed from the seventeenth century onwards, and this was sustained during the nineteenth century. It was the reformers, among them Abraham Geiger and Ludwig Philippsohn, and later Moritz Lazarus, Hermann Cohen, and Leo Baeck, who developed a systematic critique of Christianity and set out to prove the superiority of Judaism.

At a later stage it was a succession of deeply estranged Jews— Moses Hess, Leon Pinsker, Max Nordau, and Theodor Herzl— who were radicalized by anti-Semitism into a new affirmation of Jewish identity in the form of secular Zionism. The dialect of Jewish courtship and Gentile refusal led, in other words, to new Jewish affirmations among those who were least disposed to maintain a traditional Jewish identity.

The same process had been at work in more recent times among secular Jewish intellectuals. The model here is Franz Kafka, and the group includes writers and critics like George Steiner, Leslie Fiedler, and Lionel Trilling. For them the very feeling of marginality, of belonging nowhere, becomes the content and basis of a new mode of Jewishness. The paradox was best expressed by the writer Frederic Raphael who declared, "I feel myself alien from everyone. This is my kind of Jewishness."

The dialectic was to have a further turn. For it was to those who had experienced these schizophrenic identities that the completely non-Westernized Jew had made a powerful impact as a figure of wholeness, vigor, and authenticity. Already in 1862 the secularized Moses Hess was contrasting German Jewry unfavorably with the *chasidim*, whom he held up as models of Jewish vitality. The process became more marked during the early decades of the twentieth century, partly because East European Jews were beginning to arrive in Germany in increasing numbers, and partly because the First World War took Jews serving in the German army eastward, where some encountered the *shtetl* for the first time. The *Ostjude*, or Eastern Jews, became a powerful symbol in the imagination of assimilated Jews, as an antidote to the rationalized, diluted, acculturated Judaism they saw among their parents and peers.

Among those who were affected by this mood of anti-Westernization were Franz Rosenzweig, Martin Buber, Gershom Scholem, and Jiri Langer. In Rosenzweig's case it led to a partial return to tradition; in Langer's yet more so. But it generated a more fundamental intellectual turn, away from the rationalism and universalism that had held a previous generation captive, towards a reassessment of the Jewish mystical tradition and the value of an unapologetic assertion of Jewish differentness. In Buber and Scholem it led onward to Zionism.

The religious history of European Jewry between the First and Second World Wars has been insufficiently studied, dwarfed as it was by the cataclysms of the nineteenth century on the one hand and the Holocaust on the other. But it was a period of Orthodox revival, one in which many new *yeshivot* were opened and in which the Orthodox community became more self-confident and politically active. The circle around Franz Rosenzweig was not the only one in which *teshuvah*—a return to Jewish roots and sources—was in the air. Had the *shoah* not killed the movement in its infancy, a major shift of sentiment might have gathered momentum. As it was, in the wake of the destruction, Jewish life shifted to Israel and America, two relatively new Jewries institutionally and demographically. The *teshuvah* movement did not make its appearance there until the 1960s, where it took observers by surprise.

In retrospect, though, this now appears to be part of the inner dynamic of modernization, in which assimilatory forces are countered in later generations by the search for authenticity. Sociologists have formulated this elegantly as Hansen's law: the third generation seeks to remember what the second generation labored to forget. Earlier gestures of acculturation now come to be seen as compromises. Jews who had avoided or resisted the modernization process now stand out, not as anachronisms but as archetypes of integrity and wholeness. Counterassimilation as well as assimilation is part of the dynamic of modernity.

The Limits of Secularization

But the revival of Jewish identity has been part of a more widespread phenomenon. Sociologists, until the 1950s, had widely held to a cluster of assumptions about the effects of modernization on religious and ethnic behavior. The "secularization thesis" predicted a gradual decline of the role of religion in society. The growth of scientific knowledge meant, or so it was assumed, that religious beliefs would no longer be needed to explain the universe and the place of the individual within it. As industrialization and bureaucratization changed the face of the economy and government, decisions would be increasingly taken on rational grounds, with tradition playing a diminishing role. The very notion of human progress which so dominated the nineteenth century implied a revolution of thought from a tradition-bound to a future-oriented society. These and other factors combined to signal the marginalization of religion and its eventual eclipse.

What no one predicted was that by the late twentieth century, religion would continue to dominate political conflict in Northern Ireland, Lebanon, the Middle East, and Latin America. Nor was it forseen that there would be a resurgence of conservative or what is sometimes called "fundamentalist" religiosity in both Christianity and Islam. The strength of fundamentalist evangelical Christianity is particularly striking in the United States, a society that has undergone advanced secularization. The same is true about another feature of American society: the growth, especially since the 1960s, of new sects and cults, some utopian, some concerned with the search for mystical experience.

Sociologists are divided as to how to interpret these phenomena. Do they signal the return of religion to a place of prominence, or are they its last death throes? Both cases have been argued. Indeed, Will Herberg, in his *Protestant–Catholic–Jew* (1955) argued that both were true. American society was becoming more religious and more secular at the same time. Religious affiliation and observance was rising but religious belief was declining. Churches and synagogues now had less to do with traditional faith than with social belonging and a celebration of the American way of life. This trend has since been labeled "civil religion," and long before it was identified as such, it had its Jewish theoreticians.

Emile Durkheim (1858–1917), the son of a rabbi and one of the fathers of modern sociology, argued that the function of religion was to create group solidarity. Achad ha-Am (Asher Ginsberg, 1856–1927), the proponent of "cultural" Zionism, applied this to Judaism. Jewish faith and practice were to be reinterpreted as expressions, not of the Divine but of the national will. One of his famous remarks was that "more than the Jewish people has kept the Sabbath, the Sabbath has kept the Jewish people." Judaism could in effect be rewritten with the word "God" deleted and in its place the phrase "the Jewish nation." Mordecai Kaplan (1881–1982), influenced by both Durkheim and Achad ha-Am, proposed a new definition of Judaism as the "evolving religious civilization" of the Jewish people. Religion could fulfill its social function without reference to a supernatural God. He called his philosophy Reconstructionism, and it has organized its own synagogues and rabbinical seminary in America.

Achad ha-Am and Kaplan, in their drastic secularization of Judaism, reveal how traditional forms persist even in the absence of religious belief. But belief itself has not been dethroned to the extent that was once foreseen. The secular state leaves a vacuum in the lives of its citizens. John Stuart Mill foresaw a situation in which the state did not attempt to legislate morality but left it to the private choices of individuals, insofar as they did not harm others. To a large extent this has occurred in Western societies. What he did not foresee was the deeply unsettling effect of the collapse of a shared public morality. Again it was Durkheim who first charted the personal disorientation that ensued. He called it "anomie."

The loss of community, moral absolutes, and a sense of personal meaning have been among the major discontents of secular society. Peter Berger notes that "Modernity has accomplished many far-reaching transformations, but it has not fundamentally changed the finitude, fragility and mortality of the human condition. What it has accomplished is to seriously weaken those definitions of reality that previously made that human condition easier to bear." Here lie some of the roots of the unexpected present strength of religious movements—among them Orthodox Judaism—that emphasize authority, discipline, and objective truth. To the extent that they refuse to admit "modern consciousness" and its pluralism, relativism, and individualism, they become compelling alternatives in a society marked by alienation, confusion, and personal anonymity. They offer clear moral guidance. They give direction to personal life. They allow the individual to inhabit a meaningful universe. They recreate the institutions—above all, the local community and the family—in which life can be lived with a sense of continuity, purposefulness, and historical depth.

To be sure, sociology is not theology. The truth of religious beliefs is unaffected by their attractiveness or otherwise in a given age. But the Jewish believer may well feel that there is a more than accidental relationship between a religious life, personal fulfillment, and the strength of community. Revelation and creation proceed from the same source: therefore, there is an inner connection between the life of the commands and human flourishing. The discontents of secularization, seen from this perspective, point to the impossibility of constructing a social order on human values alone. To say this is, of course, to have made a leap of faith. But even without it, the available evidence points to the striking persistence of religious institutions, some highly secularized, others resolutely not so, long after a previous generation of social theorists had predicted their extinction.

Enduring Ethnicity

The same is true about ethnicity. Just as the secularization thesis envisaged the eclipse of religion, so the "melting pot" theory of the modern state assumed that within three or so generations, the distinctive subcultures of immigrants would be lost as the children and grandchildren progressively acculturated. This process was particularly poignant for Jews, for whom ethnicity and religion are closely intertwined.

Early on in the nineteenth century, French Jews had observed this happening to their own society. "The grandfather believes, the father doubts, the son denies. The grandfather prays in Hebrew, the father prays in French, the son does not pray at all. The grandfather has remained Jewish, the father is assimilated, the son no longer identifies." The problem was compounded by the unique ambivalence many Jews had and still have toward social integration. On the one hand, they wished to retain their group identity. They opposed conversion and intermarriage. On the other hand, they did not seek to be publicly identifiable. Charles Liebman remarks that "Jews incessantly demand that they be treated as if Jewishness does not exist. Nothing pleases most Jews more than to be told that they don't look Jewish or behave Jewishly." The comedian Jackie Mason, who specializes in Jewish ethnic humor, comments on the ambivalence of his audiences. They laugh loudly, then complain at the end of the performance: "Too Jewish." Sidney Morganbesser formulated the axiom of diaspora Jewishness in a memorable phrase: *Incognito, ergo sum.*

Jewish acculturation took place in all societies that opened the doors of emancipation. In America, Jews relentlessly pursued an upward path on the social ladder. The process occurred three times over, first to the early Sefardi immigrants of the eighteenth century, then to the German Jews who arrived between 1815 and 1880, and then to the vast wave of Eastern European immigrants—more than 3,000,000 of them—between 1880 and 1920. Their desire to be Americanized was passionate. Some of the best known anthems to the American dream were written by Jews: Emma Lazarus's poem inscribed on the Statue of Liberty and Irving Berlin's "God Bless America." The route involved a progression from small to larger businesses and from there to management and the professions; a university education; a move to the outer suburbs; and often a change of name. In the late 1940s and early 1950s, some 50,000 Americans each year made court applications to change their family name. Eighty percent of them were Jews.

Part of the process, perceived as such, was an abandonment of Judaism. Religion was a barrier to social mobility. To the second generation, parental piety was part of an Eastern Europe they had left behind. The very secularity of America and its rigid separation of church and state was integral to its openness as a society. Jews became and remain measurably the most secular of all ethnic groups. In a Gallup survey published in 1984, in answer to the question, "Is religion very important in your life?" 61 percent of Protestants and 56 percent of Catholics, but only 25 percent of Jews, answered in the affirmative. A succession of surveys has showed synagogue attendance among Jews to be markedly lower than church attendance among Christians.

If there was one proposition on which the several nineteenth-century approaches to the Jewish future were agreed, it was that there could be no such thing as secular Jewish survival in the diaspora. Jewish identity might be religious in the *golah* or secular in Eretz Yisrael, but these were exclusive alternatives. There could be no persisting ethnic identity outside Israel. This view was expressed well into the second half of the twentieth century by Jewish secularists like Arthur Koestler, Karl Popper, and Georges Friedmann. For the Jew who was not religious, there was a choice between individual assimilation in the diaspora and collective assimilation in Israel.

Recently, however, evidence has been accumulated by American-Jewish observers like Charles Silberman, Calvin Gold-scheider, and Steven M. Cohen to show that Jewish ethnicity survives in surprisingly vigorous forms. Jews, argues Cohen, "may indeed represent the single white refutation of the universality of the melting pot thesis." To be sure, the conclusion depends not only on the evidence but on a particular way of interpreting it. Traditional indicators of Jewish continuity—synagogue affiliation, religious observance, and resistance to intermarriage—show a steady decline. This, for sociologists like Charles Liebman, points toward the undeniable fact of American-Jewish assimilation. The "transformationists," though, argue that new modes of Jewish ethnicity are emerging and it is by these that the community must be judged.

The question, Goldscheider insists, is: Do Jews hold together as an identifiable group? If ethnic strength is to be measured by "the number and intensity of in-group interactions," then the answer is Yes. What emerges from his studies is the paradox that Jews have been so successful in their pursuit of Americanization that they have become more like one another and less like everyone else. They go to college, pursue postgraduate studies, and enter the professions more than any other religious or ethnic grouping. The educational and economic gap between Jews on the one hand, and Protestants and Catholics on the other, has grown larger over time. "The growing occupational similarity among Jews," he argues, "implies greater similarity in lifestyle, residence, values, schooling, family, and economic and political interests. These patterns mesh together in ways to reinforce Jewish cohesion and distinctiveness." If Judaism no longer unites Jews, overachieving does.

Jewish identity, in this analysis, has no definitive content. But it persists. It is measured by relatively loose associations: Jewish friends, Jewish attitudes—in particular, support for the State of Israel—and an occasional religiosity on major Jewish festivals and life-cycle events. There is also evidence to show that the major upheavals associated with assimilation stabilize by the fourth generation, at which point children tend more closely to resemble their parents' behavioral patterns. These newly optimistic forecasts are very recent: they date from the 1980s. As late as 1976, a report of the Harvard Center for Population Studies was predicting a decline of the American Jewish community within a century, from 6,000,000 to 944,000, or in another estimate, 10,420 Jews. The newer perception suggests that just as contemporary urban and suburban culture does not extinguish religion so it does not eliminate ethnicity. Instead it leads to a subtle dialectic of accommodation and resistance, to new modes of Jewish expression, and to the revival, after an initial period of adjustment, of an affirmative Jewishness.

The End of Normalization

These are sociological factors. But perhaps the most notable change that marks the late twentieth century as a significant turn in Jewish modernity lies at the level of consciousness. Throughout the nineteenth century, as we noted at the beginning of the chapter, Jews were profoundly affected by the universalism of Enlightenment thought. This was the intellectual equivalent of the social process of assimilation, and it left little room for Jewish particularity. Humanity, ethics, and religious truth were universal concepts, arrived at by reason and accessible to all. Where, in this scheme of things, was there room for the ideas on which Judaism and Jewishness rested: revelation, a chosen people, and a code of conduct that embodies Jewish singularity and the desire *not* to be like everyone else?

Almost all Jews who entered into an inner dialogue with these Enlightenment assumptions were deeply affected by the conflict. At one level it led to the many visions of the disappearance of Judaism and of Jews as an identifiable people, with the possible exception of a "saving remnant" in the small enclaves of the yeshivot and the chasidic circles. At another level it led, in Reform Judaism, secular Zionism, and among Jewish immigrants to America, to a profound desire for the "normalization" of Jewish existence.

In Reform it led to a negation of religious differentness in favor of a universal ethical mission. In the newly emancipated European Jews and immigrant Americans, it led to a kind of strategic social invisibility. Jews learned not to speak with a Yiddish accent, wear headcoverings in public, or display the indiscreet familiarities of the ghetto. John Murray Cuddihy described this as "the ordeal of civility," and Maurice Samuel reflected that "the Jews are probably the only people in the world to whom it has been promised that their historic destiny is—to be nice." In secular Zionism it led to a negation of the whole ethos of the Jewish past and a desire to be *ke-chol hagoyim*, like all the nations. The Israeli secularist Amnon Rubinstein put it bluntly: "'To be a goy' was . . . the dominant theme of Zionist philosophy in its formative period."

Though these attitudes persist, two seminal events in Jewish history have brought about a revolution in Jewish sensibilities. The first, the Holocaust, was a murderous assault on the Jewish people in its irreducible singularity. Regardless of their faith or lack of it, their nationality, their degree of acculturation or their utility, Jews as such were scheduled for destruction. The second, the birth of the State of Israel, was marked not by harmony but by conflict and immediate war. Israel has not been normalized within the international political arena, and increasingly the phrase that seems to encapsulate her destiny has not been "like all the nations" but *am levadad yishkon*, "the people that dwells alone."

The shift in consciousness was not immediate. But it came with stunning force in the weeks surrounding the 1967 Six Day War. Isolated and under threat, Israel seemed in danger of the unthinkable: a second holocaust. It was then that the trauma of the *shoah*, long repressed, came to the surface both in Israel and the *golah*. The sudden and unexpected victory, and especially the reunification of Jerusalem, seemed to many to be a moment of almost messianic significance. A long-accumulated burden of self-doubt and stigma was lifted. Throughout the world Jews walked with a new pride. Headcoverings, especially the *kippah serugah* or knitted skullcap associated with religious Zionism, reappeared among the young.

Deep connections were made where there had previously been dissociation. American Jewry, which until then had been somewhat passively Zionist, was energized into political and fundraising support for Israel. In Israel itself there was a new consciousness of the diaspora. Hitherto almost all Zionist thinkers had seen Israel as *shelilat ha-golah*, the negation of the diaspora. Israel would end anti-Semitism. As Ben-Gurion argued, hostility to Jews was purely the result of statelessness, of "our peculiar status that does not accord with the established framework of the nations of the world." In the early years of the state, memories of the Holocaust had been deliberately suppressed as a shameful episode of Jewish passivity.

Now many of these attitudes were revised. Diaspora Jewry became suddenly prominent as Israel's sole unconditional ally.

Gentile hostility began to be seen as an enduring feature of Israel's existence. The words of the Haggadah came to mind: "In every generation they rose up against us to destroy us." Memories of the Holocaust, which had been stirred by the Eichmann trial in the early 1960s, surfaced in 1967 in the form of the imperative, "Never again."

The Return of Jewish Particularism

The Six Day War was a unique moment which gave dramatic focus to trends that had been slowly forming before: the emergent ethnicity of Jews in the diaspora and a search for identity among a new generation of Israelis. In retrospect it may yet emerge as the most significant catalyst of Jewish identity since the events of 1789. A period of history was over. Jews had passed through the fires of emancipation. In America they had acquired acceptance and social standing. In Israel they had achieved statehood. The battles of the nineteenth century no longer needed to be fought.

The Jewish people had survived the lure of assimilation and the onslaught of attempted genocide. The *shoah* taught that Jews could not hide their singularity. After 1967 it seemed that Israel too was being forced into a special destiny. Writing in the wake of the Six Day War, Milton Himmelfarb perfectly described the mood that came over Jews throughout the world: "Each Jew knows how thoroughly ordinary he is; yet taken together, we seem caught up in things great and inexplicable. . . . The number of Jews in the world is smaller than a small statistical error in the Chinese census. Yet we remain bigger than our numbers. Big things seem to happen around us and to us."

A. Roy Eckardt has described the change as the "new Jewish stand," a determination to stand up to the world, assertive and unashamed. Its most significant feature is a revival of particularism. Jewish concerns have turned inward, toward Israel and Jewish survival. Jews in the diaspora have become more activist and high profile. Though the religious meaning of the Holocaust and the State of Israel remains elusive and much debated, their existential impact has been clear. Israel is the affirmation of life over

Auschwitz's shadow of death. Jewish survival has become charged with a vast resonance.

Emil Fackenheim, again writing in 1967, gave these ideas their most famous formulation: "I confess I used to be highly critical of Jewish philosophies which seemed to advocate no more than survival for survival's sake. I have changed my mind. I now believe that in this present, unbelievable age, even a mere collective commitment to Jewish group-survival for its own sake is a momentous response, with the greatest implications." It translates itself, he said, into a 614th commandment. "The authentic Jew of today is forbidden to hand Hitler yet another, posthumous victory." Whether frustrating Hitler is an adequate or healthy basis for Jewish continuity is open to question. But the quest for normalization was over. The concern was now for the survival of the *am segulah*, the people that with or against its will has singularity thrust upon it.

The effects have been evident in several directions. In American Reform Judaism there has been a gradual turn back toward traditional forms. Bar mitzvah ceremonies have reappeared in place of or in addition to "confirmation." There has been renewed interest in halakhah. Hebrew plays a larger part in the liturgy. The Reform movement has begun creating its own day schools. Hitherto it had insisted that religion, not peoplehood, was the essence of Judaism. But in its latest major statement, the "Centenary Perspective" of 1976, it declared that "the survival of the Jewish people is of the highest priority." In 1885 it had been frankly anti-Zionist. By 1976 it was asserting that "we consider the State of Israel vital to the welfare of Judaism everywhere." Collectively, these represent a Copernican revolution when compared with the universalist and antiritual Pittsburgh Platform of 1885.

In Israel too, as Charles Liebman and Eliezer Don-Yehiyah have documented, the new "civil religion" has reversed many of the assumptions of the Zionist-socialist founders. Religious symbols and concepts are more widely used. There is a convergence of Israeli and Jewish identities. In part this had been due to the increasing demographic impact of the Oriental Jewish immigrants, more traditional than the East European secularists who constituted the majority of the pre-state *yishuv*. But the politics of the last twenty years have also been significant. Surrounded by enemies, in a world perceived to be hostile, Israelis have found traditional images of the tense relationship between Jacob and Esau more relevant than Zionist-socialist universalism.

The destinies of Israel and the *golah* have become more closely interlinked. Far from negating the diaspora, Israel has provided it with a focus of identity. The either/or of the nineteenth century— either Judaism as a religion in the diaspora or as a nation in Eretz Yisrael—has been transcended. They have emerged not as two exclusive alternatives but instead as a complex symbiosis, each supporting the other in a variety of ways. Perhaps the single word that best describes the new Jewish focus is not religion or nationalism but *peoplehood*, understood as an identification with Jews throughout the world and their shared history, culture, and traditions. This is not necessarily expressed in terms of religious belief. Still less is it reflected in a widespread return to halakhic observance. But it marks the end of the chapter opened by emancipation, and the beginning of what one might call Jewish post modernity.

Prediction and Promise

A new era in Jewish history, one that we have charted in the last three chapters, began with Voltaire's prediction of the disappearance of the Jews. Emancipation posed a fateful choice for Jewish identity and initiated a series of redefinitions which deeply fragmented the Jewish people. It induced widespread doubts about the internal capacity of Jews to survive. There were external fears too. Racial anti-Semitism was rising throughout Europe. It exploded in the Russian pogroms of the 1880s. There were Jews who were aware that this was only the beginning. In Leon Pinsker's *Auto-emancipation* (1882), one of the seminal documents of the nineteenth century, the shadow of death already hangs heavily over the Jewish people. Jews are "ghosts," "no longer alive, and yet moving about among the living," a chosen people only in the sense of the people chosen for universal hatred "For the living, the Jew is a dead man."

Voltaire, a man of enlightenment, had believed that Jews would disappear of their own accord. "We ought not," he said "to burn them." That was in 1756. By 1833, a German writer using the name Dominicus Haman Epiphanes was less patient. After contemplating several alternatives for making the world *Judenrein*, he concluded that "the total extermination of Jewry would be incomparably easier." Jews, he wrote, could be turned into "tallow candles, iron medals, or pretty milk-white glass." Next, "a competition in the field of economics would be announced, whose subject would be according to which principles the total massacre of Jewry could be used to improve the soil." The unthinkable had been uttered. A century later it began to be planned. Enlightenment ended in Holocaust. Jewish children were burned to the music of string quartets.

By its close, the Central and Eastern European Jewries who had given the Jewish world its revolutionary new identities and its most spirited defenses of tradition, had been reduced to ashes. The Reform Temple in Hamburg, the Russian centers of the "Lovers of Zion," Hirsch's Frankfurt, the great yeshivot of Pressburg and Volozhyn were ruins populated by the ghosts of a murdered dream. The great experiment of European humanism, Jewish emancipation, died in the ovens of Auschwitz.

The new Jewish affirmation—the determination after the Holocaust to survive, to defend, to face the world as *Jews*—is therefore a momentous response and one that must evoke religious wonder. Whether our vision is secular or religious, we stand in the presence of a miracle, human or Divine. It is difficult not to feel beneath the surface of contemporary Jewish peoplehood the touch of the *Shechinah*, the Divine presence. And it is hard to avoid that sense of a prescripted destiny which lies at the heart of the Jewish idea of providence. For pre- and post-Holocaust Jewish existence has traced out the oldest and most haunting theme of the Bible: the improbability and yet the certainty of the survival of the covenantal people.

The first Jew was almost the last. The first promise to Abram was, "I will make you into a great nation." Immediately thereafter Abram experiences exile, a family quarrel, and a war, events that were to become continuing motifs of Jewish existence. There then follows the most poignant motif of all. Abram's first recorded words to God are, "O Lord, God, what will You give me if I remain childless?"

Judaism is the story of the covenantal family, the children of Abraham, Isaac, and Jacob. The Torah begins with humanity as a whole, with man made in the image of God, and with Noah with whom God makes a covenant. From then on it narrows its attention to one family singled out to keep the way of God, doing charity and justice. In its history and inner life God makes His Presence known in a peculiarly manifest way.

The survival of the Jewish people is therefore a continuing paradox. On the one hand, as bearers of the Divine presence, the people of Israel is eternal as God Himself is eternal. As Jeremiah was to prophesy: "Thus said the Lord, who established the sun for light by day, the laws of the moon and stars for light by night. . . . If these laws should ever be annulled by Me,— declares the Lord—only then would the offspring of Israel cease to be a nation before Me for all time." Israel will last as long as the sun and the stars. But on the other hand, its survival from one generation to the next is never assured or natural. It exists in and by a faith in the supernatural. It suffers exiles and wanderings. As a nation in its land, it is always surrounded by larger and hostile empires. In dispersal it is a fragile minority, not knowing whether more to fear oppression or embrace, persecution or assimilation. Its continuity is never mere survival. It is a miracle, repeatedly taking both Jews and non-Jews by surprise.

The first words of Abram to God thus announce a recurring theme. Abram has no children. He can see no future generation. The end of the covenantal people is in sight. The text continues: "God then took him outside and said: Look at the sky and count the stars. See if you can count them. He then said to him: Thus shall your descendants be." Why "outside"? The rabbis interpreted the word to mean that God took Abram outside the laws of nature and historical process. The driving tension of the Jewish people would be the conflict between the prediction and the promise. On the basis of prediction, the family of Abram would come to an end. On the basis of promise it would revive and be as eternal as the stars. That, too, has been the story of Jews and Judaism in modern times.

5

The State of Survival

The last chapter surveyed the good news about contemporary Jewish affirmations. But there is bad news too. The Jewish people, both in Israel and the diaspora, face a present and future crisis. Jewish continuity is far from assured. Jewish observance continues to decline. There is the possibility of demographic disintegration. Jewish identities are tracing out conflicting paths. The possibility of schism, deep and wounding, is real.

It is important to confront these issues openly but without despair. Jews are used to crisis. As we have seen, the literature of the nineteenth century was dominated by it. Some of it was justified. On anti-Semitism, the fears early expressed by Moses Hess and Leon Pinsker were all too accurate. Had they been heeded, there might have been fewer Jews in Europe in 1940, and fewer lives lost in the Holocaust.

Other fears proved unfounded, particularly those which related to the survival of Jewish identity. Even so, this does not imply that the sense of crisis was unjustified. It may simply be that exaggerated fears for the Jewish future are part of what it is to take Jewish survival seriously. The transition from one generation of Jews to the next can and may never be taken for granted. It needs a massive

self-sacrificing effort of education and commitment—unprecedentedly so in the modern age—to ensure that the tradition is
handed on.

Kabbalah and *mesirah*, receiving from the past and transmitting to
the future, are the essential covenantal acts. Judaism is less a set of
truths to be discovered than it is a set of commands to be learned
from parents and handed on to children. Judaism therefore has
much to fear from any break in generational continuity. The
language of crisis may be a symptom of how deeply modern Jews
took their responsibilities toward an uncertain future. It may have
energized them into creating a Jewish future against the probabil-
ities. It may, in short, have been a "self-refuting prophecy."

Raising the alarm is part of the function of those who see beyond
the present. As the sociologists Peter Berger and Hansfried Kellner
amusingly describe it:

> If we take our minds back many millennia, back into the dawn of
> history, we may imagine the appearance of the very first
> intellectual. After centuries during which people did nothing but
> rhythmically bang away with stone implements and keep the
> fires from going out, there was someone who interrupted these
> wholesome activities just long enough to have an idea, which he
> or she then proceeded to announce to the other members of the
> tribe. We can make a pretty good guess as to what the idea was:
> "The tribe is in a state of crisis."

But there is a Jewish approach to impending crisis, one that
marks the difference between prediction and prophecy.

In telling the story of the Jewish past—in relating the Haggadah on
Pesach—the sages laid down the rule: *Matchil bi-genut umesayyem be
shevach*, "Begin with the bad news; end with the good." In thinking
about the Jewish future the opposite rule applies. We begin with the
good news and only then contemplate the bad. The good news is that
both Jewish survival and revival are certain. That is promised in the
last chapters of the book of Deuteronomy. Faith in the messianic age
is, Maimonides ruled, one of the essentials of Jewish belief. "The
Torah has already promised," Maimonides further explained, "that
ultimately, at the end of their exile, the people of Israel will return to

God and immediately they will be redeemed." The sages interpreted the biblical phrase "the God of faith" to mean "the God who had faith in the world He was about to create."

Precisely because he shares this ultimate faith, the prophet is able to look on future crisis with open eyes and without despair. He knows it can be averted. He speaks in order that it be averted. A prediction is successful if it comes *true*. A prophecy is successful when it proves *false*, when it has alerted the community to avoid catastrophe. The task of prophecy is to be self-refuting.

The point is important. An emphasis on prediction over prophecy can lead individuals and institutions to see trends as inevitable. The only available policy is then accommodation, adjustment to what is certain to happen anyway. That approach, which has in one way or another marked most Jewish responses to modernity, is unjustifiable by Jewish sources. Fate is a concept that figures in Greek, not biblical and rabbinic, thought. Providence, by contrast, rests on the interaction between Divine promise and human choice. Whatever the present trends in Jewish life, their future direction is chosen, not given. What, then, are those trends?

Intermarriage

Perhaps the most serious trend in the diaspora, relates to intermarriage. Jewish history is the story of the covenantal family, the children of Abraham, Isaac, and Jacob, ramified and extended across time. Jewish continuity depends critically on the strength of the Jewish family. Intermarriage is therefore a direct threat to Jewish survival and was seen as such from earliest times. There are biblical prohibitions against marriages between Israelites and their idolatrous neighbors. Ezra and Nehemiah, on their return from Babylon, instituted drastic measures against those who had "been unfaithful to our God by marrying foreign women from the peoples around us." The rabbis enacted protective decrees against behavior that might lead to too close a social interaction between Jews and Gentiles. Their explicit concern was to prevent intermarriage.

It worked. Until the modern period there were internal and

external forces keeping Jews and non-Jews socially apart. The laws of *Shabbat* and *kashrut* and the alien quality of other faiths preserved Jewish distinctiveness. So too did the confined space, territorial, political, and economic, allocated to Jews by Christian and Islamic states. Jews saw themselves as a chosen people. They were seen by others as a pariah people. Benign or malign, these factors created boundaries between Jews and their neighbors that were hard to cross or to want to cross.

With modernity, much of this changed. Jews were now participating in all aspects of non-Jewish society. Traditional observance was being abandoned. So too was the traditional Jewish self-image. Jewishness, from being a source of pride, was becoming a sense of stigma. In the opposite direction, where there was Gentile tolerance, Jews were welcomed where once they had been shunned. The barriers were down.

More than this. The very conceptions of religious identity on the one hand, marriage on the other, were changing. In traditional society, Jewishness was what one *was*. In secular society, Jewishness might be a fact of birth, a set of memories, or a religious affiliation, but it is merely one aspect of a complex identity, not its totality. In traditional societies, too, marriage is firmly set in a wider social matrix. Its function is to transmit the shared values of the community to the next generation. The kind of person one may marry and the subsequent roles of husband and wife are highly circumscribed by law, custom, and social control. The scope of individuality is relatively small.

Only in the early nineteenth century, after the American and French revolutions and the rise of Romanticism, did love and personal compatibility become the main grounds for marriage. The shift in consciousness is encapsulated in a famous scene in *Fiddler on the Roof*. One of Tevyeh's daughters wants to marry for love. The idea astounds and then intrigues Tevyeh. He asks his wife, "Do you love me?" She replies, "For twenty-five years I've washed your clothes, cooked your meals, cleaned your house, given you children, and milked the cow. After twenty-five years, why talk about love right now?"

In 1908 Israel Zangwill wrote a play, *The Melting Pot*. It was performed before large and appreciative audiences throughout

America and in London. It captured the imagination of a generation. It was a latter-day version of *Romeo and Juliet* without the
tragic ending. In it two Russian-born immigrants meet in New
York and fall in love. The boy is Jewish, the girl Christian. They
discover that the girl's father, a colonel in the Tsarist army,
had been responsible for the murder of the boy's family in the
Kishinev pogrom. But the bitterness and prejudice of Russia
disintegrate in America's freer air. Love and tolerance triumph
over religion and hate. Marriage across the divide is here portrayed as an ethical achievement. The social consequences were to
follow.

Intermarriage came relatively late to America. The immigration
from Eastern Europe between 1880 and 1920 was sufficiently large
to maintain its own subculture for two generations. For the first
two decades of the twentieth century the rate was two percent. By
the midcentury it was six percent. In the early sixties it rose to 17.4
percent. By the late sixties it stood at 31.7 percent. Since then it has
stabilized somewhat. A precise figure is difficult to determine. The
rates differ from town to town and vary according to educational
levels and degree of Americanization. Most, though, would put it
at between one in three and four in ten. By 1980 research yielded
the proposition that some 350,000 Jews were or had been married
to non-Jewish partners. If their children are taken into consideration, almost a million individuals have been directly involved in
intermarriage.

The current American situation merely recapitulates the experience of two earlier waves of Jewish immigration, Sefardi and
German. European Jewry, too, had undergone the same process in
the pre-Hitler years. By 1929 three Jews in ten were marrying out
of the faith in Berlin and Bohemia. In 1927 the intermarriage rate
in Trieste was 56.1 percent. "A generational clock has ticked over
and over again in the open society," Arthur Hertzberg has written.
"Whether in New York and Philadelphia in 1840, in Paris and
Bordeaux in the 1850s, in Budapest around the turn of the century,
in Berlin and Vienna in the 1920s, and now in the United States in
the 1970s, it tells the same frightening time. The third generation
in the open society intermarries and erodes out of Jewry at a rate of
one in three."

The Jewish Family: Size and Stability

But intermarriage is not the only problem confronting Jewish survival. Low birthrates are another. The Jewish people has not repopulated itself after the Holocaust. Immediately prior to their encounter with emancipation, Jewish communities, especially those of Eastern Europe, generally had higher fertility rates than the surrounding non-Jewish population. The eighteenth and nineteenth centuries were periods of rapid Jewish demographic growth. Arthur Ruppin estimated that the world Jewish population grew from 1.5 million to 10.5 million in that period.

Emancipation suddenly and sharply reversed this pattern. Jewish fertility declined to a level below the general rate. In France, for example, Jewish women age 26–30 had an average of 2.88 children in 1808. By 1872 the figure for the same group had dropped to 1.78. Between 1926 and 1930, births per thousand in Poland were 32.3 among non-Jews, 19.6 among Jews. In her study of Jews in a German village community, Alice Goldstein has traced a similar trajectory, a sudden drop in Jewish reproduction rates around 1880 from above to below the general population.

American-Jewish demography is typical in this respect. Since the 1880s the Jewish birthrate has been consistently below the national white non-Jewish average. Jews have the lowest birthrate of all the major religious and ethnic groups. Even from this low level there was a dramatic fall in the 1970s, to an average family size of 1.2 children, a figure that suggested a rapidly shrinking and aging Jewish community. The rate has since risen, but the fear remains. Acculturation even without intermarriage leads to a Jewish population in decline, in absolute and relative terms.

Simple explanations fail. Jews are more highly educated than other groups in America, and education in general has a depressing effect on fertility. But research by Calvin Goldscheider on the Boston Jewish community shows that the better educated expect to have larger families. Samuel Heilman suggests that Jewish women became increasingly reluctant to bear the roles of wife, mother, and homemaker as households changed from extended to nuclear families. But though this may be true of contemporary America, it fails to account for similar falls in family size in rural European communities. Others have argued that low fertility is a measure of Jewish dislocation and insecurity. If so, it should have risen as Jews became more established. Instead it has fallen.

Most analysts, though, are agreed that a fall in birthrate is a feature of all societies that pass from tradition to modernity. Jews have simply been like everyone else, only more so. Peter Berger has pointed to the fact that in modern societies, people tend to see their future in terms of a "life-plan" in which the "biography of the individual is apprehended by him as a *designed project*." Jews have become master-practitioners of this art which involves a high capacity for "delayed gratification." They go to college more widely and for longer periods than other groups. They enter careers that call for high levels of prior training. The small size of Jewish families is not a function of nonmarriage, nor is it the case that childless or one-child families are particularly common among Jews. It is, instead, that they marry later than non-Jews, and are less likely to have four children or more. It seems, then, that they are adept at planning as such, and this includes birth-control and family planning.

There is by now evidence of a direct correlation between Jewish religiosity and family size. Samuel Heilman and Steven Cohen discovered that as against an average family size of 2.0 among the non-Orthodox, the figure for the "nominally" Orthodox was 2.1, for "centrist" Orthodox it was 2.9, and for "traditional" Orthodox it was 4.2. Similar correlations have been observed by Calvin Gold-scheider and Paul Ritterband. The same pattern, incidentally, obtains among Catholics. This suggests another factor. As we saw in the last chapter, Jews in America are more secularized than other groups. They are less likely to attend religious services or cite religion as an important factor in their lives. Low birthrates, then, may be another symptom of the rapid flight of Jews from Judaism.

The Jewish family used to be a symbol of stability. But this too has changed. Rates of divorce have risen generally in Western societies, and as Jews have become more like their neighbors, they too have been affected. In 1971, for example, the National Jewish Population survey in America revealed that among the 25–29 year-olds, 15 percent of households were separated or divorced. In Anglo-Jewry, the divorce rate doubled between 1965 and 1980.

One child in six can expect to experience family breakup by the age of 16. Here, even the Orthodox community is not immune.

There are two special causes for concern, apart from the tragedy itself and its impact on the institution of the Jewish family. Firstly, Jewish divorces occur more frequently among the 35–44-year olds, at a time when children are most likely to be affected. The effects of divorce on children are now known to be significant, negative, and lasting, often not revealing themselves until many years later. Secondly, the American Jewish community has been relatively slow in adjusting to the problem. It does not yet have a strong support network of parents-without-partners groups, single-parent organizations, and a marriage market for the divorced. There have been problems in rabbinic counseling skills, and in the provisions made by congregations. As a result, the divorced often feel alienated from the Jewish community and its representatives and tend to seek non-Jewish partners when remarrying.

Israeli Dilemmas

These patterns were, however, expected. They form the very heart of the secular Zionist case against the diaspora. Jewish life could not long survive an exposure to an open society in which it was an increasingly indistinct minority. In Israel, the Jewish future would develop naturally without fear of either cultural or social assimilation. Since 1948, or at least since 1967, this explicit argument has become tacitly accepted in the *golah* as well. "A young state," as Hillel Halkin put it, "is taking over the burden of Jewish history from an old diaspora." Israel would discharge the duty of Jewish survival, while the diaspora would perform a supportive and enabling role.

This is, surely, as it should be. While some philosophies of the nineteenth century, secular, Reform, and modern Orthodox, idealized the diaspora and the Jewish mission within it, this was hardly the mainstream of Jewish thought since biblical times. Jewish life is lived towards Israel, at once a land, a society, and a destiny. The Hebrew term *galut* is far less neutral than the words diaspora or dispersion. It signifies exile, punishment, alienation, dislocation.

Nachmanides even raised the question, as had the sages before him, of how the covenant could still be in place and the commandments binding outside the land. Israel was where Judaism became lucid, where Jews had a direct relationship to Providence. In the sixteenth century, the Maharal, R. Judah Loewe of Prague, saw exile as a precarious imbalance. The order of nature itself was disturbed and would remain so until Jews returned to their land. Until the nineteenth century no thinker saw the Jewish future as anything other than directed toward Israel. Secular Zionism and the negation of the diaspora therefore have deep roots in the Jewish tradition as well as their support from recent Jewish demography.

Three features, though, remain disturbing from the perspective of Jewish survival. The first is that birthrates in Israel itself, though they remain well above replacement levels, have also declined. This is particularly noticeable in the Sefardi population, who had generally arrived in Israel without first going through the modernization process that had been experienced by the European and American settlers. Initially they had had large families, but by the second generation their fertility patterns had rapidly approximated those of other Israelis. Birth control was only part of the problem. The high rate of abortion was another. The issue is acute because of the sharp disparity between the birthrates of Jews and Israel's Arab population. In the late 1970s, for example, the fertility rate for Jewish Israelis was 3.4, for Israeli Arabs, 7.7, and among Arabs in the territories, 8.0.

The second is the continued failure of Jews outside Israel to undertake *aliyah*. Of the 1.4 million immigrants from the birth of the state to 1970, the overwhelming majority were in flight from persecution in Eastern Europe and Arab lands. Only one in nine came from Western Europe, the United States, South Africa, or Australia. The paradox of diaspora Zionism is seen most clearly in the case of American Jewry. There Israel is the most widespread focus of Jewish identity, to the extent that some have called Israel the religion of American Jews. At the same time, its *aliyah* rates are proportionately among the lowest in the world. The Lakeville study, conducted before the Six Day War, showed that while 91 percent of the respondents approved of fund-raising for Israel, only one percent would consider living in Israel or encouraging their children to do so.

Aliyah from the United States reached a peak in 1971 and has been progressively declining since. Equally problematic has been the fate of South African Jewish emigrés. The South African community has been signally Israel-oriented in its communal attitudes and educational structure. Nonetheless, many Jews who left South Africa in the 1970s and 1980s settled in Australia and Canada rather than in Israel. The phenomenon that has most disturbed Israelis has been the choice of a large number of Soviet Jews to settle in America, not Israel. The revival of Jewish consciousness among the Jews of Russia had largely been inspired by the events of 1967, so that the preference for America seemed to indicate a significant reversal of attitudes. These are, hopefully, temporary trends, the result of a period of external and internal turmoil in Israeli life. But for the first time it has seemed not only as if Israel was failing to attract Jews from free societies but that it was also being displaced as the first point of refuge. There were safer and easier places to be a Jew.

Undoubtedly the most psychologically traumatizing, though not numerically the most significant, has been the third phenomenon: *yeridah.* Israelis have chosen to leave Israel. The significance of *yeridah* is that it runs directly counter to the assumption that has dominated both Israel and the diaspora since the state's foundation. Israel is a place one moves toward, not a place one leaves. So disturbing is *yeridah* that there has been a deep reluctance to recognize, quantify, and analyze it. Estimates of the number of Israelis living in the United States vary from a half to a quarter of a million, although Paul Ritterband has argued that the figures are an exaggeration. He suggests a figure of some 40,000 in New York, with perhaps another 20,000 elsewhere.

Moshe Shokeid has recently published a full-length study of *yordim* in New York, and it makes salutary reading. Israelis leave Israel to pursue higher education or professional advance, or to start small businesses. What is unique about them, in sharp distinction to earlier generations of Jewish immigrants, indeed to all other ethnic groups, is that they have established no voluntary organizations, no social meeting places, and no economic enclaves. For the most part, they avoid contact with American Jewish institutions and with official Israeli bodies. Their contact with one another is sporadic and ambivalent. They are perhaps the first Jews since the lost ten tribes to have no strategy for survival in the diaspora.

The reason is that in terms of the secular Zionist orthodoxy which they have internalized, they do not exist. The term *yeridah* carries with it a profound stigma. Israeli public opinion has frequently denounced those who leave as traitors, deserters, and mercenaries. In 1976, Prime Minister Yitzchak Rabin described them as "the leftovers of weaklings." The *yordim* themselves, if they are secularists, see Jewish identity in strictly geographical-national terms. To be a Jew is to live in Israel. Living outside Israel creates an identity crisis which cannot be solved. The American Jewish community is organized primarily along religious lines. But this, to *yordim*, is a mode of Jewishness they have rejected. As a result, they cling tenaciously to the idea that they are in America only temporarily—though often their economic and social situation suggests otherwise—and they make no provisions for establishing a group identity or for educating their children.

In the meanwhile, in Israel itself there has been deep soul-searching among a small group of writers on the implications of the "wandering Israeli." The *sabra*, the native-born Israeli, planted in his own soil, was to have ended a millennial history of the "wandering Jew." The figures explored by novelists like Aharon Megged, Amos Oz, and A.B. Yehoshua are not the *yordim* of the public image, materialists in search of a more affluent society, but spiritually restless individuals driven to leave Israel through a sense of claustrophobia. They feel constricted by the pressures of apparently endless war and Arab-Jewish hostility and by the ideals of the early settlers which now seem impossible to fulfill. One of the characters in Amnon Jackont's *Borrowed Time* says, "Anyone who stays here has to choose between a war that will eventually end up in disaster or a peace that will lead to assimilation and make all these wars that we've fought and will fight totally meaningless." In these novels, leaving Israel does not solve the problem. The characters are as plagued by doubts abroad as they are at home.

Renewing the Dialogue with Destiny

Political and military considerations aside, therefore, new thought is needed about the character and destiny of Israeli society and of the relationships between Israel, the diaspora, and Jewish survival. The question that drove Jews in the wake of emancipation was: what *place* could be carved out for Jews and Judaism in a world order that seemed to welcome neither? That place now exists, both in Israel and the diaspora.

A new question has become suddenly urgent. Given that place, what next? Why and how shall Jews survive? In modern times this has become the ultimately unanswerable question, yet the one most frequently asked. A consideration of the future of the Jewish people cannot avoid it.

We do not live in the nineteenth century. Yet contemporary Jewish thought seems locked in nineteenth-century terms. Liberal and neo-Orthodox philosophies were concerned about the modes in which Jews might become integrated into open diaspora societies. Zionism, religious and secular, was preoccupied with the question of creating a Jewish state. Both have been achieved. The question, What next? has become imperative. But it has thus far generated no new and larger visions.

Jewish thought in the late twentieth century has been marked by its attention to the immediate. How to resolve the problem of the Palestinians? How to create a momentum for peace in the Middle East? How to encourage *aliyah*? How to reduce the rate of intermarriage and divorce? How to increase the size of Jewish families? These are undeniably pressing concerns.

But Jewish thought was traditionally marked by its attention to the ultimate. Paradoxically its present was secured by a deep conviction about the future. If there is a crisis in the contemporary Jewish world, it lies at the level of thought no less than at the level of pragmatic strategy. Jewish survival has rarely been more prominent on the agenda of discussion. But Jewish survival has rarely before been so difficult to define or flesh out with substantive content. Its meaning and purpose seem to vanish as soon as attention is turned toward them.

Paul Johnson ends his recent *History of the Jews* with the question a historian must ask in reflecting on Jewish survival across almost four thousand years. Does it reveal the guiding hand of Providence? A believer would say Yes. But the historian is bound by the terms of his craft to "beware of seeking providential patterns in events." There are, then, two ways of interpreting the Jewish past.

On the one hand there is the perspective of faith. "If the earliest Jews were able to survey, with us, the history of their progeny, they would find nothing surprising in it. . . . That the Jews should still survive, when all those other ancient people were transmuted into the oubliettes of history, was wholly predictable. How could it be otherwise? Providence decreed it and the Jews obeyed." On the other hand there is the perspective of history, which sees human events in terms of human acts and their human consequences. "The Jews believed they were a special people with such unanimity and passion, and over so long a span, that they became one. They did indeed have a role because they wrote it for themselves."

But this either/or is, from a traditional perspective, a false dichotomy. Providence cannot guarantee the Jewish future without the free, unconstrained, and unpredestined assent of Jews. Nor, surely, could Jews have willed their own survival without a deep, even obstinate, faith in Providence. The concept of covenant is mutual. God takes Israel as His people. Israel takes God as its destiny. Israel believes in the one God in heaven. God chooses *goi echad baaretz*, "one nation on earth." Jewish history is their interactive relationship. Divine revelation commands human response. Human action creates a providential reply. Mutuality lies at the heart of the Jewish religious-historical drama.

Josephus tells us that this idea became problematic in the last days of the Second Temple period. The Sadducees, he says, believe that there is no such thing as Providence. History is made by man. The Essenes believe that there is no such thing as free will. History is made by God. The Pharisees, however, maintain that there is an interaction between man and God, a complex dialectic of decision and destiny. "It was God's good pleasure that there should be a fusion and that the will of man . . . should be admitted to the council-chamber of fate." The Sadducees and Essenes disappeared.

The Pharisees survived and shaped the Judaism that persisted to modern times.

Johnson is surely correct in suggesting that it was Jews' faith in their own destiny that led them to write their unique story, and merely wrong in assuming that this is a secular interpretation of events. That faith, lucid and enduring, was itself the clearest expression of the *Shechinah*, the Divine Presence, that accompanied them in their exiles and returned with them to their land. A sense of their own identity—historical, personal, collective, above all covenantal—was crucial to Jews' survival. They kept the Torah. The Torah kept them. That reciprocity of faith and endurance, Divine command and human commitment, is the very pulse of the body of Israel as a people.

Doubts, dissents, and indecisions about Jewish identity are therefore no mere intellectual quandary. They threaten Jewish continuity at its most fundamental level. To be sure, the Divine Presence will bring it about that there will always be a Jewish people. But only to the extent that the Jewish people always continue to believe in the Divine Presence. In Jewish history, identity and endurance are inextricably linked.

The question posed by Judaism in the late twentieth century therefore is: Can there be Jewish survival without a clear sense of how and why Jews should survive? Strategy begs the question of meaning and purpose. What answer shall we give to the question: What is a Jew?

6

What Is a Jew?

In 1946, writing in the wake of the Holocaust, Jean Paul Sartre surveyed the state of Jewish-Gentile relationships. His book was entitled *Anti-Semite and Jew*. It was an attack on anti-Semitism, and not surprisingly, given Sartre's existentialist commitments, it was a powerful plea for "authenticity." The anti-Semite is inauthentic in projecting his fears and discontents onto the Jew. Gentile authenticity would end anti-Semitism. But what of *Jewish* authenticity? This is, says Sartre, for the Jew "to live to the full his condition as a Jew." Inauthenticity is "to deny it or to attempt to escape from it." The essay is, in short, an encouragement of Jewish self-affirmation. What then follows is perhaps the bleakest analysis of the Jewish situation since Spinoza.

Jews, argues Sartre, "have neither community of interests nor community of beliefs. They do not have the same fatherland; they have no history." What then do Jews have in common that constitutes their Jewishness and by which they are bound, in authenticity, to live? "The sole tie that binds them is the hostility and disdain of the societies that surround them. Thus the authentic Jew is the one who asserts his claim in the face of the disdain shown toward him."

To be Jewish, for Sartre, is to be the object of anti-Semitism and to face this fact unflinchingly. This analysis, provided by one of the great philosophers of the age, is remarkable. It is not merely barren; it contradicts itself on two counts. Firstly, to be authentic in Sartre's terms is to "let existence precede essence." It is to make oneself, to be one's own "author." Uniquely, though, Jews do not make themselves. They are made by others. They exist as such only because they are singled out for hatred. As one commentator concluded on Sartre's analysis, "The Jew is the inauthentic being *par excellence*, essentially defined by the glance of the other." Secondly, since Jews exist only by virtue of anti-Semitism and since anti-Semitism would not exist in a society of authentic individuals, the Jewish destiny is ideally self-liquidating.

Sartre himself drew the second conclusion. "Thus the authentic Jew who thinks of himself as a Jew because the anti-Semite has put him in the situation of a Jew is not opposed to assimilation any more than the class-conscious worker is opposed to the liquidation of classes . . . The authentic Jew simply renounces *for himself* an assimilation that is today impossible; he awaits the radical liquidation of anti-Semitism for his sons." In an ideal world there will be no more Jews. It is difficult, at this distance, not to see the deep inner connection between Sartre's philo-Semitism and the Nazi ideology it opposes.

For this was an argument shared by friends and enemies alike since the eighteenth century. It had been Spinoza who first argued that anti-Semitism had been the most potent factor in securing Jewish survival. "As to their continuance so long after dispersion and the loss of empire," he had written, "there is nothing marvelous in it, for they so separated themselves from every other nation as to draw down upon themselves universal hate. . . . That they have been preserved in great measure by Gentile hatred, experience demonstrates." If only anti-Semitism keeps Jews Jewish, then an era of true tolerance would lead to total Jewish assimilation.

Sartre was not an anti-Semite. His warmth toward Jews and Judaism grew over time, as interviews given shortly before his death make clear. He was simply, as Steven Schwarzschild and others have argued, describing a reality. The French Jews he knew at the time were assimilated to the point that exposure and resistance to anti-Semitism was the sole content of their identity. They knew that they were Jews because society so regarded them. But beyond this their Jewishness had no substance. It had neither historical consciousness nor religious faith. It was translated into neither a distinctive way of life nor a concrete vision of a Jewish future. They were Jews without knowing why or how.

Something of that analysis remains true today. If Jewish survival is problematic it is because Jewish identity itself is problematic. Nineteenth-century Jewish thought was directed toward two specific goals: social integration in the diaspora and the creation of a Jewish home in Israel. Those goals have been realized. What remains as the motivating dynamic of Jewish survival in the late twentieth century? How do contemporary thinkers answer the question: What is it to be a Jew?

Defying Hitler

Emil Fackenheim is one of the outstanding Jewish philosophers of the second half of the twentieth century. His work is a continuing dialogue between Judaism, Christianity, and secular thought in the wake of the Holocaust. It is a deep and sophisticated attempt to explore the possibility of "mending the rupture" of a shattered world. But as we recall from an earlier chapter, he has offered a striking definition of Jewish existence after Auschwitz. He argues that the "authentic Jew who faces up to his singled-out Jewish condition" is now bound by a 614th command. He is "forbidden to hand Hitler yet another, posthumous victory." Fackenheim continues:

If the 614th commandment is binding upon the authentic Jew then we are, first, commanded to survive as Jews, lest the Jewish people perish. We are commanded, second, to remember in our very guts and bones the martyrs of the Holocaust, lest their memory perish. We are forbidden, thirdly, to deny or despair of God, however much we may have to contend with him or with belief in Him, lest Judaism perish. We are forbidden finally, to despair of the world as the place which is to become the kingdom of God, lest we help make it a meaningless place in which God is dead or irrelevant and everything is permitted. To abandon any of these imperatives, in response to Hitler's victory at Auschwitz, would be to hand him yet other, posthumous victories.

Fackenheim's thought as a totality is subtle and complex. But what is of interest is the fact that this particular formulation captured a widespread feeling. It articulated, as one reviewer wrote, "the sentiments . . . of Jewish shoe salesmen, accountants, policemen, cabdrivers, secretaries." What, on this reading, becomes of Jewish identity?

It is turned into a defiance of Hitler. This is only a hairbreadth away from Sartre's definition of Jewish authenticity. Fackenheim has in one sense gone further, for even were there no anti-Semitism, it would be a Jewish duty to remember it. God Himself only lives in Jewish minds in order to frustrate the Nazi attempt to murder His people. In his more recent work, Fackenheim's thought stays within these lines. In answer to the question "What is a Jew?" he answers that "We, the Jews of today, would either have been murdered or never born. . . . We are an accidental remnant." But a Jew who is murdered simply because he is a Jew has, according to some authorities, fulfilled the command of *kiddush ha-Shem*, "sanctification of God's name." He has become, in his death, holy. Since any Jew *might* have been a victim of the Final Solution, every Jew is holy, and in this sense "our holiness is ineluctable and brooks no honest escape or refusal." Here Jewish holiness has been equated with being singled out as a potential victim.

Jewish identity cannot be built on such a foundation. Jews in the past did indeed preserve a memory of their sufferings at the hands of Pharaoh, Amalek, and Haman. They remembered, in *kinot* and *selichot*, the victims of the Crusades, massacres, inquisitions, and pogroms. They even, in one dazzling insight into rabbinic consciousness, saw suffering as part of the essence of Jewish peoplehood. A Gentile who comes to convert to Judaism is asked, according to the Talmud, "What reason do you have for wishing to convert? Do you not know that Israel at the present time is persecuted and oppressed, despised, harassed and overcome with afflictions?" The Talmud adds, "If he replies, 'I know and yet am unworthy,' he is accepted immediately."

Despite this, no Jewish thinker prior to modernity saw suffering as a source of Jewish identity. Even Judah Halevi, who was able to rescue a vestige of pride from persecution, nonetheless saw suffering as a trial of faith, not as a substitute for it: Jews, he said, suffered more than others because they were more sensitive. "Israel among the nations is like the heart among the organs of the body." Michael Wyschogrod, in a penetrating critique of Fackenheim's work, has insisted that "There is no salvation to be extracted from the Holocaust, no faltering Judaism can be revived by it, no new reason for the continuation of the Jewish people can be found in it." Judaism survives *despite* Auschwitz, not *because* of it.

The Holocaust and Jewish Identity

Fackenheim's definition of Jewish purpose is more than mere theory. It articulates a major orientation of contemporary Jewish life. Consciousness of anti-Semitism, past, present, or anticipated, remains a dominant strand of present Jewish identities. Worse: while Jewry in the wake of emancipation tended to see hatred of the Jew as a temporary phenomenon, to be overcome by individual or collective "normalization," post-Holocaust ideology sees it as an enduring feature of the Jewish condition. "Jews," writes George Steiner, "are a people whom totalitarian barbarism must choose for its hatred." To be a Jew is to place on one's children "a burden of ancient loathing." "That fear," he adds, "lies near the heart of the way in which I think of myself as a Jew."

John Murray Cuddihy has argued that this creates "a kind of Manichean view of the world in which a small, weak, good group (the Jews) is dispersed among a large, strong, bad group (the nations, the *goyim*). This small, good group is self-defined as a victim of the large, strong, bad Christian group that victimizes it." A harsh analysis, but not an inaccurate one.

In America the Holocaust has become a new and primary symbol of Jewishness, a source of survivalism and political and philanthropic endeavor. Holocaust memorial centers have proliferated.

Holocaust programs dominate Jewish studies on campus. The *shoah* has become one of the primary themes of Jewish literature—one writer recently estimated that one in four new books on a Jewish subject are about it. It is a key element in teenagers' Jewish education. It is recalled in *Yom ha-Shoah* services. Its functional value is clear. It unites an otherwise denominationally divided community. It links American Jewry to Israel without negating the diaspora. It provides a logic for secular Jewish survival.

But, as a number of commentators have recently pointed out, the Holocaust points everywhere and nowhere. It has been used by secular Zionists to "refute" the diaspora. It has been used by religious anti-Zionists to indict Zionism: the nations, they argue, would never have turned against Jews had Jews not sought prematurely to leave. It has been cited by Americans to justify democracy. It has been cited by Jewish activists, driven by the call of "Never again," to denounce democracy. The Holocaust has been taken as proof of Jewish uniqueness. It has been taken, too, as proof that a sense of uniqueness, of the "chosen people," is a vicious concept and leads in the end of the idea to the "master race." As an instrument of Jewish survival its value is deeply ambiguous. One of the great scholars of the Holocaust, Lucy Dawidowicz, has spoken of her distress at the "almost obsessive, ceaseless attention" given to it by American Jews. "If we're a people that gets murdered, the young will flee from us. We have something more than that."

The Holocaust and Israel

The *shoah* figures prominently too in Israel's view of the diaspora. A.B. Yehoshua voiced a widespread sentiment when he wrote that "The Holocaust proved to us the danger of our abnormal existence among the nations. It is," he writes, "the final, decisive proof of the failure of diaspora existence." To one of the characters in Amos Oz's *In the Land of Israel*, written in the aftermath of the Lebanon War, the hostility to Israel displayed by Western media was part of the "cunning of history." It would increase anti-Semitism and thus force Western Jews finally to leave and make *aliyah*. This too is a significant shift in consciousness. Most of the early Zionists believed that the existence of Israel would end anti-Semitism. Instead it has transmuted it into anti-Zionism. But this, rather than being analyzed, tends to be seen in fated, apocalyptic terms. It is part of *seifa de-galuta*, the process of the end of exile. Israel fulfills a quasi-providential role when it increases the discomfort of Jews in and with the diaspora. It hastens the ingathering.

Charles Liebman and Eliezer Don-Yehiyah have charted the rise in Holocaust imagery in Israelis' description of their own situation since 1967, and especially since 1973. Here again we face a revolution of thought. In the early years of the state, the Holocaust and Israel tended to figure as opposite archetypes. The *shoah* symbolized diaspora suffering and passivity; Israel represented a new identity, powerful, proud, and assertive. But more recently the Holocaust has come to "reflect the eternal condition of the Jewish people—isolated and beleaguered."

Liebman and Don-Yehiyah are disturbed by the possible consequences of this image. They warn that "Israel's sense of isolation and distrust of its allies is profoundly influenced by the Holocaust symbol, resulting in behavior that could antagonize allies and become, in the end, a self-fulfilling prophecy." That analysis has been echoed by the secularist Amnon Rubinstein.

Since modern times, Jews have had a deeply ambivalent attitude toward anti-Semitism. On the one hand it is something to be detested, opposed, and fought. But on the other hand, though few have been as explicit in this respect as Sartre and Fackenheim, it provides substance for an otherwise perplexing identity. Leonard Fein has written that "Deep down—and sometimes not so very deep—we still believe that we depended on the pogroms and persecutions to keep us a people, that we have not the fiber to withstand the lures of a genuinely open society. It is seduction, not rape, that we fear the most." It is as if, in resisting hostility, the Jew discovered himself.

Yet as the basis of an identity, it has fearful consequences. Internalized, it can become self-hatred. Externalized it can be used to justify stances of unwarranted suspicion and aggression. Though Jews in the Middle Ages explained their suffering in terms of an enduring tension between themselves and the world—in R. Shimon bar Yochai's phrase, "Is it not well-known that Esau hates

Jacob?"—this was counterbalanced by the conviction that, in Malachi's phrase, "Nonetheless, God loved Jacob." Indeed, the very notion that the hostility of "the world" had its roots in the distant past helped to deprive non-Jewish perceptions of their sting, and make them marginal to the Jewish self-image.

What is harmful about taking anti-Semitism as the basis of identity is that it is an *imposed* identity. It takes as definitive, not the Jew's encounter with his historical past, his religious present, or his messianic future, nor even his chosen kinship with other Jews, but instead his encounter with non-Jewish society. As an identity it is, to use David Riesman's terminology, neither tradition-directed nor inner-directed, but other-directed. It turns destiny into fate. It sees Jewishness as something thrust upon the Jew. It is the product of a complex and interlocking set of alienations, of the Jew from the traditional content of Jewishness on the one hand, and of Jews from social and political neutrality on the other.

Having sought "normalization" either in the diaspora or Israel, Jews find themselves still and unpredictably bearing a high public profile. If Charles Liebman is right in seeing American Jews as "torn between two sets of values—those of integration and acceptance into American society and those of Jewish group survival," we need look no further in understanding the role of anti-Semitism in identity. For in fighting it, the Jew simultaneously asserts his right to acceptance in the wider society and establishes his differentness as the object of prejudice. The ambivalence is momentarily resolved. But at the cost of a love-hate relationship with both Jewishness and the non-Jewish reference group. A long history of ambivalence can be traced from Spinoza to Sartre and onward to Fackenheim. That surely is one price of the secularization of Jewish identity. The hatred of the world is no substitute for the love of God in explaining the Jewish "singled-out condition."

Diaspora or Exile?

If anti-Semitism is one component of contemporary Jewish identity, identification with Israel is another. Charles Liebman suggests that "concern for Israel, efforts in its behalf, and the symbols of Israel increasingly represent the content of American Judaism." Leonard Fein concurs. Since the Six Day War, he writes, "Zionism has been the collective religion of the Jews, and the needs of Israel rather than the demands of the halakhah have provided the norms for communal behavior."

But here too lies a deep ambivalence. The consensus on the centrality of Israel is unaccompanied by either a sense that Jews ought to leave America in favor of *aliyah*, or by a perception of America as *galut*, exile. To the contrary. The category of "exile" seems radically inapplicable to the American situation. "American Jews," writes Charles Silberman, "now live in a freer, more open society than that of any diaspora community in which Jews have ever lived before." As Jacob Neusner puts it, "American Jews politically, socially, and economically stand within the corporate limits of society; they do not see themselves as temporary residents, people who really belong somewhere else. Their homeland is America; its turmoil is theirs; so too is its tragedy and triumph. To allege that in the eschaton they will be magically lifted up and transported on eagles' wings to some other place is to present American Jews with a useless fantasy." America is home.

What are the consequences of a secularly Israel-oriented diaspora? The most serious is that it creates a form of *vicarious* identity. Authentic Jewish life takes place elsewhere. Charles Liebman has penetratingly defined the role of Israel for American Jews as the new *heim*, the substitute for the "old home" of Eastern Europe, now vanished in the Holocaust. The *heim* is a place one visits occasionally, feels nostalgia for, and about which one wants to feel that life goes on there as it always has. But the "characteristic of the *heim* . . . is that one doesn't live there." Jewish continuity is guaranteed by someone else, somewhere else. It is delegated away to a surviving elite. For the rest, to be Jewish is to enable other Jews to be Jews.

The most critical voice within American Jewry of this vicarious identity has been Jacob Neusner. "The rebirth of the Jewish people takes place through the achievement of the Zionist movement, and that is true. But it is true for someone else. It is not true for ourselves. We are not there." The categories through which diaspora Jewry explains itself to itself relate to events that take place elsewhere and to other Jews. "Ours is a mythic situation in which we talk about what other people go through, but then we find ourselves unable to explain the world in which we live, the things through which we pass, the life we choose for ourselves and our children. We are spectators at someone else's drama."

Beyond this, vicarious identity masks a deep disparity between the way American Jews see themselves and the way they are seen through Israeli eyes. For Americans, Israel is a source of diaspora renewal. It strengthens the sense of collective Jewish peoplehood. It provides a focus of identity and activity. For the majority of Israeli thinkers, however, this is dangerous self-delusion.

Natan Rotenstreich, A. B. Yehoshua, and Eliezer Schweid among others have continued to argue the classic Zionist case that there can be no true Jewish creativity in the diaspora, nor ultimately can there be secure Jewish survival. Schweid argues against Achad ha-Am's thesis—central to diaspora Zionism—that Israel represents "a spiritual center" for Jews throughout the world. This ignores, says Schweid, the way culture is transmitted. "Participation in a culture means direct involvement in the process of creativity." Jews outside Israel cannot absorb its inner vitality at one remove. "The superficiality of Jewish culture among the vast majority of the Jews of Europe and America is irrefutable proof of the validity of this assertion." Gershom Scholem applied to American Jewry the chasidic maxim that the greatest exile is not to know one is in exile. Arnold Eisen concludes, from his survey of recent thought of the themes of exile and homecoming, that "Negation of the diaspora, including America, stands at the very center of contemporary Zionist reflection."

Paradoxes of Interdependence

This conflict of perceptions has led to a series of ironies and paradoxes since 1967 that have shaken the axioms of secular Zionism. First, Israel was to be the "sole secure refuge" for Jews in flight from persecution. In the light, though, of Israel's recent wars and inner turbulence, Yeshayahu Leibowitz has argued that Jews who seek safety could find it more effectively in Australia and Canada. Eliezer Schweid calls Israel an "embattled fortress."

The sharp dichotomy between the security of a homeland and the insecurity of the diaspora has been ironically inverted. For to the extent that Israel is a safe refuge, it makes the diaspora safer too. Mordecai Kaplan, one of the architects of American Zionism, defined the sense in which Israel was home using words taken from the poet Robert Frost: "Home is the place where, when you go there, they have to take you in." Home thus understood is not where one lives. But it is what makes exile endurable.

Second, Israel was to be the sole context of a distinctive Jewish identity. The choice, as Arthur Koestler put it, was either "emigration to Israel or gradual assimilation to their host nations." What was not foreseen was the extent to which the existence of Israel, far from negating the diaspora, in fact revitalized it. Throughout the Jewish world as we have noted, there was a sudden flowering of Jewish self-expression in the wake of the Six Day War. Much of it was focused on Israel, but not all. There was religious self-discovery also, and a renewed contact with the texts and practices of tradition. Israel, far from hastening diaspora assimilation, has counteracted it.

These conflicts and ambivalences become exposed when phenomena arise that are impossible to explain or respond to on extant assumptions. What, for example, should be the diaspora reaction to the many Soviet Jewish emigrés who have chosen to live in America rather than Israel? What should be its response to the yordim who have chosen to leave the promised land for the "land of promise?" Should it be supportive or critical? Both groups confound established archetypes. Israel, not America, is the natural refuge for Jews fleeing oppression; and Israel is not a home one leaves. To that extent, Russian and Israeli arrivals in America are often regarded as disturbing anomalies. Yet both groups have chosen what American Jews themselves have chosen: to live outside Israel. To that extent they regard local reaction as hypocritical.

Is Israel supported or compromised by a strong and self-sufficient Jewish life in the *golah*? Is the diaspora to be educated toward its own survival, or to the view that only in Israel is there complete Jewish fulfillment? The conventional wisdom, at least in the diaspora, is that in practice there is no conflict between these objectives. As one American lay leader put it, "We must recognize that the future of the generations that follow us is inextricably linked to Israel as a source of deepening commitment to our own sense of Jewishness and spiritual identification." But, he continued, "It is not and cannot be a substitute for our own increased commitment to creative Jewish continuity at all levels in our own communities." But between these two sentences is a latent conflict that is not always avoidable.

Identification with Israel does not ease the burden of diaspora Jewish self-definition. On the contrary, it heightens it. It has meant, in recent years, taking a political stance sharply at odds with the image of Israel projected by the media. It has meant, for Jewish students at universities, running the gauntlet of anti-Zionist propaganda. It has disturbed rather than supported the harmony between diaspora Jewry and its environment. Here again we are confronted by the failure of "normalization," the project by which Israel would make Jews "like other nations." Israel, no less than the Holocaust, testifies to the Jewish "singled-out condition." But it does not of itself explain it. On secular Zionist orthodoxy, Israel and the diaspora should have gone their separate and divergent ways, the one toward integration in the family of nations, the other to disappearance through assimilation. Yet they have remained obstinately linked to one another in a state of mutual tension.

The stark alternatives of secular Zionism, between a disintegrating diaspora and a secure and normal homeland, have given way to a complex and fraught interdependence. Israel has made all Jews, both its own and those of the diaspora, feel more at home in the world. At the same time, under the impact of Israel's political isolation, it has served to emphasize the "not-at-homeness" of the Jew. Israel and the diaspora have grown markedly closer in the last two decades while at the same time holding strikingly different perceptions of one another. Out of these paradoxes it is difficult to draw a coherent picture of a diaspora identity focused on a place in which one chooses not to live.

Jewishness and Judaism

The author has suggested that a Jewish identity built around the Holocaust and Israel, the two defining symbols of diaspora Jewishness since 1967, is not in itself sufficient to give meaning and content to Jewish life. They are, to be sure, the most momentous events in Jewish history since the destruction of the Second Temple. No contemporary Jewish thought can avoid confronting and being shaped by them. But they do not in themselves yield meaning. They presuppose a prior set of meanings, a framework of interpretation. In themselves, and especially in the diaspora, they mask and to some extent embody ambivalence about being a Jew.

But there have been some American sociologists who have argued that this kind of analysis is misconceived. There is, they suggest, no such thing as a specifiable Jewish identity. As we noted in an earlier chapter, Charles Silberman, Calvin Goldscheider, and Steven M. Cohen have argued, in effect, that Jewishness is what Jews do. They grant that in America, Jewish observance continues to decline. So too does affiliation with synagogues and other Jewish organizations. They speak of "ineffective, inadequate, and unsuccessful Jewish education . . . pervasive ignorance . . . decline in temple and synagogue participation, empty synagogue schools, and unused community facilities . . . emphasis on and acceptance of minimum Jewish commitments." They concede that "mobilization of energies for fund-raising devoid of Jewish content as a goal in itself" has become a substitute for "creative Jewish commitments."

But this, they argue, does not of itself entail a *decline* in the vitality of Jewishness. It represents a *transformation* in the nature of Jewishness. And this is only to be expected. For there is no essence of Jewish identity. As Jews change, so does the character of what counts as "Jewish." At one time it might have been adherence to halakhah, at another, membership of a synagogue, at yet others, supporting Israel or Jewish welfare causes, or perhaps simply having Jewish friends. Jewishness persists so long as Jews see themselves as Jews and so long as they are measurably similar to one another and different from everyone else.

We recall Calvin Goldscheider's definition of Jewishness in terms of group cohesion: "The strength of the Jewish community reflects the number and intensity of ingroup interactions. The more the bases of interaction and the greater its intensity, the more cohesive is the community." The implications of this statement are striking. For example, as Goldscheider himself points out, Jewish education is usually evaluated in terms of success or failure in communicating Jewish knowledge or commitment. But it has another dimension. "Parents bring their children to school, have contact with other Jewish parents and with Jewish teachers and other Jewish children. The ramifications are extensive. It is clearly what community is all about." Schools are places where Jews meet. They are a setting for "ingroup interaction." The street outside the school, where parents meet, may be as important as the classroom, where children meet. As long as Jews meet, mix, and have attitudes and lifestyles in common, we need not ask about the *content* of Jewish life. Instead we must concede the *fact* of Jewish life, which changes in form from generation to generation.

These sociologists are responding to a fact best analyzed over thirty years ago by Nathan Glazer. What has happened to American Jewry, he suggested at the time, was less significant than one thing that had *not* happened. "This negative something is the strongest and potentially most significant religious reality among American Jews: it is that Jews have not stopped being Jews . . . It is not that most Jews in this country submit themselves to the Jewish law; they do not. Nor can they tell you what the Jewish heritage is." Their sense of Jewishness might consist in anything from Zionism to a love of Yiddish or Jewish food or Jewish jokes. But it persisted. There was, he found, "a stubborn insistence on remaining a Jew, enhanced by no particularly ennobling idea of what that means."

There is, though, one profound difference between Glazer and the contemporary "transformationists." Glazer distinguished between Jewishness and Judaism. Judaism represents a religious faith and a holy way of life. It is not what Jews actually do, but what they ought to do, what they are religiously called on to do and what, traditionally, they did. The significance of Jewishness, for Glazer, is that it keeps Jews at least potentially in touch with

Judaism. So long as Jews remain identifiably Jewish, "they are capable of being moved and reached and of transcending the pedestrian life that so many of them live in company with other Americans." So long as Jewish ethnicity is actual, Jewish religiosity is possible, for were there no Jews there could be no Judaism. The persistence of Jewishness "means that the Jewish religious tradition is not just a subject for scholars but is capable now and then of finding expression in life. And even if it finds no expression in one generation or another, the commitment to remain related to it still exists."

Goldscheider, by contrast, is more interested in Jewishness than Judaism. "Religiosity," he argues, "is only one of the ways in which Jews express their Jewishness." And it is this move that is open to argument on two different grounds. The first concerns the future. Can Jewish ethnicity, rooted in no more than the fact that Jews tend to have similar education, careers, lifestyles, and political attitudes, survive? The second concerns definition. Is this *Jewish* survival? Is there not some point at which Jewishness must be measured against Judaism? Is there not some point, indeed, at which Jewishness ceases to have any connection with Judaism? Arthur Hertzberg brings the two arguments together when he writes that "Judaism is neither authentic, nor can it survive, if it amounts to no more than a triumph of adjustment to suburban life."

Behind every sociology there is a theology. And behind the transformationists lies a view of Jewish life which owes much to Mordecai Kaplan, who defined Judaism as the evolving civilization of the Jewish people. Kaplan's Reconstructionism recognized that while Judaism as traditionally understood had "practically become inoperative," there was nonetheless a secondary cohesive force that bound Jews, namely "the will to maintain and perpetuate Jewish life as something desirable in and for itself." On this view there is no "essence" of Judaism. The primary function of Judaism is to express and sustain group cohesion, and there is no way of specifying in advance the forms it will take. To the extent that Silberman, Goldscheider, and Cohen evaluate rather than simply describe; to the extent that they see in the changing patterns of American Jewry not decline but a new kind of vitality, they tacitly endorse something like a Reconstructionist interpretation of Jewish life. Indeed, almost two decades ago, Charles Liebman had already described the beliefs that underlay Reconstructionism as the "folk religion of American Jews."

Who Is a Jew?

Is there anything that stands in the way of this *minimalist* conception of Jewish identity, which sees it in terms of Jewishness rather than Judaism and which attaches no normative content to Jewishness? Jews, after all, *do* survive as Jews in the diaspora, against all expectation. They have widely different conceptions of what Jewishness means, or perhaps no clear conception at all. Yet they identify, with surprising passion and sometimes self-sacrifice, as Jews. Why should this not be sufficient? A Jew is one who identifies as a Jew. Beyond that, no clarification is possible or necessary. We can measure the shifting patterns of group solidarity. What we cannot do is describe some as more "authentic" than others.

Without at this stage invoking theology or halakhah, there are nonetheless two formidable problems, one theoretical and one practical. The theoretical issue is this: The word "Jew" has a reference that is extended over space and time. Part of what it means to be a Jew is to be a member of a people that spans millennia and continents. Existentially that sense of peoplehood lies close to the heart of modern Jewish identities. To feel Jewish, as many recent observers have noted, is less to feel bound by Jewish law and belief than to feel a sense of kinship with the Jews of Israel and the Soviet Union, the Jews who perished in the Holocaust, the Jews who enacted their unique drama through the echoing centuries of exiles and wanderings, hopes, and persecutions. Presupposed in the use of a single word to describe a people divided by time and space, land and language, custom and culture, is some common content designated by the word "Jew."

That content is not given by the analyses of contemporary diaspora Jewish ethnicity. Upward mobility, advanced education, residential or occupational clustering, a taste for certain kinds of food or humor or political positions—these tell us what is American about American Jews, or English about Anglo-Jews, not what is Jewish. Jewish ethnicity has long had this character. Even in their most segregated, ghetto-bound periods, Jews borrowed manners and motifs from their surrounding culture. In large measure this is what marked the difference between Ashkenazim and Sefardim, between the Jews of Rome and Rizhin, Manchester and Mezeritch.

What was improbable, striking, and decisive is that despite these differences, Jews constituted a single people. They saw themselves and were seen by others as having a direct horizontal continuity with one another and a vertical continuity with the people of the Bible and the rabbinic age. What they held in common was definitive; what they held distinctively in their various localities was not. What they held in common was, as Saadia Gaon noted, Torah. That bound them to a shared life, a shared history, and a shared destiny. That was the "essence" detectable beneath the variegated cultural forms in which it was clothed.

Jewish peoplehood cannot survive the dissolution of that "essence." This theoretical concern comes to the fore in one burning and practical question. Who is a Jew? The answer given by tradition is unambiguous. A Jew is one born to a Jewish mother or one who has undergone a halakhically valid process of conversion. Several things have happened, especially since the 1960s, to make that answer seem out of step with the social reality of Jewish life in the diaspora.

First is the rapidly accelerating rate of intermarriage. American Jewry, as we have seen, has now reached the state of Western and Central European Jewries between the two world wars: an outmarriage rate of approximately one in three. Precise quantifications are not available for Anglo-Jewry, but it seems likely that the rate here will also rise to, if it has not yet reached, that level. Second is what we have called the new Jewish ethnic affirmation. Intermarriage was hitherto seen as both a real and symbolic exit from the Jewish community. Today a significant proportion of those with non-Jewish spouses wish to remain identified as Jews and wish their children so to be identified. Third is the rapidly growing acceptance of intermarriage as a fact of Jewish life, even among those who do not endorse it or wish it for themselves. The 1975 Boston survey, for example, showed that while 43 percent of the over-60s held strongly negative views about it, only 5 percent of those aged between 18 and 29 did so. Fourth, the lifestyles and attitudes of the intermarried and non-intermarried are growing more alike. The former are more likely to have Jewish friends and values and live in a Jewish neighborhood. The latter are less likely to have a high profile of Jewish observance and synagogue attendance. Sociologically, the two groups are becoming harder to distinguish.

This has led to the most controversial claim of the "transformationists"—that intermarriage does not significantly weaken, and may in some ways strengthen, the Jewish community. The argument mounted by Silberman, Goldscheider, and Cohen is complex and points in more than one direction. In part it is defensive. Outmarriage rates, they argue, are lower than have been estimated. The rate of increase is slowing. Only the more marginal section of the community is affected. But in part it is evaluative. If the couple stay within the community, outmarriage represents a demographic gain. If the non-Jewish partner converts, the couple is likely to be more Jewishly active than average. Acceptance of the outmarried by the Jewish community will tilt the balance from loss to gain.

But it is here that sociology and halakhah part company. Goldscheider is explicit. "The definition of the Jewishness of the family in terms of biology (or halakhah) is becoming less important for most American Jews than it was in the past and less relevant to Jewish communal continuity than how people define themselves behaviorally, communally, and culturally, and how the community defines them." Those who see themselves and are seen by others as Jews, are Jews. But historically it was in just such circumstances that schisms arose within the Jewish world. Hellenists, Sadducees, the early Christians, and the Karaites saw themselves as Jews. They did not, however, stay within the Jewish mainstream. Though the question of *what* is a Jew may, at certain times, be indeterminate and open-ended, it tends to converge on the highly specific question, *who* is a Jew? That is not a question that tolerates a multiplicity of answers, a measure of vagueness or diplomatic disattention. To the contrary, it is a question that precipitates crisis.

Religious Legitimation and Social Process

That crisis, in the context of American Jewry specifically, diaspora Jewry generally, has an additional dimension. It can be expressed thus. Already in the mid-1950s Will Herberg and Nathan Glazer were commenting on an unusual feature of Jewish life. Jews were deeply secularized, far more so than either Protestants or Catholics. Yet there were signs of what was ostensibly a religious revival. There was a stunning increase, in the postwar years, in the number of synagogues, schools, and community centers. Books and periodicals appeared on religious themes. Yet Jews did not participate in great numbers in synagogue services. They did not see Judaism as having a significant bearing on the conduct of their lives. They did not turn to rabbis for personal direction. The rabbi, indeed, was seen at this time primarily as a religious functionary and a representative figure to the non-Jewish world.

What had happened, argued Herberg and Glazer, was that Judaism as a religion had itself become secularized. For Herberg it had become a "culture-religion" celebrating not the Mosaic faith but "Americanism." For Glazer the change had taken place when Jews moved from urban to suburban settings. There, experiencing for the first time a predominantly non-Jewish neighborhood, Jews felt the pressures of conformity and "respectability." Church-going and Sunday school were the norm, and Jewish equivalents had to be created. They were to be "Jewish, but not too Jewish." Both writers pointed to the fact that in the emergent American Judaism, what dominated the agenda were human needs, not Divine commands; American integration, not Jewish "chosenness." Religion, when it spoke to the individual, was expected to provide "peace of mind" and enhance the power of positive thinking. When it spoke to the community it was expected to serve the cause of group solidarity and ethnic survival. No longer did Jews exist to serve Judaism. Judaism existed to serve the needs of Jews.

It was this phenomenon that led, a decade later, to one of the most powerful religious statements to have emerged from American Jewry, R. Joseph Soloveitchik's long essay, *The Lonely Man of Faith*. Judaism, he argued, did not bring peace of mind. To the contrary, it brought deep inner conflict between the secular and religious sides of the human personality, what he termed, respectively, "majestic" and "covenantal" man. Now, however, secularism had invaded the sanctuary. Modern man "comes to a place of religious worship. He attends lectures on religion and appreciates the ceremonial, yet he is searching not for a faith in all its singularity and otherness, but for religious culture." He wants an aesthetic, not a religious experience. He seeks community, not command. "Western man diabolically insists on being successful. Alas, he wants to be successful even in his adventure with God. If he gives of himself to God, he expects reciprocity." He thinks in terms not of covenant but of commercial transaction. He insists that "faith adapt itself to the mood and temper of modern times." The grandeur of faith—"aboriginal, exploding with elemental force"— could not, argued Soloveitchik, be reduced to a suburban sedative and a leisure pursuit.

But it was happening, and R. Soloveitchik could offer no more positive prospect than that the man of faith should withdraw from society and experience "ontological loneliness" and "social isolation." Religion was being pressed into the service of a secular culture. And here was the paradox. In America, Jews preferred Jewishness to Judaism but insisted on giving it a religious expression. The institutions of ethnicity were the synagogue and the rabbinate. Theology had become the handmaid of sociology. Judaism had become the legitimator of Jewishness.

Mordecai Kaplan had given the process its intellectual basis. But it affected not only his Reconstructionism, but American Reform and Conservative Judaism as well. This meant that, in varying degrees, all the non-Orthodox denominations had to accommodate themselves to the ethos of contemporary American Jewry, an ethos only tangentially related to classic Jewish values and beliefs. It meant, among other things, mixed seating in synagogues, an abandonment of the prohibition against a Cohen marrying a divorcée, and the ordination of women as rabbis and cantors. These have been endorsed even by the most traditional of the denominations, Conservative Judaism.

In addition, the Reform movement has accepted the creation of synagogues for homosexuals. One Reform writer, Norman Mirsky, recently noted that "the Reform rabbi has to be both gyroscope and weathervane, for while throughout the Jewish world the weather is always changing, never before has there been a Jewish clergy whose pledge to its laity has been so overt in integrating rapid social change into a recognizable Jewish liturgical and institutional framework." Reform, in short, has fulfilled the function of giving religious legitimation to the changing boundaries of Jewishness.

Issues of Status

So the tension between Jewishness and Judaism exists not only as a personal issue for individual Jews, nor as an intellectual argument among sociologists, but as a religious argument between Orthodoxy and others, Reform in particular. Inevitably the most intractable issues turn on the question of personal status. One relates to divorce. Since the 1840s, radical Reformers in Germany, Samuel Holdheim in particular, had argued that a civil divorce was sufficient to terminate a Jewish marriage, under a radical reinterpretation of the idea that "the law of the land is law." This view had been adopted, at least de facto, by the American Reform rabbinate.

By Jewish law, however, termination of a marriage requires a halakhically valid divorce, *get*, and without this the partners remain bound to one another. Should the woman remarry on the basis of a civil divorce only, the relationship is halakhically adjudged to be adulterous and any children born from it are *mamzerim*, illegitimate, and unable to marry legitimate Jews. The issue was acute enough to lead R. Zvi Hirsch Chajes, in 1849, to propose a formal excommunication of Reform Jews and a ban against marriages with them. But the issue remained on the sidelines until recent rising rates of divorce and remarriage and the continued prominence of Reform in American Jewry made it a numerically significant phenomenon.

Sociologically, though, the central issue has been intermarriage. It is here that the religious legitimation of secular survivalism is most potentially explosive. The tacit acceptance of mixed marriage, or at least the desire on the part of Jewish parents "to keep their children Jewish, no matter how," has led to some 40 percent of

American Reform rabbis officiating at marriages between Jews and non-Jews. Half of those who refuse will refer the couple to a colleague who will perform the ceremony. Norman Mirsky adds that "there is enormous pressure placed on Reform rabbis to officiate at mixed marriages. It is rumored that some congregations will not hire rabbis who refuse. Personal correspondence seems to bear this out."

The question then arises as to the religion of the spouse. In some cases the non-Jewish partner converts to Judaism. The figures are elusive, but Steven Cohen estimates that some 23 percent of non-Jewish wives do so, and some 11 percent of non-Jewish husbands. One reliable estimate places at 10,000 a year the number of converts to Judaism in America. Most of these are performed under Reform auspices. Halakhically, conversion to Judaism requires immersion in a *mikveh*, circumcision in the case of males, and *kabbalat ha-mitzvot*, "acceptance of the commandments." In the case of Reform conversions, one or other of these criteria, possibly all, will standardly not have been fulfilled. Orthodoxy, too, sees the Conservative movement's relationship to halakhah as ambivalent, and thus questions the validity of its conversions.

But if almost a quarter of non-Jewish wives are willing to convert, more than three quarters are not. In the new climate of affirmative ethnicity, though, often the husband wishes and the wife is willing to raise the children of the marriage as Jews. This led to the notorious decision of the Central Conference of American Rabbis—the Reform rabbinic convention—in 1983, which declared "that the child of one Jewish parent is under the presumption of Jewish descent. This presumption of Jewish status of the offspring of any mixed marriage is to be established through appropriate and timely public and formal acts of identification with the Jewish faith and people."

The decision signaled a willingness to defy the millennial criteria of Jewish status. Henceforth, a child might be deemed Jewish without a Jewish mother or an act of conversion, on the basis of "patrilineal descent" and personal identification. Indeed, as a number of perceptive observers, among them Shaye J.D. Cohen and Manfred Vogel, noted, the resolution subtly changed the whole basis of Jewish status. For while it included children of Jewish fathers, it also excluded children of Jewish mothers who did not choose to identify as Jews. In effect it "Protestantized" Jewish status, shifting it from a biological endowment to a personal religious choice. The irony was overwhelming. In its pursuit of "peoplehood" American Reform had thoroughly "religionized" Jewish identity.

The shock waves were deep and immediate. A host of scholars and religious leaders outside Reform warned of what Reuven Bulka called "the coming cataclysm." Irving Greenberg posed the question, "Will there be one Jewish people by the year 2000?" The patrilineal decision had focused attention on the cumulative effect of Reform policies on divorce and conversion. Greenberg suggested that within the foreseeable future, between 15 and 20 percent of the American Jewish community would be "socially and halakhically separated from traditional Jews." Self-ascribed identity was in headlong collision with halakhic norms. The prospect was real of the greatest schism since Judaism and Christianity parted company. As Lawrence Schiffman's timely study *Who Was a Jew?* pointed out, that schism too had eventually turned on the question of personal status: "The ultimate parting of the ways for Judaism and Christianity took place when the adherents to Christianity no longer conformed to the halakhic definitions of a Jew."

Israel and "Who Is a Jew?"

The problem sharply illustrates the proposition that the word "Jew" presupposes criteria that span time and space. That continuity of definition is the basis of the continuity of Jewish peoplehood. Jakob Petuchowski put the point well: "It is . . . the halakhah dealing with 'personal status' which guarantees the underlying unity of the 'holy community.'"

Sociologists on the one hand, the Reform rabbinate on the other, may propose new criteria of Jewish identity that accord with the contemporary American experience. But Jewish status cannot be localized without fragmenting Jewish peoplehood. An American consensus might emerge that ran counter to standards that obtained in the past, and to the way Jewish status is understood elsewhere.

But it would have no effect on the meaning of the word "Jew" as determined by tradition and by other Jewries. Indeed, the precipitating point of crisis is almost certain not to come from within America itself, but from Israel where the Orthodox rabbinate exercises a monopoly of Jewish religious authority.

Several major controversies have already arisen in Israel. In 1958 the question arose of how children of mixed marriages should be registered in the national registry. The interior minister recommended a position not unlike that of the patrilineal principle: if either parent were Jewish, the child could be registered as Jewish if both parents agreed. The National Religious Party resigned from the cabinet over the issue. In the ensuing cabinet crisis Ben Gurion temporarily revoked the decision and took the views of an international group of Jewish scholars. In the light of their responses the government voted in favor of retaining the halakhic criteria.

Similar results followed in a series of test cases. The Shalit case, for example, established that a Jewish father and non-Jewish mother could not have their children registered as Jews in nationality only. To be a Jew nationally involved being a Jew religiously. The attempts to separate the two identities have thus far failed. But continuing tension surrounds the Law of Return, under which any Jew who decides to live in Israel can automatically become a citizen without undergoing a naturalization procedure. The law is central to Israel's self-definition as the state of the entire Jewish people. But, as amended in 1970, it defined as a Jew someone born of a Jewish mother or one who had been converted to Judaism. Since then there have been sporadic but intense efforts to have the phrase amended to specify conversion "in accordance with halakhah," the most recent following the November 1988 Israeli general election.

The issue has significance far beyond its immediate concern. The number of Reform and Conservative converts in America is large; the number of those directly affected by the Law of Return—those who choose to live in Israel—is small. In Israel itself the Reform and Conservative rabbinate has no official status. An amendment to the Law would therefore have direct repercussions on perhaps no more than half a dozen individuals a year. But it would, by implication, delegitimate all conversions performed by non-Orthodox rabbis anywhere in the world. Its significance for the

Conservative and Reform movements is potentially immense, given their deep attachment to Israel on the one hand, and the unity of the Jewish people on the other.

Not all Orthodox authorities are in favor of the amendment. The British Chief Rabbi, Lord Jakobovits, argued as long ago as 1974 that "the religious character of the Jewish state will be determined not by legislation or coercion, but by persuasion." The criteria of who is a Jew should in any case be determined not by secular legislation but by the religious courts. This view was recently echoed by Rabbi Norman Lamm who stated that "a secular body such as the Knesset is not the right forum to determine halakhic issues." Rabbi J. David Bleich has suggested that the Law of Return be restricted to naturally born Jews. Converts would then apply for naturalization, and there could be no objection if "State officials, without in any way passing on matters of halakhah, use objective judgment in considering even technically invalid conversion as evidence of a convert's sincere desire to identify with the aspirations and common destiny of the citizens of the State of Israel."

These are attempts to defuse the crisis, and ultimately to take it out of the purview of legislation. But the substantive issue remains. No Orthodox authority disputes the invalidity of nonhalakhic conversions. The problem persists, erupting occasionally, smoldering continually, threatening to shatter the fragile coalition of world Jewry and splitting it between Orthodoxy and the non-Orthodox, religious and secular, Israel and the diaspora.

Identity and Survival

In this chapter we have considered only a few of the leading themes of the contemporary debate on Jewish identity, its content and criteria. We have argued that neither the imposed identity created by anti-Semitism, nor the vicarious identity lent by Israel to the diaspora, represent coherent visions of a Jewish life. They embody latent conflicts and ambivalences. They hover awkwardly between a desire for normalization and an assertive singularity. They focus on Jewish survival without giving inner meaning to that survival.

We then turned to the minimalist identity traced out by a school of contemporary Jewish sociologists, and given religious legitimation in some of the policies of the American Reform movement. We raised the question of how far Jewishness could be divorced from Judaism, and how far Judaism could be subordinated to Jewishness. The issue came to the fore in the question of Jewish status: Who is a Jew? Here the possibility of eventual schism remains disturbingly real. As diaspora Jewish ethnicity is increasingly evacuated of traditional religious content, what is local in Jewish life becomes more prominent than what is universal. Whether a shared concept of Jewish peoplehood can long endure such a process is open to doubt.

We have argued that the problems of Jewish survival outlined in the previous chapter cannot be divorced from the problems of Jewish identity surveyed in this. Both are symptoms of the secularization of a religious tradition. The question that arises, therefore, is: What has been the fate of that section of the Jewish world that has held tenaciously and on principle to the classic terms of the tradition? What has been the fate of Orthodoxy in the last two decades?

7

The Reemergence of Orthodoxy

In 1929 a young American Orthodox rabbi, Oscar Fasman, had just completed his rabbinic training. He and his fellow graduates were about to set out on a career of teaching Torah and ministering to congregations in the Midwest of America. "We were not," he recalls, "overly optimistic about our chances of success." Around them, Jews had virtually abandoned *kashrut* and *Shabbat*. Reform was the dominant presence. Such Orthodox synagogues as there were, were small, poor, and largely comprised of elderly immigrants. Tradition seemed fated to extinction. Even some of the Orthodox synagogues had decided to meet Reform halfway by abolishing the *mechitzah*, the barrier between the sexes, in favor of mixed seating at services. One of Fasman's teachers at the seminary described his own role as "being available to recite, a generation or so later, the final kaddish for Orthodoxy."

If this was true of the new world, it was true also of the old. At around the same time, the outstanding scholar and saint of East European Orthodoxy, R. Israel Meir ha-Cohen, the Chafetz Chayyim, was lamenting the collapse of religious life in the wake of the upheavals of the First World War. "The sanctity of the Holy Torah is declining from day to day at a frightening pace. The new generation is growing up without Torah and faith. They are becoming wayward children who deny God and His Torah. And if, God forbid, this situation continues much longer, who knows to what condition we will fall. The mind compels one to believe that it will not be long before our righteous Messiah will come."

Orthodoxy was in retreat. In Germany it had long been threatened by the Jewish desire for acculturation. In Eastern Europe it was now being confronted by revolution. Young Jews were joining socialist or communist organizations. Jewish girls were involved in the emerging feminist movements. Those who felt their Jewishness most strongly, expressed it in a stridently secular Zionism. In America, Judaism was disintegrating in the pursuit of opportunity. Orthodoxy—everywhere, it seemed—evoked images of an old and outworn order. Such was the prevailing mood in 1933.

And if before the Second World War, Orthodoxy appeared to be dying, the war itself and its aftermath seemed to seal its fate. The last remaining hinterlands of traditional faith in Central and Eastern Europe had been destroyed in the Holocaust. An era was ended. From now on Jewish life would be focused on two centers, Israel and America, in both of which secularization had proceeded faster than anywhere else.

Since 1912, when the leaders of European Orthodoxy dissociated themselves from the Zionist movement by forming Agudat Yisrael, the momentum of Zionism had been almost wholly secular. There were small enclaves of Orthodoxy in the old *yishuv* of pre-1880 settlers. There was a group of religious Zionists, mainly represented by Mizrachi, who remained in dialogue with the secularists. But the dominant voice belonged to Zionist socialism, which, though it took over some of the language and symbolism of tradition, was either hostile or indifferent to religion.

Nachman Syrkin, one of the movement's ideologists, had written that "Zionist socialism sees in the applied Jewish religion, which is not a religion but a tragedy, the major impediment confronting the Jewish nation on the road to culture, science, freedom." The focus of Zionist Socialism was not God but the Jewish people itself. The biblical phrase, "who can tell the glories of God" became, in a popular song of the time, "who can tell the glories of Israel." History seemed to concur in its verdict. The Jews who had faith in

Heaven had stayed in Europe and been murdered. The Jews who had faith in themselves had gone to Israel and been victorious in the War of Independence. Orthodoxy was part of *galut*, exilic consciousness. *Galut* was a chapter that had ended in tragedy. Jewish history had moved on.

In America, meanwhile, Jews were on the road to achieving what they had sought in Europe, social integration and economic success. America's individualism did not sit easily with the disciplines and restraints of halakhah. Nor was there the stabilizing influence of an extant tradition. American Jewry was newborn. It had no institutions carried over from premodern Jewish life. The German immigrants of the mid-nineteenth century brought Reform with them, and they developed it in radical rather than conservative directions. By 1883, at the dinner given to honor the first graduating class of the Reform rabbinical seminary, the Hebrew Union College, the menu consisted of clams, crab, oysters, and shrimp. The pursuit of Americanness had become the new faith of America's Jews. One Jewish writer, recalling his childhood in the 1920s, describes how at the age of five he first asked his mother what his religion was. "If anyone ever asks you that again," his mother replied, "just tell them you're an American."

The Orthodox leaders of Eastern Europe advised their alumni to avoid taking rabbinical positions in America. It was a *treifa medinah*, an impure land. As a result, Orthodoxy and its rabbinate lacked organization, authority, and prestige. Jews in the urban ghettos placed their children in state schools. Jewish education, such as it was, came through *chadarim*, after-school classes, remembered by those who attended them for their ramshackle premises, arbitrary discipline, and pedagogically untrained teachers. Yeshivah scholars did arrive in America, but often left disillusioned. One observer wrote in 1910 that parents pay Hebrew teachers "only the going price for the job, which is generally not enough either to live on or to die—and thus schoolmastering has become a low, despised trade . . . chosen only by a man who has tried his luck at every trade and skill, who sees that his stars of success are extinct and that lifelong darkness awaits him."

The dynamic of congregational life rested with lay rather than rabbinic leaders. Restless with an Orthodoxy that seemed not to understand America, not yet ready for a Reform that seemed Germanic, exclusive, and cold, the second generation created its own pragmatic compromise. The Conservative Judaism that emerged was marked by a sharp divergence between theory and practice. Theory was taught at the Jewish Theological Seminary; practice was dictated by the conventions of Jewish suburbia. The younger members of the congregation observed neither *kashrut* nor *Shabbat*, but they expected their rabbi to do so. The rabbi's contract came up for regular renewal, so major confrontations on religious principle were ill-advised. In such an environment, the march of acculturation seemed inevitable. Orthodoxy was for the immigrants, the old, the undereducated, the poor. It was the lowest rung on the social ladder which all were expected to climb.

Caught between a secularist Israel and a secularizing America, the end of Orthodoxy was in sight.

Orthodoxy in America

So Charles Liebman's conclusion in 1965 seemed eccentric, if not wishful thinking. For he ended his study of "Orthodoxy in American Jewish Life" with the judgment that "The only remaining vestige of passion in America resides in the Orthodox community." There is, he said, "a recognition and admiration for Orthodoxy as the only group which today contains within it a strength and will to live that may yet nourish all the Jewish world."

By the 1980s that prognosis had been fully vindicated. Orthodoxy flourishes in both America and Israel. In America Jewish day schools, overwhelmingly an Orthodox phenomenon, had increased from some thirty establishments after the war to 587 by 1986. The Jewish day school had initially been opposed as a barrier to Jewish integration in America. But between 1962 and 1986, the enrollment at such schools more than doubled, from 60,000 to 130,000.

Yeshivot, too, have proliferated and expanded. Prior to the war, the tone of American Orthodoxy had been set by the combination of Jewish and secular study represented by Yeshiva College, now Yeshiva University, and its *bet ha-midrash*, the Rabbi Isaac Elchanan Theological Seminary (RIETS). The pragmatic character of American Jewry demanded such a synthesis. An institution devoted exclusively to talmudic study for its own sake seemed untenable. Today, yeshivot like Lakewood, Ner Yisrael, Torah va-Da'at, R. Chaim Berlin, Telshe, and Mir dominate Orthodoxy, to the extent that the authority of the congregational rabbi has been displaced by that of the *rosh yeshivah*, or yeshivah head. Increasing numbers of students continue their yeshivah studies past marriage, in the *kollelim* attached to yeshivot or scattered, as outposts of learning, throughout the country. The Lithuanian tradition has been transplanted in America.

So too has the chasidic tradition. Fleeing from Europe in the 1940s, two groups in particular made their home in New York: Lubavitch and Satmar. Under its present rebbe, R. Menachem Mendel Schneersohn, Lubavitch has grown into a worldwide movement of active outreach to uncommitted Jews. It has changed the profile of American Jewry with its *mitzvah*-mobiles, *tefillin* campaigns, Chabad houses, and its use of cable television, local radio, and international telephone links. Initially almost alone in its program of seeking out the alienated and estranged, it has won widespread support and emulation, and has created a strong presence in many hitherto neglected areas of Jewish life.

Satmar, a more inward and enclosed movement localized in Brooklyn's Williamsburg, is deeply opposed to modern culture and to the State of Israel. But it too has grown rapidly through its own high birth rates, estimated at an average of between eight and ten children per family. There are currently some 28,000 students registered in Satmar educational institutions.

The demographic implications are stunning. Conservative Judaism had seemed likely, in the 1960s, to be the future of American Jewry. But despite its nominal attachments to tradition, it has been weakened by the nonobservance and defections of its members. The chasidic community, meanwhile, has grown apace and through its intense social and educational structures has reversed the current of assimilation among its young. The demographic perspective was put arrestingly by Daniel Elazar: "It may be hard to believe," he wrote, "but it is important to note that at the late 1984 wedding of two scions of the Satmar dynasty, the number of

Jews packed into a single Long Island stadium for the nuptials equalled the whole body of authentic Conservative Jews."

The old equation of social advance with acculturation and de-Judaization has been broken. Today there are successful Orthodox scientists, lawyers, psychiatrists, academics, and businessmen. Talmud classes take place at lunchtime in executive suites. The new Orthodox affluence is channeled into funding for its own educational institutions and their students. Recent surveys have shown that within the American Orthodox community, unprecedentedly, levels of observance increase between the third and fourth generations.

Already by the mid-1970s, non-Orthodox observers were sharing Charles Liebman's perception. The sociologist Marshall Sklare declared that "in less than three decades Orthodoxy has transformed its image from that of a dying movement to one whose strength and opinions must be reckoned within any realistic appraisal of the Jewish community." The radical thinker, Leonard Fein, confessed himself shaken by the turn of the tide. "Look at the astonishing capacity of people who have entered—and conquered—the most modern precincts of the modern world, and who continue to celebrate the ancient tradition. And look also at the degree to which the rest of us have become defensive in the presence of the Orthodox. For now that we see that Orthodoxy cannot only make its peace with modernity, but actually thrive in the modern world, we are bound to confront the obvious question: is not the Orthodox way the authentic way?"

Orthodoxy in Israel

A parallel development has taken place in Israel. There are, admittedly, deep differences between Israeli and American Judaism. There is, in Israel, no official Reform or Conservative presence. Orthodoxy exercises a hegemony over the religious establishment, and thus far Israel has resisted America's split into denominations.

The religious Jews who came to the land in the century prior to the state were Orthodox; the other settlers were secularists. Agudat

Yisrael, abandoning its opposition to the state under the impact of events in Europe in the 1930s, eventually came to an agreement with David Ben Gurion. In return for their support of the state's proclamation, Ben Gurion guaranteed that certain religious conditions would be met in public life. *Shabbat* would be the official day of rest. *Kashrut* would be maintained in public institutions. The state would fund a school system for the religious. Matters concerning personal status would be the province of religious courts.

This, the so-called status quo agreement, has projected religious issues into the political domain where they are often fought with high contentiousness and publicity. Necessarily so, since at stake in Judaism in Israel are issues directly relating to the ethos of the state: among them the allocation of government expenditure, the creation of new settlements, and exemptions from military service. There are recurring tensions between secularists and religious groups. Each new social development—archaeological digs, postmortems, cinema clubs open on *Shabbat*, immodest advertisements—tends to be assessed against the status quo, with each side suspicious of the other's incursions across the established boundaries.

Orthodoxy in Israel is itself highly differentiated, between the religious establishment, the *charedi* or ultra-Orthodox community, the religious nationalists associated with Gush Emunim, and the traditionalists who make up the majority of the population. Each of these groups is in turn segmented. The *charedi* community is divided, for example, between the extreme antistate Neturei Karta, the more moderate Agudat Yisrael and the various chasidic circles. The religious nationalists are divided between territorial maximalists and a more accommodating wing. The fundamental issue in Israel is not, as it is in the diaspora, religious compromise with or resistance to a non-Jewish culture. It is the shape of a Jewish culture in a Jewish state. Between those who see Israel as the fulfillment of an ancient religious destiny and those who see it as a distinctly new chapter in Jewish history, the argument goes deep. Religion in the diaspora is a matter of private life and personal decision. In Israel it belongs to the public domain and to law.

Judaism in Israel is not Judaism in the diaspora. But the same revival of Orthodoxy has taken place over the same period. The ultra-Orthodox groups have grown through their large families and their ability successfully to resist secularization. In 1947 the *charedi* community was lamenting, as Menachem Friedman has documented, "that the sons do not carry on the traditions of the fathers." By 1982 it was declaring that "a youth has arisen here, great in numbers and high in quality, with an unprecedentedly erect spiritual bearing and an extremely firm self-awareness." The numbers of students at yeshivot has eclipsed Eastern Europe at its height. The growing political strength of the *charedi* community has been evident in Israel's last two general elections.

Two developments in particular have shaken the assumptions of secular Zionists. The first was the *teshuvah* or religious return of many young and previously irreligious Israelis after the Six Day War. The numbers were relatively small, but they included one or two prominent figures, and the development shocked parents by its unexpectedness. Janet Aviad, in her researches among the returnees, found that they made repeated reference to disillusionment with secular Israeli society. They criticized its materialism, emptiness, dishonesty, and hypocrisy, its absence of moral standards, and lack of authority. The events of 1967, as we have noted, produced a general awareness in Israel of the long history of anti-Semitism and its connection with anti-Zionism, and of the failure of the early dream of "normalization." This too figured in the minds of the *baalei teshuvah*. They criticized Israel for seeking to be "like all the nations" and leveled against Zionism the phrase first coined by Isaac Breuer, that it represented "collective assimilation." Judaism as halakhah represented an antidote to individualism and amoral behavior. Judaism as historical faith gave positive meaning to Israel's unique destiny as a "people that dwells alone."

The second development sent deeper shock waves through Israeli society. After the euphoria of the Six Day War subsided, it became clear that many intellectuals among the kibbutz movement, hitherto Israel's pioneering vanguard, were suffering from deep self-doubt about war, militarization, and the persistence of the Israel-Arab conflict. Their internal conversations were published in a book, *The Seventh Day: Soldiers Talk*, which received widespread attention. At the same time that this soul-searching was taking place, there was an opposite reaction on the part of a group of religious Zionists, many of them disciples of R. Avraham Kook's son, R. Zvi

Yehudah Kook. For them the war marked another stage in the redemptive process by which the whole of the biblical land would return to Israel's jurisdiction. The Divine hand was once again evident in history. What was called for was courage in resisting any abandonment of destiny, induced by a secular interpretation of events. New settlements should be established in the territories of Judea and Samaria. R. Kook's mysticism suddenly became actualized as a radical political program. Gush Emunim was born. *Chalutziyut*, the traditional Zionist mantle of the pioneering elite, had moved from the secular kibbutz to the new religious settlement.

These two phenomena, together with the gradually increasing political power of the *charedi* community, have overturned many secular Israelis' deepest conceptions of the nature of Zionism and the state. Amnon Rubinstein and Yehoshafat Harkabi, among others, have felt obliged to mount extended attacks on religious nationalism: oblique testimony to its power over the current popular imagination. Rubinstein charts the corresponding collapse of an earlier image of the secular Israeli as a new being, indomitable, the product of the soil, unbeset by *galut* hesitations, collectively minded, and courageous. He calls it "the end of the sabra myth." Amos Oz, Israel's leading novelist, reflects on the strength of *charedi* life, still resurgent after the Zionist revolution. "In a conversation twenty years ago, my teacher . . . said that Zionism was nothing more than a passing episode, a temporary mundane phenomenon of history and politics, but that Orthodox Judaism would reemerge, would swallow Zionism and digest it." Then Oz dismissed the remark; now he can no longer do so. Leonard Fein's remark that "the rest of us have become defensive in the presence of the Orthodox" applies equally to secularists in Israel.

Leadership and Followership

Why the transformation? Partly it has to do with the extraordinary determination with which the survivors of the Holocaust set about rebuilding the lost world of Eastern Europe on American and Israeli soil. Here the full irony of Emil Fackenheim's theology becomes clear. The determination not to hand Hitler a posthumous

victory was most evident in those whose commitment to Jewish
survival had nothing to do with anti-Semitism and everything to do
with revelation, command, and religious vision. It was the chasidic
leaders on the one hand, and the yeshivah heads on the other, who
determined a policy of encouraging large families, building strong
communities, and creating the educational institutions to support
them.

Their influence on America, in particular, was decisive. Never
before had the community experienced Orthodox leadership of this
stature. The Eastern European figures arrived determined to make no
concessions to acculturation. The transformation of American Orthodoxy was in large measure due to the extraordinary inspiration and
dedication of a handful of remarkable figures like R. Menachem
Mendel Schneersohn of Lubavitch, R. Joel Teitelbaum of Satmar, R.
Aaron Kotler, founder of Lakewood Yeshivah, and R. Shraga Mend-
lowitz, driving spirit of the Jewish day-school movement.

In many cases, too, the leaders arrived along with their disciples.
A certain community coherence and strength was possible from the
outset. The new immigration was quite different from those that
had preceded it. The East European Jews who had arrived in their
millions after the pogroms of the 1880s had been in search of
physical survival. Those who arrived in the 1930s and 1940s were
bent on spiritual survival. They, the last to leave, had been the most
tenacious in their determination to stay with their religious leaders.
When they finally reached America they proved equally tenacious
in helping their leaders build the old *heim* in a new land.

We referred in a previous chapter to the unprecedented and
quasiparental authority of chasidic leaders over their followers and
of yeshivah heads over their students and alumni. That authority
proved crucial to the strength of their institutions in Europe, and it
was to prove no less significant in America. It is most clearly
embodied in the development of the concept of *daas Torah*. Literally
this means "*a* or *the* Torah view" of a particular problem. It has
come to mean, though, something more specific: the capacity of a
gadol or "great Torah sage" to penetrate unerringly to the heart of an
issue and deliver an almost prophetic judgment on it. "It assumes,"
wrote one commentator, "a special endowment or capacity to
penetrate objective reality, recognize the facts as they really are,

and apply the pertinent halakhic principles. It is a form of *ruach ha-kodesh* (Divine inspiration) as it were, which borders, if only remotely, on the periphery of prophecy."

In some respects this idea is at odds with halakhic tradition. Maimonides, for example, sharply distinguished between the prophet and the sage, as did R. Zvi Hirsch Chajes. A famous talmudic narrative describes how R. Eliezer ben Hyrcanus, though he was supported by a "heavenly voice," was nonetheless defeated by the majority consensus of his colleagues. For this reason, *daas Torah* in its modern sense tends to be opposed by many within Orthodoxy who see halakhah as a rational discipline operating in the empirical world, open to argument and counter-argument and the development of consensus. They also see the new charisma with which the yeshivah head has been invested as subverting the traditional authority of the *mara d'atra*, the local rabbi.

Argument aside, *daas Torah* has a specific function within the *charedi* community. It replaces the external power which the autonomous Jewish community once had over its members with an internalized equivalent. This too proved crucial in resisting the effects of secularization. To have large families, support children for an extended period in yeshivah and *kollel*, resist the blandishments of secular culture, and stay in close proximity to the Rebbe or yeshivah instead of moving to suburbia involves a massive series of sacrifices on the part of ultra-Orthodox Jews. Only a deep mutual relationship between leader and follower could support such patterns of obedience, and this has been the special strength of these communities. Alongside the gift of leadership, in other words, has gone the art of followership. No religious group which has made concessions to the individualism of contemporary culture and the consequent diffusion of religious authority can mobilize such adherence to the advice of its sages.

The Environment of Orthodoxy

These are perhaps the most important internal factors. But there have been external factors as well. Until relatively recently, all Jewish groups—all minority ethnic groups generally—were under social and cultural pressure to conform to a national archetype; in a word, to assimilate. The modern state has tended, more recently, to recognize the value of indigenous cultures. Forcing the pace of assimilation often disrupted family life among immigrant populations and caused more problems than it solved. Most Western societies are today culturally pluralist. The distinctive dress of *chasidim*, for example, is no more exceptional than that of other ethnic groups, let alone of the more outré styles of dress among the young. Ethnic affirmation has become part of the diversity of urban life and has supported, instead of undermining, Jewish differentness.

The residential patterns in the modern city also allow for the physical creation of the voluntary ghetto. In Jerusalem, for example, new suburbs are often religiously self-segregating. In New York, high mobility has meant that previous areas of Jewish concentration have been occupied by other ethnic groups. Only those committed to a particular chasidic community stay behind. The differences between such Jews and their neighbors reinforces their sense of isolation and togetherness which in turn strengthens community ties.

Perhaps the most important single factor has been economic. Welfare provisions, rising standards of living, and the general extension of schooling has meant that families are able to support their children in yeshivah for increasing lengths of time. The availability of work for religious wives as teachers within the *charedi* school system allows them to serve as breadwinners while their husbands continue to study in *kollel*. The strong group loyalties within the community often facilitate the employment of yeshivah alumni in businesses in which there is a strong *charedi* presence, and compensate for the narrowing of career options for those without university degrees. As a Satmar *chasid* put it, "Many of our *yunge leit*, young people, make more money than your college graduates."

Contemporary culture, then, has been more open to the distinctive life-style of Orthodox Jews than was the case a half century ago. But these considerations alone do not begin to explain why Orthodoxy has come to have a prominence in the contemporary Jewish world out of all proportion to its numbers. Here we approach the heart of the matter. Jewish survival has come to seem to many Jews—Reform, Conservative, ethnic, and secular—to be a primary value. After the trauma of the Holocaust and the travails of Israel, the Jewish people has gone through too much simply to disappear through its own indifference and slow disintegration.

Charles Liebman has spoken of "the sense of many non-Orthodox Jews I know that the Orthodox are the real Jewish survivors." That sense is well-justified in terms of the evidence accumulated in this chapter. In this century the chasidic and yeshivah worlds have risen, phoenixlike, from the ashes of the Holocaust. Though it is less often noted, the same was true of earlier crises. Hirsch's Frankfurt, R. Sofer's Pressburg, and R. Chaim's Yeshivah of Volozhyn were powerful responses to cataclysmic social change. In each case, after an initial period of defensiveness and disarray, Orthodox leadership evolved survival strategies which, if they did not save a generation, preserved at least a minority intensely dedicated to safeguarding the tradition. The revaluation of Orthodoxy was already taking place in enlightened German circles in the 1920s, and it is taking place today for the same reason. When survival heads the Jewish agenda, Orthodoxy takes on a significance far beyond its own ranks. What, then, is the secret of its endurance in an open society?

Tradition, Marriage, and the Family

The question takes us directly to the concerns of the previous two chapters. How has Orthodoxy resisted the processes by which Jewish identity is diffused and diluted in contemporary culture? The first factor concerns intermarriage. Running through all the alternatives to Orthodoxy that surfaced in the nineteenth century was a profound desire for "normalization," whether individual or national, most clearly expressed in the programs of radical Reform on the one hand, secular Zionism on the other. To this, Orthodoxy could not accede, for it went against the fundamental thrust of tradition in which to be a Jew was to be a member of a singular, different, and chosen people.

Reform in particular has paid a heavy price for its accommodation to assimilation, its abandonment of *kashrut* and the disciplines

of *Shabbat*. High rates of intermarriage were the inevitable consequence. There is something approaching bad faith in the pursuit of
social integration on the one hand and the disapproval of mixed
marriage on the other. Recent surveys of New York Jews have
highlighted the importance of the religious factor in marriage
decisions. In families with a "high" level of ritual observance,
children are one-fifth or one-sixth as likely to intermarry. In those
with a "medium" level of observance, they are about half as likely
to do so. The highest rates are in those where the level of
observance is "low." No other variable shows as close a correlation.
The most effective barrier against intermarriage is the discipline of
distinctiveness and distance embodied in Jewish law.

Second is the question of birthrates. Here too we noted a direct
correlation between religious observance and the size of family. In
America at present, Orthodoxy is the only group that is experiencing population growth. Within Orthodoxy itself the rate varies in
direct proportion to commitment. Why should this be so? Here we
can only speculate. Part of the answer is likely to be negative.
Declining birthrates were a universal phenomenon in the wake of
the industrial revolution, urbanization, rising standards of living,
and a lowering of infant mortality rates. Jews responded to the
times, only more so than others. Low birthrates are a general
feature of modern society, due in part to the collapse of the
extended family and a change in women's role and self-perception.
To the extent that Orthodoxy resists modernity—particularly in
enclosed chasidic communities—it resists the complex social pressures toward small families.

But there is surely more to it than this. *Peru u-revu*, the
imperative of having children, is the Torah's first command. There
are halakhic reservations about birth control and abortion. Generational continuity—handing on the tradition to one's children—is a
primary religious duty and one that figures largely in the patterns
of Jewish life. These are all factors within Judaism that militate in
favor of demographic growth.

No less significant is the degree of importance attached to Jewish
concerns when making major choices of lifestyle. To have large
families involves couples in economic sacrifice and restrictions of
personal freedom and mobility. For the wife, it may interfere with

a career. How the choice is eventually made will depend not only on what the couple value, but on the degree of priority some values hold over others. Orthodoxy is predicated not only on a high level of ritual observance, but on a willingness to forego other considerations in favor of religious demands. In modern societies where religious behavior is voluntary, Orthodoxy has tended to be self-selecting in favor of those willing to make those sacrifices. Inevitably, then, it contains a higher proportion of those willing to place the imperative of raising children ahead of personal, economic, or career goals.

Perhaps, too—and here we approach the unfathomable—part of the explanation lies in the different role of children in tradition-bound and modern societies. In traditional societies, the family was closely tied, economically, politically, and religiously, to the community. It transmitted shared values. It communicated established roles. There was, by modern standards, a close integration between communal and private life. Personal relationships played a less prominent role. As Edward Shorter has shown, "the traditional family was much more a productive and reproductive unit than an emotional unit . . . lineage was important, being together at the dinner table was not."

Peter Berger has written of the "invention of childhood" as one of the major revolutions of modernity. Philippe Ariès has documented the emergence of this new concept of childhood as part of the rise of the European bourgeoisie. As the family was gradually separated from the work environment, it became instead a protected enclave away from the harsh outside world. The family was privatized and, in Berger's words, "bourgeois childhood became sheltered, tender, even 'sentimental'." Berger has also pointed to the effect of the sharp decline in infant mortality. Until relatively recently, most children died. The fact that this shadow of potential anguish has been largely removed has, he argues, freed parents to "invest expectation in their children from the moment of birth that would have been quite unrealistic before."

The impact of these changing patterns on Jewish consciousness was immense. It left its traces on the literature—even the jokes—of several generations. Jews projected their intense expectations of economic, cultural, and social advance onto their children. In some cases, the strain was overwhelming. It is significant that the two major modern assaults on the family have come from within the Jewish world: Freud's analysis of parent–child relationships as the source of neurosis, and the kibbutz vision of the family as the source of capitalism. Bruno Bettelheim, in his study of communal child-rearing in the kibbutz, *Children of the Dream*, notes that the early settlers feared that the family unit would disrupt the sense of community and would transmit "exilic" attitudes—sentimentality and individualism. There was also, he notes, a deep anxiety on the part of the early kibbutz women that they could not match their own mothers' example of devotion to children.

These reactions are the obverse side of the preternatural child–centeredeness of modern Jewish families, a phenomenon that would take several studies to document. Diaspora Jews are notable not for their number of childless families, but for the preponderance of small families. Might this not be related to the high level of individuation within the Jewish family, and the degree of emotional investment in each child? If so, the greater community-centeredness of chasidic and yeshivah families might represent an important defusion of family stress and a release of some of the anxieties of child-raising. Paradoxically, the larger family size of the extremely Orthodox may be due to the fact that they are in some ways less child-oriented than the Jews of suburbia.

Be this as it may, the Orthodox community represents the one striking exception to a general Jewish demographic decline. The fact is significant in itself, all the more so in light of the accumulating evidence that government pronatalist policies have no significant effect on fertility decisions in the long run. Again, the religious factor has proved the most decisive.

Orthodoxy and Diaspora Zionism

Equally striking is the impact of Orthodoxy on the relationship between Israel and the diaspora. As we noted, one of Israel's continuing concerns has been the low levels of *aliyah* from secure and prosperous diaspora communities. Since the Six Day War a clear trend has emerged. Prior to that time, research indicated that religious motivation did not play a significant part in the decision of those who chose to leave America for Israel. Since then, it has done so. Calvin Goldscheider found that among those who made *aliyah* in years 1969–1970, 37 percent defined themselves as Orthodox. More recently, Chaim Waxman found that this had risen to more than half of those who chose or were contemplating *aliyah* in 1986. The percentage is remarkable given the fact that Orthodoxy is usually estimated as the affiliation of only some 10 percent of American Jews. Orthodox Jews are, in other words, highly and increasingly overrepresented among those who move to Israel.

Waxman suggests why this has occurred. Orthodox boys and girls, particularly the alumni of Jewish day schools, are likely to spend a year or more in Israel at yeshivot and seminaries. This period in Israel, at an important time for making life-decisions, may be one factor. Many of the yeshivot themselves stress the importance of *aliyah* as a religious obligation. In addition, Waxman argues, Orthodox Jews are more likely than others to place Jewishness at the center of their lives and as a result seek a more completely Jewish environment than can be found in the diaspora. Of great importance is Waxman's conclusion. The secular Zionist argument for *aliyah*, he suggests, has become untenable. It rests on the premise that Jewish life is insecure and unsupportable in the diaspora. This simply conflicts with American Jews' perception of their own reality. "The Jew who views the state of American Jewry positively and therefore does not subscribe to an imperative of *shelilat ha-golah* [negation of the diaspora] will not view *aliyah* as an imperative without religious backing. The Orthodox Jew, on the other hand, can view the state of American Jewry positively and nevertheless subscribe to *aliyah* as a religious imperative."

Orthodoxy is important to the Israel–diaspora relationship in another way, which became apparent during the Lebanon war in the early 1980s. Israel had hitherto loomed large in the identities of many secular and non-Orthodox Jews in the diaspora. It had been a source of pride and self-respect. The critical reaction of Western media, beginning with television pictures of the bombing of Beirut, and culminating recently in the Palestinian *intifada*, imposed a severe strain on the relationship. To be sympathetic to Israel's policies, Jews in Europe and America had to discount much of what they read and saw in the media, and to take a stance against the mood of public opinion. It was noticeable that much of the Jewish criticism of Israel came from Reform and secularist quarters, and that Orthodox Jews were generally more supportive.

This is not to suggest that Jews of any denomination or none were equivocal in their attachment to the state and its people. But it nonetheless points to an important dimension of diaspora attitudes. Jews tend to assume, for the most part, a principled harmony between their own and others' interests. This is a central component of postemancipation diaspora ideology. Orthodoxy, by contrast, is more ready to assume a measure of dissonance between Jewish and non-Jewish attitudes. It embodies a kind of "hermeneutic of distance" from its surrounding culture. Thus, when public opinion is hostile to Israel, this accords more readily with Orthodox than non-Orthodox expectations. At such moments, Orthodox Jews may find it easier than others to identify with Israel's plight.

Rethinking Modernity

Ultimately, though, the current salience of Orthodoxy has to do with a profound reevaluation of the Jewish experience of modernity, a cumulative and revolutionary shift in attitudes away from assumptions that had prevailed for almost two hundred years. The disappearance of Orthodoxy, we recall, was predicted on three different grounds. First, with emancipation, Jews were entering a new era of universalism, tolerance, and enlightenment. The traditions of Judaism, particularist as they were, seemed radically inappropriate to this unfolding world. Second, with the development of secular Zionism, Judaism seemed to represent all that was lamentable about the Jew in exile. Israel would produce a new human type, free of the burden of an ancient and emasculating religious heritage. Third, and more generally, religion was destined for eclipse in the modern world. The commanding past held no resonance for a society turned toward the future. Religious authority was out of place in a culture that encouraged individualism. Religious belief was no longer needed to make sense of a universe mapped by science and mastered by technology. In the last two decades, each of these beliefs has been shaken if not displaced.

The first, belief in the power of enlightenment to enlighten, was broken by the Holocaust. George Steiner and Emil Fackenheim have charted in searing detail the failure of high German culture to stand as a barrier against attempted genocide. "We know now," writes Steiner, "that a man can read Goethe or Rilke in the evening, that he can play Bach and Schubert, and go to his day's work in Auschwitz in the morning." The Orthodox critique of secular humanism, evident even in a thinker as positively disposed toward emancipation as Samson Raphael Hirsch, has come to seem tragically justified. The Reform theologian Eugene Borowitz frankly admits that "as long as confidence in human-kind and in Western civilization remained high, devout Orthodoxy seemed out of the question. Entering the 1980s, that optimism has been shattered." The result has been "Orthodoxy's emergence as a living option for modern Jews."

The second belief, that a secular Israel would be a radical break from the religious past, has become progressively untenable since 1967. Israel's isolation, the continued hostility of her Arab neighbors, and the rise of anti-Zionism were inexplicable in the classic premises of Israel's secular founders. So was the persistence of diaspora Jewry. Nor did American Jewry accord with the archetype of the *galut* Jew" constructed by Herzl, Jabotinsky, and Syrkin. There was, too, what Liebman and Don-Yehiyah call a "legitimacy crisis" after the Six Day War as a new Palestinian voice was heard challenging Israel's right to the land. Increasingly, Israelis turned toward the Bible as the source of the Jewish right to the land of the promise to the patriarchs.

In the new vocabulary of public discourse Israelis rediscovered their links with the Jewish past and the diaspora, symbolized by the opening of *Bet ha-Tefutsot*, the Museum of the Diaspora, in 1979. The connecting factor was Judaism, and its symbols became correspondingly more prominent. Discontent with secularism and materialism, of the kind that lay behind the *teshuvah* movement, also confounded an assumption stated most forcibly by Jacob Klatzkin. "In longing for our land," he had written, "we do not desire to create there a base for the spiritual values of Judaism. To regain our land is for us an end in itself . . . living in the land is ipso facto the national life." By the 1970s this answer was no longer sufficient. Something more was needed to explain the uniqueness of life in Israel. Those who sought "normalization," anonymity, and material affluence were finding it in *yeridah*, not *aliyah*. As Israelis were challenged to redefine the character of society and state, classic religious terminology increasingly displaced the language of secularism.

The third belief, in modernity itself, has suffered a similar retreat. Liberal individualism, since the 1970s, has seemed an inadequate basis for personal meaning, lasting relationships, stable institutions, or moral coherence. A search for tradition and historical depth has been apparent across a wide range of disciplines, in the cultural critiques of George Steiner and Allan Bloom, the ethics of Alasdair MacIntyre, Stuart Hampshire, and Michael Walzer, and the biblical scholarship of Brevard Childs. Belief in the unlimited power of technology has given way to concern for the future of the environment. Belief in the power of political revolution has yielded to the realization that the twentieth century has witnessed tyranny and oppression on an unprecedented scale. The authors of the recent survey of American society, *Habits of the Heart*, conclude that "there is a widespread feeling that the promise of the modern era is slipping away from us. . . . Progress, modernity's master idea, seems less compelling when it appears that it may be progress into the abyss."

It was on this point, perhaps more than any other, that Orthodoxy parted company with other Jewish identities in the nineteenth century. The belief in revelation and tradition is belief in the power of the past to command the present. That orientation was profoundly at odds with the enlightenment assumptions of evolution and progress. Orthodoxy demanded a sense of human finitude, of humility in the face of mystery, of obedience in the presence of the Divine word, that ran counter to a century of confidence in the power of human reason and autonomy. In the late twentieth century these perceptions have acquired a new urgency and relevance.

Coming Home

We have argued, in this chapter, two propositions, the first straightforward, the second controversial and contestable. The first is that Orthodoxy is at the height of a renaissance, one that was unforeseen, perhaps unforeseeable half a century ago. The second is that Orthodoxy raises questions that must be confronted by anyone concerned with Jewish survival.

Can intermarriage be stemmed other than by a renewal of the disciplines of Jewish law? Can the Jewish demographic decline be reversed other than by relocating the family within the structure of religious community? Can the links between Israel and the diaspora be sustained on a secular base? Can Israel explain itself to itself other than through the categories of tradition?

Implicit in these questions is the judgment that the terms on which Jewish identities have been constructed since the emancipation have become, in the last two decades, increasingly inadequate to the challenge of Jewish survival. The conventional Orthodox view would be that they were in error from the outset. The more mystical view, to be found in the work of R. Avraham Kook, is that they were part of a providential process, necessary to their time, the antithesis to Orthodoxy's thesis, ultimately to merge in a new synthesis. Either way, retrospective judgment is not our present concern. The future is.

One word has recurred periodically throughout twentieth century Jewish thought, in the work of R. Avraham Kook and R. Soloveitchik, the philosophy of Emil Fackenheim, the literature of religious Zionism, and language of modern yeshivot. The word is *teshuvah*, "return" or "coming home." It has meant many things in different contexts: the return of Jews to their land, language, and political independence, to their sense of peoplehood and particularism, and to their religious tradition.

Our underlying thesis has been that these senses are essentially connected, fused more than linguistically in a single word. The concept of a covenantal people, constituted by the terms of the revelation at Sinai, and bound thereby to a way of life, a land, and a religious destiny, gives Jewish identity a coherence and compelling power unrivaled by any contemporary alternative. Judaism paid a heavy price for the complex set of alienations from that vision induced by European emancipation. Jewish identity became problematic. Jewish survival was questioned. The Jewish people was fragmented.

There is no immediate way of undoing the effects of modernity. But there is a path that leads away from it, slow, tentative, and tense though the journey may be. The path is that of *teshuvah*, a renewed dialogue with the terms of tradition and its unified vision of a people, a way of life, and a land. That dialogue, we believe, will be the theme of Jewish postmodernity.

PART IV
FUTURE

8

Assimilationism and Assimilation

J acob Neusner, not an Orthodox scholar himself, poses the fateful question:

> When you consider the power of Judaism, realized most fully and profoundly in Orthodoxy, you must wonder why every Jew should not be Orthodox and Judaic—not merely Jewish. The grandeur of the Judaic perspective on humanity, the extraordinary relevance of that perspective to everyday practice, the ineffable beauty of the consequent way of living, a holy way of living, separate and distinct, in full measure congruent with the profound meaning of our mortality and our human striving—what is life without that vision? And how can people turn their backs on it?

He continues, "And yet, the great majority of North American Jews who choose to be religious also choose not to be Orthodox, and a near majority of them choose not to be religious at all." For this is the paradox. A new and surprisingly widespread set of attitudes has emerged in the last two decades, sharply at odds with assumptions that had governed most of Jewish life since the emancipation. We have charted the transformation through a series of unexpected developments that were brought into sharp and revelatory focus around the Six Day War. That transformation ought to have brought about a turn toward Orthodoxy. But apart from the much publicized but numerically insignificant *chozrim bi-teshuvah*, religious returnees, the shift has not taken place. Orthodox parents have more children than others, and they are more successful in retaining or even increasing their commitment. What Orthodoxy has not succeeded in doing is generating a large scale move by Reform, Conservative, or secular Jews to its ranks.

Why not? Jewish thought has, after all, turned inward and particularist, and Orthodoxy was the most particularist of nineteenth-century Jewish identities. Jewish concern has centered on survival, and Orthodox Jews are the virtuosi of survival. Jewish reflection has become more traditional and more textual. It has sought to make connections with the past. All these attributes point to Orthodoxy. Jews have been concerned to establish firm and coherent links between Israel and the diaspora. Again, as we have shown, those links are most lucidly made within an Orthodox perspective. Above all, Jews have found meaningful the concept of Jewish peoplehood, the shared history and destiny that links Jews throughout space and time. That concept, as we have shown, is fraught with ambivalence when stated in terms of radical Reform, transformationist sociology, or secular Zionism. Orthodoxy, with its principled identification—substantive as well as sentimental—with the collective body of Jews, past, present, and future, is the natural vehicle of peoplehood.

Thus Orthodoxy, for almost two centuries militantly or defensively at odds with prevailing Jewish attitudes, has become the most cogent expression of Jewish aspirations. But it has not become the dominant affiliation of either American or Israeli Jews. Figures drawn from the 1980s show that only 13 percent of Jews in New York identify as Orthodox, 11 percent in Miami, 6 percent in Chicago, and 3 percent in Washington. The most recent and thus far unpublished national survey, conducted by Paul Ritterband and Barry Kosmin, shows that 9 percent of Jews across nine cities identify as Orthodox, 30 percent as Reform, and 34 percent as Conservative. To be sure, Orthodox Jews are more likely to join synagogues than others: among synagogue members, the Orthodox percentage rises to sixteen. Equally important is that the outflow from Orthodoxy, so dramatic in the past, has ceased. A survey conducted in New York in the early 1980s showed that 56 percent of first generation Americans were Orthodox, 20 percent of the second generation, 10 percent of the third, and 13 percent of the fourth. American Orthodoxy, having lost three generations, is retaining the fourth. But it remains a marginal and minority presence.

America, as the saying goes, is different. In Anglo-Jewry a full 75 percent of Jews are still affiliated with Orthodox synagogues. In Israel there are no official denominational alternatives: no recognized Reform or Conservative rabbinate. Unlike diaspora communities, Jewish identity is not primarily expressed in religious forms and synagogue membership. To be Jewish is to live in a Jewish state. Nonetheless, the broad majority of the population is not "Orthodox" but "traditional." An increasing number of Israelis describe themselves as "religious," but in a loose sense that comprises folk customs, observance of the major festivals, and identification with Israel's new "civil religion." These vast differences are more institutional than substantive, for it is clear that "Orthodoxy" means different things among the different countries. The average Jew in America, Israel, and Britain might well display a similar profile of religious observance. But in America he would probably be affiliated with the Conservative movement, in Britain, a member of a mainstream Orthodox synagogue, and in Israel he would define himself religiously without reference to a synagogue.

Secularism and Secularization

The situation can be summed up thus: the return to Orthodox attitudes has not been accompanied by a return to Orthodox affiliation or faith or religious practice. Why so? Firstly, the institutional forms that emerged in the nineteenth century have proved surprisingly persistent. Nineteenth-century German and American Reform was universalist, antiritual, anti-Zionist, and antiethnic. Late twentieth-century American Reform, as described by its leading exponent Eugene Borowitz, is particularist, interested in ritual, pro-Zionist, and ethnic. Yet it remains Reform, and its membership is high and rising. Its social function, too, has changed. A critical observer might say that in the nineteenth century it gave a religious legitimation to acculturation and social integration. He might say that in the present it gave a religious legitimation to intermarriage. Reform scholars themselves have said both these things. But a function remains: not one that could ever be acceded to by Orthodoxy, but one that self-evidently meets the wishes of a large percentage of American Jews.

Institutions persist beyond the causes that brought them into being. And Jewish thought in the modern age has tended to be institutional. The irony is that while the aims of radical Reform and secular Zionism—diaspora integration and the State of Israel—have long since been achieved and no longer need to be argued, thought tends to be conducted within the lines of those ideologies. Some of the most arresting modern Jewish thought—the work of Michael Wyschogrod, Irving Greenberg, David Hartman, and Eliezer Schweid, for example—is a conscious attempt to break down the dichotomies between Orthodox and non-Orthodox, religious and secular. But because it lacks an institutional base, it remains intriguing rather than influential.

The institutional persistence of nineteenth-century Jewish forms is one reason for the failure of a return to Orthodoxy. The other is the continued secularization of Jewish life in both Israel and the diaspora. Here we must distinguish between process and intent. There is a difference between assimilation*ism* and assimilation, secular*ism* and secularization. The one signifies a conscious goal, the other an unplanned, even an unwanted tendency.

In the nineteenth century there were significant numbers of Jews who sought deliberately to merge into non-Jewish society. They were assimilationists. There were others—among them culturalists, Yiddishists, Bundists, and Zionists—who sought to eradicate the religious component from Jewish identity. They were secularists. One of the great ironies of that time is that the assimilationists failed to assimilate and the secularists were not secular. As Theodor Herzl noted on the one hand, "We have sincerely tried everywhere to merge with the national communities in which we live . . .

[but] in our native lands where we have lived for centuries we are still decried as aliens." As R. Kook noted on the other, the great East European secularists were often deeply religious figures—one thinks here of Bialik's love of tradition, Syrkin's utopianism, A. D. Gordon's mysticism of land and labor. Many of them came from distinguished rabbinic families, were alumni of the great yeshivot and had their intellectual roots in the traditional learning and literature. They were rebels dialectically related to the religion they rejected.

In contemporary Jewry the irony has been compounded, for the situation has been reversed. Jews no longer seek to assimilate, but they are increasingly assimilated, measured against a whole range of indices: intermarriage, high social and economic profile, low rates of religious observance, a decline in residential clustering, and all the other registers of diaspora Jewish integration. Nor do they seek to be secular. To the contrary, as documented by Jonathan Woocher in America and Liebman and Don-Yehiyah in Israel, even highly secular Jewish contexts—fundraising, political activism, and the symbols of statehood—have become infused with religious symbolism. But this does not mean that they have thereby become religious. To the contrary, what has emerged is "civil religion," a process whereby a set of symbols, values, and rituals—often borrowed from a religious tradition—is used to integrate and legitimate a social order. The language of civil religion is religious. But its focus is secular. At its heart is not God but society.

Thus process stands opposed to intent. There are few Jews today, fewer still among the young, who endorse a conscious strategy of assimilation or a principled Jewish secularism. Yet assimilation and secularization proceed apace. As religion becomes more marginal to the practical concerns of society and is relegated to the status of one among many leisure-time activities, both processes take place. Thus it can come about that Jewish attitudes grow more Orthodox, while Jewish behavior grows less so.

Institutional Logic

There is a further irony. One word often used to describe the contemporary Jewish situation is "polarization." The term is misleading. Jewry, as we have seen, was effectively polarized in the nineteenth century, not the twentieth. It was then that the fierce intellectual battles were fought between protagonists and opponents of enlightenment and emancipation, Orthodoxy and Reform, Zionism and diasporism, between those who saw Jewish identity in religious terms and those who gave it, instead, national, political, cultural, or ethnic interpretations. Those confrontations have to a large extent abated. But what is fought in one generation as a clash of ideas is enacted, a century later, as sociological reality. And one legacy of the past is particularly disturbing.

A tacit assumption of almost all strands of nineteenth-century Jewish thought was that the revolutions that were shaking Jewish life were the equivalent of an ecological upheaval. A Darwinian natural selection was taking place in which only the fittest would survive. The early radical Reformers tended to see Orthodoxy as an archaic survival of the ghetto that would be eclipsed by the forces of modernity. Many Orthodox observers, for their part, saw Reform as a barely disguised form of assimilation that would be the instrument of its own demise. It was too diluted to secure Jewish continuity against the pressures of intermarriage. The early Zionists, with few exceptions, saw the diaspora as doomed, whether as Pinsker and Herzl thought, through anti-Semitism, or as Klatzkin argued, through assimilation. The anti-Zionists were no less negative in seeing Zionism as politically dangerous, religiously subversive, and practically unworkable.

The rhetoric of nineteenth- and early twentieth-century Jewish thought, with its internecine hostilities and undertones of selective survival, is distasteful to a post-Holocaust age. More importantly, it has simply proved false. Israel exists. The diaspora survives. There are still Reform Jews. Orthodoxy flourishes. This is a consequence no one had foreseen. The various philosophies and ideologies that animated Jews had been couched in terms of an explicit or implicit negation of alternatives. Each school of thought profoundly believed that only it would survive. As a result, few contemplated the complex plurality that is contemporary Jewry. Coming to terms with the existence of alternatives was not an item on the intellectual agenda of Jewry a century ago. The word "pluralism" has only been heard relatively recently in a Jewish context.

The result has been that the various segments of the Jewish world have defined their futures in terms of institutional logic rather than through sustained reflection on the Jewish people as a whole. From such a narrow perspective, strange and incompatible conclusions can be drawn. Diaspora sociologists, for example, have evolved a concept of ethnicity that allows American Jewry to conclude that it is surviving, even reviving. At the same time, and on the basis of the same evidence, Israeli sociologists have concluded that it is fast assimilating and disintegrating.

Orthodoxy, contemplating its own remarkable growth, has concluded rightly that its future is secure, and wrongly that the future of other dimensions of Jewish life is insecure. For Conservative and Reform leaders in America note that Orthodoxy has made few inroads into their own ranks, and that they remain overwhelmingly the majority affiliations. The Reform movement in particular can take comfort from the results of a recent New York Jewish survey which showed that while only 9 percent of first generation Americans identify with it, 40 percent of the third generation and 51 percent of the fourth do so. That halakhic doubts exist about the Jewish status of a significant proportion of these members is, from the point of view of institutional logic, of minor concern. For it is precisely Reform's openness to mixed marriages and other problematic identities that has secured its growth. As for Orthodox delegitimation, Reform scholars have argued that since it is unlikely that Reform would be legitimated by Orthodoxy under any circumstance, no particular policy can make matters worse than they already are.

Once Reform has thus severed its links with halakhic criteria of Jewish identity, it can claim, in the recent words of Norman Mirsky, to be "the only American Jewish religious movement that truly has the religious survival of the Jew and Judaism at heart." These are sobering words in light of the fact that the policies that lie behind them have been described, by Conservative, Orthodox, and even some Reform thinkers, as threatening the entire structure of Jewish peoplehood. They serve to show quite how differently the same reality can be viewed from different perspectives.

Pluralism

In short, a situation can arise in which Orthodoxy, Reform, Israel, and the diaspora can each claim, within their own terms of reference, that the Jewish future is bright and that they are its inheritors. Each can argue that the others are insecure and under threat. These four ways of interpreting the present are radically incompatible with one another. But they reinforce the reluctance of each to come to terms with the existence of the others. Why should they? They will survive; the others will not. Thus, a way of thinking that had its origins in the nineteenth century still controls contemporary perceptions despite the fact that it has become radically inappropriate.

The situation arises because each group has a different definition of what Jewish existence is. An even more paradoxical phenomenon can occur. Each group can subscribe sincerely to a public rhetoric of Jewish unity, even while making that outcome increasingly less likely. For what Jewish unity means to Orthodox and Reform Jews are two quite different things. One endorses pluralism; the other does not. Each can speak of peoplehood, covenant, revelation, and *mitzvah*, seeming to have much in common, while differing profoundly in their understanding of those words. Israelis and Jews in the diaspora, for their part, can speak of Israel as home in two radically different senses.

Meanwhile Orthodoxy and Reform, Israel and the diaspora, and the religious and secular publics in Israel itself have simply drifted apart in terms of culture, life-style, and intellectual assumptions. Their respective perceptions reinforce the fragmentation. Jewish peoplehood, even as it becomes more important to all four groups, becomes increasingly incoherent. The result is that the mirage of Jewish unity vanishes, the closer it is approached.

None of this would necessarily signal collision were pluralism possible within a Jewish framework. It is not. For Judaism is defined in terms of revelation and tradition. It cannot embrace interpretations that, for example, reject the binding authority of halakhah. The classic beliefs of Judaism are not merely beliefs: they are constitutive of the covenant and thus of Jewish peoplehood. Orthodoxy, faithful to those beliefs, cannot admit a pluralism that

would in effect legitimate their denial, secularization, or subjectiv-
ization. It is no accident that while there have been Orthodox
rabbinic authorities who have placed a high value on tolerance,
unity, and Jewish kinship, none since the birth of Reform has been
willing to confer on it legitimacy as an interpretation of Judaism.

Specifically, matters of personal status require a global consensus. As Michael Walzer has pointed out more generally, "The
primary good that we distribute to one another is membership in
some human community." He adds, "Admission and exclusion are
at the core of communal independence. They suggest the deepest
meaning of self-determination. Without them there could not be
communities of character, historically stable, ongoing associations of
men and women with some special commitment to one another and
some special sense of their common life." Who stands within and
who outside the Jewish community is the criterion on which the
existence of the community depends. If there are multiple answers,
there are multiple communities, not a single people. The criterion
admits of neither ambiguous nor plural answers. Pluralism at this
primary level is impossible, even incoherent.

There is, then, an asymmetry between Orthodoxy and Reform.
Reform can concede legitimacy to Orthodoxy; Orthodoxy cannot
do so to Reform. The same asymmetry exists between Israel and
the diaspora. The *golah* can concede centrality to Israel; Israel
cannot do so to the *golah*. This has nothing to do with secular
Zionism, which based its negation of the diaspora on empirical
premises: in one sense or another, diaspora Judaism could not
survive. Instead it has to do with something deeper than Zionism:
the place of the land of Israel in the Jewish imagination since
Abram was first commanded to leave his father's house and travel
to "the land that I will show you." Israel is home. Elsewhere is
exile.

Exile is dislocation, not only geographical but spiritual. Though
the Jewish people experienced its greatest religious heights in
exile—the revelation in the desert, the Talmud in Babylon, the
poetry in Spain, the piety of medieval France and Germany—it
remained conscious that it was in exile. Not until the nineteenth
century did it seek to redefine exile as either mission or home. That
was an aberration, tragic in retrospect, even as it is perpetuated in

contemporary diaspora ambivalence about the meaning of the word *galut*. For Jewish peoplehood to be a concept that embraces a continuity of Jewish life, past, present and future, there must be an asymmetry between Israel and the diaspora: the asymmetry between a permanent home and a temporary dwelling. That Jews have spent the vast majority of their history away from home and that most Jews today do not live there neither compromises nor contradicts the fact that Jewish life is a life lived toward Israel. A pluralism of "centers" of Jewish life is as unavailable as a pluralism of "truths" of Jewish faith.

Identifying Home

We arrive, then, in the late twentieth century at a series of paradoxes. Tradition has become more important to Jewish identity than any time since the birth of emancipation, while traditional behavior continues to decline. Israel is central to diaspora identity, while *aliyah* continues to decline. Jewish peoplehood is affirmed by all groups, but in different and incompatible ways. Jewish unity has come to seem both necessary and impossible. The various groups in the Jewish world are, by comparison with the nineteenth century, growing ideologically closer and existentially further apart. These are dilemmas which must surely be confronted. But by whom? And in what terms?

At the beginning of the twentieth century, the Zionist movement made a fateful decision. Joseph Chamberlain had proposed to Theodor Herzl that a Jewish settlement be created in East Africa. From many perspectives, the scheme had overwhelming merits. Jews in Russia were in desperate straits in the wake of the Kishinev pogroms. Here was a secure refuge, a place where Jews could exercise autonomy and create their own society. The Uganda proposal, as it was called, had the support not only of Herzl but of a secularist like Israel Zangwill and a religious Zionist like R. Isaac Reines.

Had it proceeded, it would have split the Zionist movement in two. It was rejected. The complex politics of the decision are one thing; the collective verdict of the Jewish people was another. Only the land of Israel is home. Not all Jews live in Israel, but the overwhelming majority of Jews live toward Israel. That fact creates mutual responsibilities between Israel and the diaspora, which constrain each, at times, from actions that would benefit themselves but harm the other. It supplies Jewish identity with a content and direction and an overarching unity. Nowhere else would have served this function; because nowhere else has for so long and so universally exercised its hold on the Jewish soul.

In the late twentieth century, Jews face another fateful decision. Jews in the diaspora assimilate, even against their will. They abandon Jewish law. They absorb the ethos of their environment. They develop new conventions of sexuality and role-expectation. They marry out. The proposal, made in varying degrees of radicalism by Reconstructionist, Reform, and Conservative thinkers, is that a home be found for these behaviors within a redrafted Judaism, one that embodies new conceptions of revelation, authority, *mitzvah*, and halakhah. The proposal has many merits. It creates a home for Jews who want to be Jews. It creates a religious refuge. It promises to enlarge the Jewish community at a time of demographic crisis. The integrity of those who advocate it is not to be questioned.

But were it to proceed, it would split the Jewish people in two. The complex politics of mending the extant rift is one thing; the fate of *knesset Yisrael*, the collective entity of Israel, is another. Only revelation and tradition, the line that leads through however many inflections to the Oral and Written Law and Sinai, has the power to unite the Jewish world into a coherent people. Not all Jews live by tradition; but all Jews might live toward tradition. That fact would create mutual responsibilities between Orthodoxy and the non-Orthodox, which would constrain each from policies that would benefit themselves but alienate the others. It would supply Jewish identity with a shape and ultimate destination: a holy, distinct, commanded way of life. Not all would live it, but it would be normative: an endpoint if not an immediate achievement. That most Jews in America live outside Orthodoxy is no more normative than the fact that most Jews in the world live outside Israel. Ultimately only one land is geographical home; only one tradition is spiritual home.

No one making such an assertion can expect it to do other than generate deep controversy. But in this case, it must be all the deeper, for it will come from all sides. Our argument is that convergence toward a common destiny can only come about through a normative reinstatement of Judaism as traditionally understood. There is evidence that, at least attitudinally, the Jewish people as a whole has turned toward tradition in the last two decades. The question is: has tradition turned toward the Jewish people?

Here we must take up the narrative where we left it in the third chapter: the history of Orthodox attitudes to modernity. What has happened to the visions of Samson Raphael Hirsch, R. Avraham Kook, and R. Moses Sofer in the last two decades?

9

The Radicalization
of Orthodoxy

The revival of Orthodoxy has not been evenly distributed between the various traditional alternatives examined in the third chapter. The yeshivah and chasidic communities are experiencing rapid growth. Samson Raphael Hirsch's philosophy of *Torah im Derekh Eretz* is currently out of favor. R. Avraham Kook's religious Zionism has been taken in new and unexpected directions by the Gush Emunim. As elsewhere, so with Orthodoxy: events in the last two decades have been ironic. The two broad movements within Orthodoxy that welcomed modernity—Hirsch's and Kook's—have been outflanked by modernity. The strategy that most consciously resisted the spirit of the age—that of R. Moses Sofer—has emerged as the approach that best captures the spirit of the age.

To be sure, we speak of a mood rather than a majority. In Anglo-Jewry, for example, some 70 percent of synagogue members belong to the mainstream, moderate Orthodox congregations, while only 5 percent belong to the so called right-wing or ultra-Orthodox communities. In Israel, the *charedi* presence is somewhat larger and more politically prominent. In America, where Orthodoxy as a whole is only a small section of Jewry, the yeshivah community has a proportionately larger influence on its attitudes.

Nonetheless in both countries, the majority of Orthodox Jews are participants in secular society along the lines envisaged by Hirsch. They see religious significance in the State of Israel along the lines suggested by R. Kook. But mood is significant. It suggests a disenchantment with, or a failure of confidence in, the philosophies that inspired an earlier generation.

That sense was recently expressed by the British Chief Rabbi, Lord Jakobovits. "Personally," he wrote, "by upbringing and by conviction I am deeply committed to the philosophy of *Torah im Derekh Eretz*. It is my way of life, my ideology. But I am realistic enough to appreciate that such a religious-secular fusion as a movement is not likely to prevail in our generation for a whole variety of reasons, certainly not by juxtaposition, or in opposition to the rest of the Torah camp. . . . We must recognize the growing ascendancy of these yeshivah/chasidic worlds and come to terms with them."

This view is widely shared. The journal *Tradition* published a symposium in 1982 on "The State of Orthodoxy." While most of the contributors agreed that "the vigor as well as the image of Orthodoxy has been completely revitalized," they were equally struck by what they termed the "move to the right." The yeshivah and chasidic communities were buoyant. "Modern" Orthodoxy was not. This consensus was all the more remarkable for the fact that its authors were all broadly within the modern or centrist camp, even if they were unhappy with these labels. The journal's editor, Walter Wurzburger, spoke of the "religious inferiority complex" felt by the moderates or modernists. In another context, R. Aharon Lichtenstein noted that the "right-wing faction has aggrandized even more than it has grown." Its profound self-confidence and "at times, excoriation of [its] opponents" was having an effect on Orthodoxy as a whole. It was "increasingly dictating Orthodox life-style and axiological norms [even] for many not affiliated with this camp." Its influence was out of all proportion to its numbers.

As a result, certain attitudes associated with modern Orthodoxy are in eclipse. They include the idea of a synthesis between Judaism and contemporary culture; a commitment to religious tolerance and to at least some cooperation with other groups; the value of moderation as a religious ideal; and a positive approach to Zionism.

Other views, more rejectionist in their approach to secular culture, the non-Jewish and non-Orthodox world, and the State of Israel, are in the ascendancy. How and why has this occurred?

Torah and Secular Culture

Hirsch, we recall, believed that Jewish and secular studies should be combined. "We maintain," he asserted, "that a familiarity with all those elements which lie at the root of present-day civilization, and a study of all those subjects required for such an acquaintance, is of the highest necessity for the Jewish youth of our day as it was in fact in all times, and should be looked on as a religious duty." Truth, he believed, was unitary. There could be no conflict between history and science on the one hand and Torah on the other. To the contrary: a knowledge of science would deepen religious understanding of creation, while a sense of history would increase awareness of the Jewish role in civilization. Two peoples, the Greeks and the Jews, had been the educators of the world. The Greeks had given mankind aesthetics, Jews had taught it ethics. The two cultures were therefore complementary.

Hirsch formed his views in the 1830s. Common to his and R. Kook's understanding of secular culture was the view that Torah was sovereign among the disciplines. The secular was in itself neutral. It could be given shape and direction by Judaism. It was not intrinsically hostile to or destructive of Torah. Judaism, for Hirsch, would give the secular ethical content; for R. Kook it would give it unity and sanctity. But by the 1960s, R. Soloveitchik was suggesting that, far from being neutral, the secular approach was now actively infiltrating Judaism and recreating it in its own image. Secular studies actively secularized.

The implication was that the ultimate harmony of human knowledge assumed by Hirsch and R. Kook did not exist. R. Soloveitchik did not document the thesis in detail. But we can infer something of what he may have meant. Secular history is resistant to the idea of revelation and miracle. Post-Darwinian natural science does not lend itself easily to the idea of purposive creation. Sociology tends to relativize religious belief by seeing it in terms of context and function. Secular ethics tends to be either Kantian or utilitarian, built, that is, on rational rather than revealed foundations. None of these disciplines is incompatible with religious faith, but none is obviously harmonious with it. Each, as R. Soloveitchik pointed out elsewhere, incorporates a different perspective on reality. They cannot be combined into a single unified vision. Just as one cannot view an object from several different points of view simultaneously, so one cannot view the world secularly and religiously at the same time. The most one can do is oscillate between them. This creates tension and ceaseless dialectic, not harmony.

Hirsch and R. Soloveitchik do not necessarily disagree. They speak to different ages. The idea of a unified body of knowledge with which Hirsch was familiar had been replaced, by the time R. Soloveitchik came to study at the University of Berlin, by a far more complex and fragmented culture. The Galilean-Newtonian view of nature had been supplanted by non-Euclidean geometry, relativity theory, and quantum mechanics. Philosophy and science no longer spoke the same language. Academic study had split and parcelled knowledge into a multiplicity of subjects and methodologies. As Stephen Toulmin put it, "The broad and general questions about 'cosmic interrelatedness' which were the focus of earlier debates about nature have been superseded by other, more specialized, disciplinary questions." R. Soloveitchik's thought, with its conflicts and disharmonies, mirrors this disintegration. Science did not, as Hirsch hoped, teach one to see nature "with the spirit of David." Nor did academic study reveal, as R. Kook wished, the essential unity of creation.

So it became and remains unclear as to what a *Jewish* approach to secular study might be. The point was made in a significant remark by Rabbi Norman Lamm, president of Yeshiva University, an institution dedicated to *Torah u-Madda*, a synthesis of Torah and secular knowledge. Speaking at its fiftieth anniversary, he recalled that as a student he had complained to the president, "Why don't you tell me how to combine the two worlds?" He was told, "Our job is to give you the materials, your job is to let them interact within you." Rabbi Lamm added: "I disagreed then. But I agree now." The synthesis, in other words, could not be made programatic. It was personal. It did not take place in the curriculum. It took place in the mind of the student. There are numerous institutions which teach both Jewish and secular studies, but none—despite many experiments—where the two are fully integrated. Nor is it hard to see why. Academic study is detached; Torah study involves commitment. Academic study is value-free; Torah study is value-laden. The one is universal, the other particular. These dichotomies do not always exist. Maimonides, for example, was able to integrate science, philosophy, ethics, theology, and halakhah into a single system. But with such dichotomies is how our culture is presently organized.

Educational Models

There is more to the eclipse of *Torah im derekh eretz* than this, however. The retreat from the Hirschian position began in his own community almost immediately after his own death. *Torah im derekh eretz*, it was argued, had been advocated only as a temporary emergency, or only for the specific circumstances of German Jewry, or only as a means of preparing oneself for a career. Hirsch himself had argued otherwise. But his successor and son-in-law, R. Solomon Breuer, had been influenced by the Hungarian model of Orthodoxy. He had studied under R. Moses Sofer's son Avraham at the Pressburg Yeshivah. That model, quite different from Hirsch's, was to exercise its influence over successive generations of German Jews, as it has done more recently to American Jewry.

The question was not so much intellectual as practical. What, to put it at its simplest, was the best way to train Jewish character? Was it in an institution in which Jewish and secular studies were taught side by side? Or was it in a yeshivah, where secular studies were totally excluded? In a yeshivah the student was immersed, at a critical stage in his identity formation, in an intense, exclusive atmosphere of talmudic learning and piety. Even when he left the yeshivah and entered the secular world, the memory of his days there would be a constant reminder of Jewish authenticity. Having once felt the full intellectual and spiritual grandeur of a complete Jewish environment, he would find the world outside pale and untempting in comparison. His mind and body might be else-where, but his heart would still be in the yeshivah.

Hirsch and those who adopted his educational philosophy believed otherwise. The student had to be prepared from the very outset to meet the intellectual challenges of the outside world. Otherwise he would be overwhelmed. The new culture with which he was confronted would seem to him to conflict with everything he had learned at yeshivah. He would be forced to make a choice. And the secular world was seductive. It offered success and excitement. If the choice was all or nothing—Judaism without secularity or secularity without Judaism—Judaism would be the loser. It was necessary from the very start of schooling to train children to combine rather than make a choice between the two worlds.

As a practical question, it had a practical answer. Which system worked? In fact, both had their successes and failures. It depended on the individual, the place, and the time. In Frankfurt, *Torah im Derekh Eretz* was attractive in the 1860s, less so in the 1930s. In America, "synthesis" was popular in the 1960s, out of favor in the 1980s. When secular culture is highly attractive, the Hirschian model seems appropriate and necessary. When it is less so, the yeshivah model is more powerful. In general, a Jewish sense of isolation—induced by the anti-Semitism of the 1930s and the anti-Zionism of recent decades—leads to a search for a total Jewish identity which distances the non-Jewish world. That is found, *par excellence*, in the yeshivah, and it is this that has made it so powerful a presence in contemporary Jewish life.

It is not, then, that there has been a move away from secular study. To the contrary. Most American yeshivot accept de facto that the majority of their students—86 percent, according to William Helmreich's researches—will go on to a university. But secular study is seen as purely instrumental, a career qualification. And, according to Helmreich, yeshivah leaders tend to prefer their students to attend secular colleges rather than a Jewish institution like Yeshiva University "precisely because they believe that the distinctions between the Orthodox life-style and that pervading the college are so clear that the student will not be tempted or confused by them." The important thing, from this point of view, is contrast rather than synthesis. One "learns" Talmud; one "studies" economics or medicine. College teaches a student a technical skill. The yeshivah teaches him who he is.

Integration or Compartmentalization

More, though, is at stake than the best way to form character. For the question is: What *kind* of character does one seek to form? The Hirschian ideal was *Mensch-Jissroel*, "man-Israel," an integrated fusion of ethical citizen and religious Jew. The yeshivah ideal tends to be somewhat different. The ultimate aim is "to sit in the house of God all the days of my life." Perfection is a life of study, unencumbered by the need to make a living. Clearly this is possible only for a few. But a career is not an end in itself. It is a necessary distraction. For Hirsch, just as secular study was part of Torah, so secular involvement was part of the service of God. For the yeshivah alumni, both tend to be seen as *bittul Torah*, neglect of the primary duty of Torah learning. Hence both, if possible, should be kept to a minimum.

Both positions have their precedent in Jewish tradition. Indeed Maimonides himself could be cited on both sides of the argument. Again, though, which model is the more compelling depends on the time and place. A number of developments have made the Hirschian paradigm increasingly less convincing. From Moses Mendelssohn onward we find Jewish thinkers of all shades assuming the idea that ethics are universal. "Jews may have a special way of actualizing ethics in their lives, or a special ethical mission, but what is right and good is essentially the same for all humanity." So long as this is believed, the idea of *Mensch-Jissroel* makes sense. The "moral revolution" of the 1960s, however, broke this assumption for a generation. Ethics were not universal but individual. "Doing your own thing" became the existential imperative. There were experiments with sex, drugs, and cults. This offended and frightened many Jews. Jewish ethics were not the same as, they were the antithesis of, secular ethics. In the backlash that followed in the 1970s, it became important that Jews should be insulated from, not integrated with, the "new morality."

This was the popular expression of a deeper development that has been charted by philosophers and political and social theorists. The liberal state draws a sharp distinction between public and private life. The public domain is ethically neutral. The state does not legislate morality; it merely prevents harm. Ethics becomes the free and private choice of individuals. "Modernization," as Peter Berger puts it, "has entailed a progressive separation of the individual from collective entities, and as a result has brought about a historically unprecedented counterposition of individual and society." When this occurs, public involvement comes to seem less close to identity than private life. A job is less who one is than what one does. Relationships become roles. Activities become functions. Meaning is provided by the private, not the public sphere.

This leads to *compartmentalized* identities. And as Charles Liebman has noted, "Orthodox Jews, by and large, do not search for consistency between their Jewish and non-Jewish life. On the contrary, they make a virtue of their inconsistency." This, he argues, is their great strength in contemporary society, their "survival strategy." They "have retained their ritual tradition and belief system virtually intact and at the same time have acculturated in language, dress and education to American styles because they have been able to separate these two aspects of life so that they impinge on one another as little as possible." This approach to identity sees only Jewish contexts as "real"; work, socializing, and secular culture are concessions to necessity. This is closer to the yeshivah ethos than to Hirsch. The point is that contemporary culture supports and even demands compartmentalization.

To be sure, Jews who live in two worlds tend to feel uncomfortable about their lack of integration. Samuel Heilman concludes his study of a modern Orthodox congregation in America, *Synagogue Life*, with the perception that the members "are forever trying to engage in 'passing' behavior." To their more traditional Orthodox friends "they must appear strictly Orthodox." To their colleagues at work they must "seem to be completely engaged with the present and with downplaying their Orthodoxy and the anachronism it connotes." This is the prosaic equivalent of the kind of conflict which R. Soloveitchik elevated to the level of philosophical drama in "The Lonely Man of Faith." It was precisely this that Hirsch, and in another way R. Kook, sought to avoid. But what are the alternatives?

The Vacation Paradox

One is to follow R. Soloveitchik and see tension, or what Adin Steinsaltz calls "strife of the spirit," as a religious experience. But, their powerful argument notwithstanding, most modern Jews turn to faith for security, not inner struggle. The other alternative is indeed to search for synthesis. But synthesis in the late twentieth century is not what it was in the early nineteenth. It would have to incorporate, among other elements of "modern consciousness," the idea that morality is chosen, not given; that religious truth is a function of history, society, or the individual mind; it would have to present within an Orthodox framework what Mordecai Kaplan called "Judaism without supernaturalism." But "modern Orthodox" thinkers of the 1960s, most notably Eliezer Berkovits and Emanuel Rackman, were controversial. Their successors in the 1980s, David Hartman and Irving Greenberg, are several degrees more radical. The synthesis of two life-styles may simply not be available.

An amusing illustration was provided by a recent scholarly exchange in the journal *Tradition*. Across twenty-five pages of dense argumentation two modern Orthodox thinkers debated whether taking an exotic Club Mediterranean holiday away from other Jews—careful nonetheless to observe the laws of *kashrut*, daily prayers, and so on—was an example of synthesis or compartmentalization. One argued that it was the epitome of synthesis. What, after all, could be a better example of "the creative blending of the best elements of Jewish tradition and modern culture" than saying *Minchah* on a sun-soaked tropical beach? The other argued that it could only be considered synthesis if it was evidence of an integrated life and was conducive to spiritual growth. This in the circumstances seemed unlikely.

The problem is, of course, that the concept of a vacation is a peculiarly modern one, dating from the 1870s. And as Michael Walzer notes, "What is crucial about the vacation is its individualist (or familial) character." Central to the idea is that vacations are "individually chosen and individually designed." Walzer notes that the vacation is in a sense the exact opposite of the idea of *Shabbat* rest which is "enjoined on everyone, enjoyed by everyone." *Shabbat* is an institution of law, vacations are a matter of choice. *Shabbat* is communal, vacations are personal (hence the appeal of "getting away from other Jews"). The vacation is a phenomenon of modern consciousness, part of its rich emphasis on private as opposed to public life.

Hence the place of a vacation in an "integrated Jewish life" becomes impossible to solve. One side of the argument sees it as synthesis, thus incorporating into Judaism an individualism entirely foreign to tradition. The other side rejects this and instead defines synthesis as a unified life. But what proof-text establishes that "a unified life" is a Jewish value? The author derives his proof from the nineteenth-century Christian existentialist Kierkegaard: "Purity of heart is to will one thing." Both sides are driven many miles from tradition.

Neither scholar quotes Maimonides, who deals with the issue in the fifth of his *Eight Chapters* as something quite self-evident. All of man's conduct should be directed to a single goal, the service of God. In this way all his deeds will be "for the sake of heaven." Since he cannot serve God while exhausted or depressed, he may sometimes need to take a break "by walking in gardens and fine buildings, by sitting before beautiful forms and by things like this which delight the soul." Leisure is thus dealt with under the rubric of medicine which is part of the perfection of the body which is needed for perfection of the soul. For Maimonides, leisure is part of a unified world. For moderns, a vacation is an escape from a pluralized world.

Faced with such philosophical conundrums, *chasidim* take vacations en masse, refusing to admit individualism into the social structure. For the modern Orthodox Jew getting away from it all, it is just another insoluble problem of synthesis, to be agonized over or ignored according to temperament. Compartmentalization is the victory of fact over theory. It is a way of life that seems to work even if it cannot be philosophically justified. Thus, many observant Orthodox Jews live a life that is Hirschian in practice but not in principle. They study both Torah and secular disciplines. They attend yeshivah and university. They keep halakhah and have professional careers. Their dual life is neither a noble conflict nor a creative synthesis: it is just what one has to do in the modern world. *Torah im derekh eretz* is widely practiced but rarely preached. This is troubling to many modern Orthodox Jews. But that is the dilemma. Orthodoxy cannot be translated without remainder into modern consciousness. This is one of the unsolved problems of contemporary Orthodoxy, and why there has been no clear intellectual heir of either Hirsch or R. Kook.

Religious Zionism and Wittgenstein's Ladder

It was precisely this kind of problem that led R. Kook to believe that a full and consistent Jewish life could only be lived within a Jewish land. He stated his objections to diaspora Judaism in somewhat mystical terms, but we can put the case more prosaically. Judaism is more than a religion. It embraces the totality of life. But if most of life is conducted on non-Jewish terms, there are only three alternatives: segregation, compartmentalization, or "synthesis." Segregation artificially restricts Jewish life. Compartmentalization artificially restricts Judaism. And "synthesis" is simply not available. Judaism is natural only in Israel, where it can shape a total culture. This, expressed nonmystically, is the core of R. Kook's religious Zionism.

However, religious Zionism is currently undergoing the same eclipse as *Torah im derekh eretz*. In the early 1980s, R. Aharon Lichtenstein noted that "twenty or thirty years ago the overwhelming majority of the Orthodox community, its yeshivah component included, was suffused with pride in the State and identified with its character and symbols." This frame of mind was today receding. In 1985 Bernard Rosenzweig could write that religious Zionism is "at the crossroads of its existence, threatened with extinction organizationally, or at best with being consigned to a marginal role in the scheme of things." Reuven Bulka spoke of the growing influence of the extreme anti-Zionist attitudes of Neturei Karta within the yeshivah world and its consequent impact on Orthodoxy as a whole.

Why? Again the reasons are complex. One way of focusing on the problem is to ask what religious Zionism actually is. The phrase "religious Zionist" can mean two things. It can refer to someone who is two separate things, religious and a Zionist. Or it can refer to someone who is a Zionist on religious grounds: who sees Zionism as an essentially religious phenomenon. R. Kook was a religious Zionist in the second sense. For him, Zionism was *atchalta de-ge'ulah*, the beginning of the process of redemption. The events that led toward the messianic age began with the ingathering of exiles and the return of Jews to their land. This had been the view, too, of earlier religious Zionists like R. Zvi Hirsch Kalischer and R. Yehudah Alkalai.

But this was bound to be a highly contested position. After all, surely redemption was something brought about by God, not man. Had Moses not said, "Even if you have been banished to the most distant land under the heavens, from there the Lord your God will gather you and will bring you back." Moses seemed to speak of a miracle brought about by Heaven, not a political process engineered by man. What is more, the Talmud in *Ketubot* had spoken about two oaths taken by Israel in exile, not to return en masse to the land, and not to rebel against the nations of the world. In return the nations had agreed "not to oppress Israel excessively." This seemed to suggest that the task of the Jewish people was to wait passively in exile and rely on prayer and piety to bring the promised return. Hirsch himself had said that "actively to accelerate" the end of exile "is prohibited to us." Zionist activism looked suspiciously like an attempt to preempt Providence. Moreover, the Zionist movement was led by notoriously assimilated Jews like Nordau and Herzl. Could one associate with non-Orthodox Jews in general, let alone in so sacred a task? Even in the early days of the movement, there were many Orthodox Jews who argued that, if it aimed at bringing redemption, Zionism was heresy.

In response to this challenge, a new type of religious Zionist emerged. The most prominent figures were R. Isaac Reines (1839–1915) and R. Samuel Mohilever (1824–1898), and they were religious Zionists in the first sense. They were religious and they were Zionists, but they argued that the two were independent. The attempt to create a Jewish settlement in Eretz Yisrael had nothing

to do with bringing the redemption. It had to do instead with
piku'ach nefesh, the command of saving lives. Jews throughout
Eastern Europe were suffering from a wave of anti-Semitic attacks.
They were fleeing in their millions to America. A refuge could and
should be built in Israel.

This approach countered the two objections to Zionism in R.
Kook's sense. Firstly, it separated Zionism from the question of the
messianic age. Secondly, it provided a basis for working with
nonreligious Jews. As R. Reines put it: religious intention is
required only for commands between man and God. But saving life
is a command between man and man. If an irreligious Jew gives to
charity, he has fulfilled a *mitzvah*. So too if he helps to rescue Jews
from oppression by building a land for them to inhabit. R.
Mohilever put it similarly: "Our attitude toward those among us
who did not observe the religious precepts must be, as it were, as
if fire had taken hold of our homes, imperiling our persons and our
property. Under such circumstances, would we not receive anyone
gladly and with love who, though irreligious in our eyes, came to
rescue us?"

The movement which emerged from their efforts was Mizrachi.
To be sure it did not confine itself to the task of settlement only. It
was committed to the idea of "the land of Israel for the people of
Israel according to the Torah of Israel." But its great strength, in
contrast to the views of R. Kook on the one hand and the religious
anti-Zionists on the other, was its demystification of the idea and
program of Zionism. To create a state, it was necessary to work
with nonreligious elements. To create a religious state, it was
necessary to influence the Zionist movement from within, rather
than criticizing it from outside. But therein, too, lay its weakness
once statehood had been achieved. For here we confront a problem
common to both religious Zionism and *Torah im derekh eretz*, what
might be called the "Wittgenstein's ladder" syndrome.

Wittgenstein once spoke of philosophy as a ladder on which one
climbed to clearer perceptions. The ladder could be thrown away
once the objective had been reached. Whether or not this is true of
philosophy, it is the fate of certain legitimating ideologies. *Torah im
derekh eretz* provided an ideological basis on which Orthodox Jews
could participate in the secular world. Religious Zionism of R.

Reines's and R. Mohilever's kind allowed them to participate in a global movement to establish a Jewish state. So long as these objectives had not been achieved, the ideologies were important motivators. But once they have been realized, so securely that they can be taken for granted, legitimation is no longer so important. A second phase ensues.

With the objectives realized, the next stage becomes suddenly less clear. Synthesizing Torah and secular culture turns out to be highly complicated and not fully realizable. Shaping Israel into a state and society "according to the Torah of Israel" is also a slow and tortuous process. It suffers occasional setbacks. It calls for tact, diplomacy, accommodation, and a long-range strategy that seems to yield few short-term gains. Instead of ideology representing a simple and dramatic goal, it now dictates a measured realism, an engagement with recalcitrant facts. Slogans that once inspired come to seem to stand for compromise and "the art of the possible." The promised land is always more promising in the wilderness than in the arrival.

Hence religious Zionism has come to suffer the same fate as *Torah im derekh eretz*: having become reality it has ceased to be ideology. Orthodox Jews are more likely than others to live or study in Israel, to speak Hebrew, to make *aliyah* and to defend unpopular Israeli government actions. At the same time they are more likely to be highly critical of the very idea of a secular state and to refuse to attach religious significance to such celebrations as *Yom ha-Atzma'ut*, Israel's Independence Day. Pragmatic religious Zionism has suffered the failure of success. Having seen the achievement of its first objective, "the land of Israel for the people of Israel," it has lost momentum on the slow and less dramatic route to the second, "according to the Torah of Israel."

Anti-Zionism

What then has happened to Zionism within religious circles? The question is complicated by the extraordinary variety of approaches to Zionism within Orthodoxy. This variety, which at times generates violent conflict and mutual delegitimation within yeshi-

vah and chasidic circles, is all the more surprising given the
impressive amount of common ground shared by almost all Orthodox Jews, Zionist or anti-Zionist.

Israel is the promised land, the land to which Jews turn in prayer
and to which they long to return. Settling in the land is a religious
duty. A home outside Israel is only a "temporary dwelling."
Orthodox authorities were universally critical of the deletion of
prayers about Zion and the ingathering of exiles from the liturgy of
the Reform temple in Hamburg in 1818. Orthodoxy rules out
anti-Zionism in the sense of an affirmation of the diaspora as home.

It is equally unanimous in its rejection of Achad ha-Am's
"cultural Zionism": the attempt to see in Zionism the basis of a new
and secularized Jewish peoplehood. Orthodox Jews are agreed in
believing that nationalism is not an end in itself, that there must be
serious reservations about working within the framework of secular
organizations, and that ultimately Israel must become a society
organized along religious lines. The common ground is substantial.
The ultimate vision is the same. But within this framework deep
divisions are possible and have become pronounced in recent years.

There have been two broad developments. The first is an
increasingly negative attitude toward the state. What had been
forgotten in the turbulent years between the 1930s and 1950s is that
the consensus of Central and Eastern European Orthodoxy before
then had been resolutely opposed to the Zionist movement. This
has been the stance of the coalition of Orthodox leaders, Agudat
Yisrael, formed in 1912, which brought together yeshivah heads,
chasidic leaders, and the successors of Hirsch in Germany, R.
Solomon Breuer and his son Isaac. The opposition to Zionism was
consistent with a positive attitude to settlement in Israel. Isaac
Breuer (1883–1946), for example, believed that the Balfour Declaration had messianic significance and that Orthodox Jews should
work toward making Israel a national home. He nonetheless
vehemently opposed their participation in the secularist-dominated
Zionist movement, which he saw as a rebellion against the sovereignty of God.

The literature of the early twentieth century contained denun-
ciations of Zionism by an extraordinary array of *gedolim*, outstanding Torah sages. R. Meir Simcha ha-Cohen of Dvinsk (the Ohr

Sameach, 1843–1926) spoke of the "conspiracy" of Herzl and Nordau and their "abominable movement." R. Meir Israel ha-Cohen (the *Chafetz Chayyim*, 1838–1933) denounced Mizrachi, declaring that "our healing will not spring from them nor will their glory be for ever." R. Joseph Rosen (the *Rogachover*, 1858–1938) condemned the work of R. Reines as "an abomination and a desolation." R. Aryeh Leb Alter, Rebbe of Ger (the *Sefat Emet*, 1847–1905), spoke of Zionism as the result of the "confusions of Satan."

Collectively they argued that political activism to bring about a state was an attempt to "force the end" and frustrate the oaths by which Jews had agreed to wait patiently in exile. Redemption would come by God, not man. Zionism was worse than Enlightenment, for instead of offering an alternative to Judaism it offered a substitute. It redefined Jewish identity. It substituted nationalism for the life of Torah. It was, said Isaac Breuer, "collective assimilation." Though these views lost their salience after Hitler's rise to power, they were bound eventually to resurface, for they represented virtually the entire spectrum of the Torah world and its leading rabbis, men of unquestioned influence and authority.

The man who carried the argument into recent times was R. Joel Teitelbaum (the Satmarer Rebbe, 1888–1979). A powerful writer and religious leader, and himself a survivor of the Bergen–Belsen concentration camp, he restated the classic objections to Zionism and raised them to a new level of cosmic significance. The secular government of Israel, composed as it was of sinners and heretics, could yield no blessing. Orthodox Jews should have no part in it. Religious Zionists, in calling the state "the first flowering of our redemption," were aiding a false messianism.

Zionism had been the cause of the Holocaust. Jews had taken an oath to not rebel against exile, and the nations had taken an oath not to "persecute Israel overmuch." Since the Zionists had broken the first, they left the nations free to break the second. Indeed, argued R. Teitelbaum, Zionists had a vested interest in stirring anti-Semitism, for it made diaspora life difficult and supported the claim that Jews were only safe in Israel. Indeed Israel's "arrogance" and "aggression" had provoked the Six Day and Yom Kippur Wars and had heightened anti-Semitism throughout the world. If Jews would only give up their state and government "they would undoubtedly remove thereby the wrath of God and all of these hardships would vanish."

These views, representing as they did the extreme Neturei Karta position of principled opposition to the State of Israel, were widely regarded as unrepresentative, even fanatical. A not dissimilar position, though, has come recently to be widely shared in yeshivah circles. R. Isaac Hutner, for example, head of the R. Chayyim Berlin yeshivah and an influential presence in American Orthodoxy, argued in 1977 that the Final Solution had been influenced by the Mufti of Jerusalem, who had met Hitler in 1941. The Mufti had become a fierce opponent of Jews under Zionist pressure for a Jewish state. Zionism thus brought about for the first time a coalition of Christian West and Islamic East to destroy the Jewish people. The implication was that Zionism had been responsible for the *shoah*.

The continuing secularism of Israeli life, dissatisfactions within Israeli society, and the oppressive sense of unending conflict between Israel, Arab states, the Palestinians, and world opinion— all these lend momentum to a disillusionment with secular Zionism that can be expressed, in religious circles, in terms of sharp oppositions. Zionism comes to seem to be the cause of all evils afflicting Jews. Politics leads to corruption and decay. The essentially apolitical stance of Judaism since the collapse of the Bar Kochba rebellion in the second century C.E. is turned into a powerful critique of the Zionist politicization of Jewish history. Among Israeli *ba'alei teshuvah* this view is particularly strong. These views coexist, we must recall, with a strong dedication to the land itself and living within it. Indeed, both the yeshivah and chasidic communities have, in recent years, been highly active and organized in the political arena, a fact lamented by supporters of Neturei Karta. Once again we are struck by the conflict between existential reality and religious ideology.

Messianic Politics

If anti-Zionism, mild or militant, has been one motif of Orthodoxy in the last two decades, messianic Zionism has been the other.

Here we return to the ideas of R. Avraham Kook. R. Kook, we recall, believed that the return of Jews to their land would set in motion a messianic process. The rift between religion and the secular would be mended. There would be a new flowering of religious creativity. From Israel would radiate forth a Divine light which would heal the tensions between Jew, Christian, and Muslim. In the wake of the Six Day War it became clear that none of these things had happened. But something else had. Jerusalem had returned to Jewish hands. So had Judea and Samaria. Israel's army had proved victorious against its assembled Arab enemies.

Throughout Israel there was a mood of religious fervor. As Eliezer Schweid, himself a secularist, noted at the time, the "storytellers and poets of the War of Independence" in 1948 "did not dare employ religious symbols or the language of religious experience." In 1967 they did. Religious symbols were "consciously perceived and fraught with meaning." There was "no sense of recoil from using them." The mood dissipated among the general population, but it was preserved among a small group of religious Zionists, who now found inspiration in R. Kook's son, R. Zvi Yehudah Kook (1891–1982). Though there were direct continuities between the thought of father and son, there were differences of emphasis also.

R. Avraham Kook, the first Chief Rabbi of Palestine, lived and worked prior to the creation of the state. His son spoke to new realities. In R. Avraham Kook's writings, the emphasis is on *aliyah*, national rebirth, and literary renewal. No political program can be extracted from it. In R. Zvi Yehudah's speeches, by contrast, there was an intense identification with the realities of statehood: the army, the boundaries of the land, and the necessity of war. One speech in particular proved decisive. It was delivered at Merkaz Harav Yeshivah on Israel's Independence Day, 1967, before the start of the emergency that eventually led to the war. In it R. Zvi Yehudah spoke of his longing for those parts of the land that were currently in Arab hands: "Where is our Hebron? Do we let it be forgotten? And where are our Shechem and our Jericho? . . . Can we ever forsake them? All of Transjordan is ours. . . . Do we have the right to give up even one millimeter?"

Within less than two months these areas were back within Jewish control. In retrospect, the speech was seen as an inspired and inspiring prophecy. Gush Emunim began on its program of settling the territories, beginning in Hebron the next year. Religious messianism had become an active political force. R. Zvi Yehudah was clear on the meaning and imperative of the hour. The transformations foreseen by his father would come in due course. In the meanwhile, redemption must proceed along the axis of conquest and resettlement of the land. "Everything connected to it, all forms of weapons, whether produced by us or by the gentiles . . . all is holy."

It is thus paradoxical, but it has nonetheless happened, that messianism has led to opposite extremes. Neturei Karta and Gush Emunim share the view that the messianic idea is central to Judaism and that the State of Israel can only be understood in relation to it. For Neturei Karta the messianic process has not yet begun; therefore the state is a heresy. For Gush Emunim the process *has* begun; therefore the state is, wittingly or otherwise, holy and the instrument of redemption. Extreme antinationalism and nationalism flow from the same concepts, even the same texts. Between these two radical alternatives, the voice of religious moderation, expressed in a variety of movements—Oz ve-Shalom, Netivot Shalom and Meimad—has lacked widespread support.

The significance of religious nationalism has gone far beyond the boundaries of Gush Emunim and embraced a wide section of the religious Israeli public. One of the key problems is the application of religious texts, halakhic and aggadic, to immediate political decision-making. The verse in Deuteronomy 7:2, "You shall make no covenant with them nor show mercy to them," has been variously interpreted to mean that no territory should be ceded by Israel as part of a peace settlement, or that all non-Jews should be expelled from Jerusalem. Translating halakhah directly into a nonhalakhic state creates precisely those conflicts that religious moderates had hoped to avoid. The point was made bluntly by Meir Kahane: "There is an absolute and irreconcilable contradiction between the State of Israel . . . and the modern nation-state that sees all of its citizens as possessing equal rights. . . . There is a potential confrontation . . . between the Zionist state . . . and modern ideas of democracy and citizenship."

Orthodox thinkers of distinction—among them, in their different ways, R. Nachum Rabinovitch, R. Aharon Lichtenstein, and R. Yehudah Amital—have argued otherwise. They stress the importance of religious education as against religious legislation, of peace as against territory, of the broad imperatives of social justice and concern for minority rights. They argue the significance, ethical and political, of international opinion. Halakhah functions in concrete social and historical contexts, they insist, not in the vast abstractions of messianism and apocalypse. Similar views have been taken in different directions by Lord Jakobovits, Mordecai Breuer, and Uriel Simon. The most sustained and controversial attack on religious nationalism has come from the idiosyncratic Orthodox intellectual, Professor Yeshayahu Leibowitz.

But the mood of the times has been against them. The conflicts with which Israel is faced have seemed insoluble; their enemies implacable; world opinion systematically hostile. Apocalyptic images speak more directly to Israeli hopes and fears than the language of diplomacy or moderation or subtle halakhic interpretation. Messianic Zionism and messianic anti-Zionism are the result. Israel seems caught in the grip of vast forces. Providence is palpable, though opinions are divided as to whether it is endorsing or negating the state. In this climate, moderate religious Zionism comes to seem too complex, defensive, and weak to chart a lucid future. Argued by intellectuals, it hovers above the storm of political passion and fails to win either votes or hearts.

Ideal as Moderation or Extreme

So, while the Jewish people as a whole has moved toward traditional attitudes, tradition has not moved toward the Jewish people. To the contrary, it has moved further away. Orthodoxy has become radicalized. The connections once made between it and secular culture on the one hand, and the collective Zionist enterprise on the other, have grown attenuated and thin. The ironies of the religious situation continue to abound. In the previous chapter it was argued that Jewry outside Orthodoxy has become more traditional attitudinally but not existentially, in terms of its beliefs, not its life-styles. In this chapter we have suggested a similar discrepancy within Orthodoxy itself. *Torah im derekh eretz* and religious Zionism are Orthodox realities but no longer ideologies. They exist de facto but are not defended de jure. This does not make relations between Orthodoxy and the rest of the Jewish world easier. For attitudes generate conflict; and conflict has increasingly dominated the Orthodox agenda.

At this stage a tantalizingly simple question comes to the fore. Which is the more authentic, the more mandated by tradition: religious moderation or religious extremism? Accommodation to a real world or the dedicated pursuit of a utopian ideal? There is, of course, no answer. For R. Saadia Gaon the ideal religious personality was marked by harmony, balance, and integration. For the *chassidei Ashkenaz*, the thirteenth-century German-Jewish mystics, it was one who lived at the very edge of human experience, in constant consciousness of martyrdom. Jewish thought is a constant dialectic between world-affirmation and world-denial.

In the pages of the Talmud, we meet R. Jose ben Kisma arguing for political compromise with the Romans, and his colleague, R. Chananiah ben Teradyon, insisting on defiance unto death. R. Ishmael argues for a combination of Torah, work, and citizenship. R. Shimon bar Yochai insists on Torah exclusively and at all times. Maimonides sees halakhah as the perfection of society. Jewish ethical treatises from *Chovot ha-Levavot* ("The Duties of the Heart") in the eleventh century to *Mesillat Yesharim* ("The Path of the Upright") in the eighteenth, see it as the perfection of the self. The argument as to whether moderation or extremism was the religious ideal has been a recurring theme of Jewish deliberation. Maimonides saw, with characteristic insight, that the tradition idealized both types: he called them the "sage" and the "saint," respectively.

To be sure, one could hardly call either Samson Raphael Hirsch or R. Avraham Kook "moderates." Hirsch favored the complete secession of Orthodox congregations and rabbis from any Jewish organization dominated by non-Orthodox Jews. It was this philosophy, promoted by Hirsch's successors through Agudat Yisrael, that increasingly today challenges any Orthodox involvement in community-wide bodies. R. Kook, ostensibly the most tolerant thinker in Jewish history, wrote that alongside any belief which is both certain and universal "goes a refusal to share with others in any collaborative pluralism." The tolerance in which he believed was one which found "a place for every form of illumination, of life and of spiritual expression." But Judaism determined that place. R. Kook would surely have agreed with Yeshayahu Leibowitz that Judaism is "totalitarian in the realm of values." As Eliezer Schweid has pointed out, R. Kook and the secularists in whom he found "hidden sanctity" talked at cross-purposes. What he and they understood as tolerance were two different, diametrically opposed things.

In a sense, this has been one of the problems of contemporary Jewish thought: that the figures who most left their mark on posterity, Hirsch and R. Kook, left an unsuspectedly double-edged legacy. Hirsch could be quoted in favor of both *Torah im derekh eretz* and Orthodox segregation. R. Kook could be cited in defense of both moderate and radical politics. The same has proved true, in recent years, of R. Joseph Soloveitchik, who is standardly cited nowadays on both sides of controversies on the role of women, pluralism, and humanism in Jewish life. Those who spoke most forcibly for moderation, among them R. Azriel Hildesheimer, R. Yaakov Ettlinger, R. Isaac Reines, and R. Chayyim Hirschensohn, were altogether less dramatic and systematic. They left no philosophy that could be summarized in a slogan and capture the imagination.

Secularization and Segregation

But the tension remains. Halakhah concerns both the individual and society. Judaism embodies a code of individual perfection on the one hand. But it remains, on the other, resolutely tied to the Jewish people as a whole. What moderated Jewish law in the past was the fact that it was the constitution of a complete society, from the righteous to the sinners and the great mass of intermediates between. The Jewish people was constituted by its Torah, said R. Saadia Gaon; but the Torah, equally, had to be interpreted in the context of the Jewish people. It was the law not of an elite, nor of a self-selecting community of those who chose to adhere, but of the biological "congregation of Jacob," those who had been born into its covenant.

This mutual bond between the Torah and the collective entity of Israel split apart with European emancipation. The structures of Jewish self-government dissolved. The environing society was itself secularized. Jews became free to be Jewish in any way they chose. They had the option, unprecedented for many centuries, of ceasing to be Jewish without becoming, religiously, anything else. Modernity, as many social theorists have pointed out, is marked by the transition from "fate" to choice. Roles and identities are no longer things given by birth. They become things one chooses. The chaos this created for Judaism we have charted throughout this study. Jewish identity and its attendant duties and relationships are primarily given by birth. Modern consciousness could hardly have done other than have the effect of disintegrating tradition. That the Jewish people still survives in a state of real, if fragile, coherence is little short of miraculous.

In retrospect, the insight of R. Moses Sofer has been stunningly vindicated. It had already been adopted by *chasidim*. It came to be taken up by Samson Raphael Hirsch as well. Judaism would survive precisely if faithful Jews took advantage of the collapse of Jewish self-government and dissociated themselves from the rest of the Jewish world. In the protected enclaves of the yeshivah, or the chasidic community, or the Hirschian school-synagogue nexus, they could pursue a life of religious intensity strong enough to resist the tide of secularization and assimilation. The world of tradition was collapsing around them. What else could be done but conserve a "saving remnant"? The more independent they were of the general Jewish community, the more free they were to develop an elite that would eventually emerge, in an age more congenial to tradition, as heirs of the Jewish future.

It took almost two centuries. But that, in the last two decades, is precisely what has happened. To these heroic figures, who guarded tradition's flame against the cold extinguishing winds of modernity, Judaism owes an eternal debt. But there was a price to be paid. The price was the atrophy of the concept of "the congregation of Israel" as an empirical reality. In the voluntary enclave, Jewish law could be interpreted strictly rather than leniently, for it was no longer bound to the constituency of all Jews. Most Jews did not observe Jewish law anyway, so whom could leniencies benefit? The more the enclave felt the need to be segregated from a secular world, the more oppositional images came to the fore. Instead of synthesis, there was dichotomy and choice. Where some had proposed an "and," religious authenticity now demanded an "or": Torah *or* secular culture, religion *or* Zionism, Judaism *or* the Jewish people.

Thus, as society drifted away from religion, religion drifted away from society. As the Jewish people moved far from Orthodoxy, Orthodoxy moved in directions that took it far from the majority of the Jewish people. The alienation was mutual and self-reinforcing. The two great attempts to span the divide—Hirsch's and R. Kook's—became increasingly untenable as the gap widened. And so the great paradox of the Jewish present was born.

Jewish peoplehood has rarely before seemed so desirable and so elusive. In the last twenty years the sense of global Jewish kinship has deepened, but so too has the sense of inner Jewish conflict. As the idea of peoplehood has become secularized, it has moved further away from Torah, the one basis on which it could be coherently constituted. Orthodoxy, the one group positioned to unify the Jewish people, has seemed to be the one group standing in the way of unity. Increasingly it has developed a confrontational stance toward secularism in Israel and Reform in America. Internally it has been riven by conflict between the various chasidic and yeshivah groups, and between both and modern Orthodoxy.

We have argued that only tradition has the power to shape the Jewish people into a coherent entity. But does it? When Judaism itself becomes a battleground, where do we seek the Torah that "was only given to make peace in the world"? Have there been other voices within Orthodoxy that have sought to bring it closer to the rest of the Jewish world? As Orthodoxy moves inward toward greater segregation from secular culture, have there been movements in the opposite direction? What is and should be Orthodoxy's relation to the Jewish people as a whole?

10

Between Two Covenants

In confronting the Jewish world, Orthodoxy faces a situation at once full of possibilities and risks. We have suggested that the Jews of many different kinds have, for the last two decades, been moving emotionally closer to and yet sociologically further away from tradition. The most enduring effect of the shift in consciousness since 1967 has been a renewed and deep sense of Jewish peoplehood. But does "the Jewish people" still exist?

At a theoretical level, its meaning, role, and destiny are understood differently by Orthodoxy and Reform, by Israelis and Jews in the diaspora, and by secularists and religious Jews in Israel itself. At the most basic level there are those who believe themselves to be Jews, having been so pronounced by Reform rabbis in America on the basis of conversion or the patrilineal principle. Yet halakhically they are not Jews. It is not accidental that the question, Who is a Jew? has provoked such bitter controversies, for it goes to the heart of the matter. If there is no clear and single answer to that question, can we speak lucidly of a Jewish people at all? And if we cannot, what becomes of the sense of peoplehood? Jews have sought unity in the late twentieth century, while still living within divisions created in the nineteenth.

Imagine a group of friends in a mountain valley. Their aim is to climb. They agree that each will take a separate route. For some time, each is fully occupied in the difficult task of negotiating, step by step, a path upwards. Each is out of sight of the others. Eventually each emerges at the top. But they then discover that each has reached the top of a separate peak. They can see one another on their separate summits. They want to be reunited, but none is willing to climb down. Yet that is exactly what they will have to do if they want to be together as a group again.

That is the nature of Jews and Judaism today. Each group can claim to have reached its particular summit, even if each has privately to admit to falls and injuries on the way. Secular Zionism can point to the State of Israel, created and sustained by secular means: through politics, diplomacy, and wars. The liberal Jewish denominations can point to a flourishing diaspora, particularly in America, affirmative in its identity which it still chooses to express through religious institutions, even if its attachment to Jewish law and observance is slender. Orthodoxy can point to its unprecedented successes in Jewish education, its burgeoning day schools and *yeshivot*, it high birth rates, its passionately committed young, its resistance to assimilation, and its growing power within the Jewish world.

But there are separate summits. And there were injuries on the way. Secular Zionism would have to admit that its initial vision does not have the power to explain and sustain Israel's character today. To find meaning in their personal lives and their internal and external confrontation with the Arab world, Israelis have turned toward religious language and in some cases toward a religious way of life. In recent years, more Israelis have chosen *yeridah* than diaspora Jews have chosen *aliyah*. Reform Judaism in America has recently been growing. But only because it has chosen to provide religious legitimation for the great numbers of Jews who have intermarried. In so doing it has consciously courted the risk of writing itself and its members out of the Jewish people. Orthodoxy has seen the biblical and rabbinic tradition, of which it has been the uncompromising defender, lose its power over the vast majority of Jews in both Israel and the largest diaspora community, the United

States. It is a successful and confident minority, but it is a minority nonetheless.

Each regards the others as a threat to itself. Secular Zionism is threatened by a Reform that legitimates the diaspora, and by an Orthodoxy that either attaches little independent value to the state or, in the form of Gush Emunim, seems to want to take it into an aggressive, risk-ridden confrontation with the Arab world. Reform is threatened by an Israel that has made life increasingly awkward in the diaspora, and by an Orthodoxy that seeks its delegitimation. Orthodoxy is threatened by a State of Israel and a diaspora Reform, both of which it sees as active agents of secularization.

And yet, more powerfully than any events since the destruction of the Second Temple, twentieth-century history has made Jews conscious that their fate is indivisible. The Holocaust, the birth of Israel and its subsequent isolation have made Jews feel that, with or against their will, they are involved, each in the destiny of all. The various sections of the Jewish world have not simply gone their separate ways. Israel retains close links with the diaspora and the diaspora with it. Reform has sought new ways of recognizing the centrality of Israel on the one hand, traditional observance on the other. Orthodoxy has been involved with the Israeli political process, and has held back from formally excluding Reform Jews from the Jewish people even if it will not and cannot admit Reform as a form of Judaism.

Having reached this set of separate summits, where does the Jewish people go from here? In facing this question, Orthodoxy bears a peculiar responsibility of leadership. To see why, we have to return to first principles.

Jewish Peoplehood

Jews and Judaism represent more than a religion accidentally tied to a people, or a people coincidentally bound to a religion. The definitive moment which brought Israel into being was the covenant at Sinai, which married a people to God, and God to a people. The conventional distinctions between religion and nation here fall away. For the people of Israel was to be constituted by a covenant which embodied the religion of Israel. The relationship between the two might be tense and troubled, but a split was inconceivable. There could be no people without a specific faith, and no faith conceived independently of a particular people.

By the covenant at Sinai, the people agreed to be bound by a distinctive, holy way of life. In return, their history would be uniquely written in moral rather than natural categories. It would be a commentary on their covenantal loyalty or betrayal. It would be seen, both by themselves and by others, as evidence of the presence of God in history, or sometimes, tragically, as the temporary "hiding of the face" of God. The people of Israel would be both *edah* and *ed*, a congregation and a witness, summoned and testifying to a Divinely endowed destiny.

They would find that their end was already written in their beginning. There would be a pattern to their fate. Jewish history would repeatedly be written in terms of exile, exodus, and glimpses of redemption. From time to time Jews would disappear. Assimilation, forced conversions, and persecutions would take their toll. But as a people they would survive. With a perfectly uncanny conviction, the prophets were certain of this: that the covenantal people would endure every persecution, and be ingathered from the furthest exile. But it would survive on the basis of the covenant. It would survive because dispersion and persecution would recall them to their singular sense of peoplehood and from there to their holy way of life.

Judaism cannot therefore coherently imagine a divorce between Torah and the Jewish people, or between either and the place of their redemption, the land of Israel. Tradition envisaged no Jewish identity that was ethnic without being religious; or that was religious without the dimension of peoplehood; or which was not, in some sense, turned toward Israel; or which was based on an Israel unrelated to the Jewish people as a whole, or to Torah. Because there was only one God and one revelation, there could be only one Jewish people, one Torah, and one land which is a Jewish home. Individuals might make their choice to live outside one or the other. But there would be no enduring or lucid Jewish identity that did not define itself in relation to these three framing realities.

Covenantal Crisis

But underlying this definition is a monumental assumption, namely that Jews would continue to see themselves in these terms. "It is not with you alone that I am making this covenant and this oath," says Moses, addressing the generation that would cross the Jordan and take possession of the promised land. "I am making it both with those who are standing here with us today before God our Lord, and with those who are not here with us today." The covenant would bind all future generations. But why would it? Why should it?

We here confront the central, if unstated, question that has hovered just below the surface of Jewish life since the beginning of emancipation. Why be Jewish? Judaism marries fact and value, birth and obligation. One is born a Jew. Yet to be a Jew involves the assumption of responsibilities, a set of commands that define a way of life. A key, or perhaps *the* key assumption of Western thought since the enlightenment is that these two propositions cannot be joined to one another. Obligation presupposes choice. Existence, in Sartre's phrase, precedes essence. How then can a Jew be bound by the terms of a covenant made somewhere else and long ago, in a lonely desert by an ancient people? As a human being, surely he is free to write his own destiny. He is free to be a Jew or not a Jew. Or, deciding to be a Jew, he is free to shape that fact as he chooses. If there is choice, how can there be fate? If there is freedom, how can there be a prescripted Jewish destiny? In one way or another, this question has haunted the history of Israel since its earliest days. But there are times when it becomes particularly acute. At such times, there is covenantal crisis.

We can identify earlier periods at which the *givenness* of the Jewish destiny became acutely problematic. In exile in Babylon after the fall of the First Temple, Jews might have gone the way of the ten tribes before them, of disappearing through assimilation into a larger culture. After the fall of the Second Temple, again Jews might have chosen the way of Rome, or even the way of Pauline Christianity, integrating themselves into and even transforming from within the dominant imperial power. In the fifteenth century in Spain, they might have chosen, en masse, publicly to accept Christianity even if they remained *marranos*, Jews in secret. European emancipation offered a similar embrace, half menacing, half benign. Each invited Jews to abandon or merge their particular identity in favor of a more universal conception of civlization, history, and faith.

Some Jews did. In not every case was it a matter of defection to another people or culture or religion. It could take the form of limiting Jewish identity so that it fitted into the space left for it by the dominant culture. It could become a Hellenized Judaism that accommodated to the eclecticism of the Greek and Roman worlds. It could become a secret Judaism that took outwardly Christian forms. It could become a denationalized and ethicized Judaism that accorded with European notions of what a religion might be in a secular state. It could become a Jewish nationalism that sought expression in a secular state of its own. Alternatively, Jews could mount an attack on both their own and the dominant faith, seeking a world of pure universalism in which there were neither Jews nor Gentiles. Such, in modern times, was the strategy of Spinoza, Marx, and Freud. In each case the assumption of Sinai was shaken, that Jews had a unique and particular destiny that accorded with no universal norms. The question ceased to be theoretical and became burningly real and personal: Why should Jews remain bound to and commanded by a remote and distant covenant?

Why Be Jewish?

We can trace, too, the answers Jews gave to that question. There was the *mystical* answer given by the sages. The covenant in the wilderness was made not only with one generation but with the souls of all Jews as yet unborn. They were there and gave their assent. Sinai is, as it were, written into the collective unconscious of the Jewish mind. Then there was the *natural law* answer given, in fifteenth-century Spain, by Isaac Arama. Jews had found safety only under the wings of Providence. Cast to the winds of chance, they had been treated savagely by every people among whom they had come to live. It was no more possible that all Jews should forsake the covenant than that all members of a particular species should commit suicide. The law of Sinai was as deeply engraved in Jewish consciousness as the law of life was written into nature. Alternatively there was the *legal-metaphysical* answer given, also in the wake of the Spanish Inquisition, by Don Isaac Abarbanel. Jews had ceded their freedom to God by becoming His servants after the exodus from Egypt. From then onward, Heaven held a title, as it were, to the Jewish people.

Each of these was an attempt to show how fate could coincide with freedom, and how a covenant could be passed on across the generations. But undoubtedly the answer that held the greatest resonance was a much older one, first given by the prophet Ezekiel. "You say: We want to be like the nations, like the peoples of the world. . . . But what you have in mind will never happen. As surely as I live, declares the Lord God, I will rule over you with a mighty hand and an outstretched arm and with outpoured wrath. I will bring you from the nations and gather you from the countries where you have been scattered—with a mighty hand and an outstretched arm and with outpoured wrath." History would recall Jews to their destiny. They might succeed individually, but not collectively, in assimilating. The nations would resist it. They would expel Jews. There would be an exodus against their will.

The question and the answer recurred again and again. The talmudic sages envisaged a line of argument that suggested that history had *broken* the covenant. They read this back into the Babylonian exile. Jews came to the prophet and said: "If a master sells his slave, or a husband divorces his wife, does he then have any further claim on them?" Having sent Jews into exile, God could have no further claim to their loyalty. It was an argument that was to be repeated by Spinoza on the threshold of modernity. Jews, he argued, had ceased to be bound by the covenant since the collapse of their national autonomy. It has been heard more recently in the wake of the Holocaust, this time from Elie Wiesel and Irving Greenberg. Greenberg argues that after the *shoah* there can be only a "voluntary" covenant. Its "authority" has ended. Wiesel explains why. "The Jewish people entered into a covenant with God. We were to protect His Torah and He in turn assumes responsibility for Israel's presence in the world. . . . Well, it seems, for the first time in history, this very covenant is broken." In this last remark Wiesel is wrong, for the words have been heard before.

And yet repeatedly the unexpected has occurred. Jews did not see their sufferings as a sign that they had been abandoned by God and that they should now take refuge in the world. Instead they saw it as a sign that they had been abandoned by the world and that they should now take refuge in God. The covenant, said Isaiah, admits of no divorce between God and His people. Attempted genocide by Haman did not lead to Jewish defections but instead, as the Talmud put it, a renewal of the covenant more miraculous, because more voluntary, than at Sinai itself. Suffering would always lead back to, not away from, the Jewish destiny. If nothing else led Jews to return to their faith at the end of days, said the sages, Heaven would send "a king whose decrees will be as harsh as those of Haman" and they will repent.

Ezekiel's words echoed through the ages. History would bring back Jews to their vocation. Isaac Arama told the *marranos*, "You will find no rest among the Gentiles, and your life will hang in the balance." Abarbanel, quoting Ezekiel, added that "though they and their descendants would do all in their power to assimilate, they would not succeed. They would still be called Jews against their own will and would be accused of Judaizing in secret and be burnt at the stake for it." Moses Hess used remarkably similar language in the nineteenth century to the assimilationist Jews of Germany. And this, above all, is what has happened to Jewish consciousness in modern times. It is how most Jews react to the impact of the Holocaust and anti-Zionism. The Jewish destiny cannot be normalized in either the diaspora or Israel. The world will not let Israel, the people or the state, be "like the nations, like the peoples of the world." More than anything else, a sense of history answers the question: Why be Jewish?

A Partial Renewal

But in the past, this was only one aspect of a two-sided process. A sense of shared history led to a sense of shared destiny. To use R. Soloveitchik's terminology, *brit goral*, the covenant of fate, led to *brit yi'ud*, the covenant of purpose. In discovering that persecution did not distinguish between Jews, the Jewish people summoned themselves to a common future in the light of their common past. When Moses, and later Joshua, and later Ezra turn to address the people of Israel in a formal ratification of the covenant, they each preface their remarks by recalling Israel's history. Covenantal renewal begins in memory, much of it painful. But the pain does not end there. Joshua calls on the people to put away their strange gods. Ezra calls on them to put away their strange wives. To move toward a covenantal future means renouncing some aspects of the past.

What makes the present moment in Jewish history so tense and fateful is that we stand midway between two processes that have never hitherto been separated. The Holocaust, Israel, and anti-Zionism stand at the very forefront of Jewish identity. There has been a renewal of the *brit goral*. Jews feel part of a shared history. They feel bound together and in some sense "over against" a hostile non-Jewish world. They feel responsible for one another. They act in concert to defend one another. But there has been no renewal of the *brit yi'ud*. There has been no convergence toward a reinstatement of revelation and tradition. Because both Reform and secular Zionism have been "traditionalized" this has seemed to take place, but in reality it has not. Instead, tradition has been used to legitimate both secularization and intermarriage, the very things that Joshua and Ezra excluded from the covenant.

In this unprecedented situation Orthodoxy is faced with an awesome challenge and responsibility. For it was Orthodoxy which, through the last two centuries of a deeply unfavorable intellectual and social climate, has been the guardian of the *brit yi'ud*. Against Reform it insisted that there could be no secularization of the idea of revelation and no abandonment of the binding authority of halakhah. Against Conservative Judaism it insisted that halakhah is not determined by the values of the age; instead it is halakhah that determines the Jewish response to the values of the age. Against secular Zionism it argued that neither a land nor a state are ends in themselves. Against some recent Holocaust theologians, it has argued that no event in history can "rupture" the covenant or "break" its claim upon Jews.

Surveying Jewish history since 1789, the Orthodox Jew—especially if he has a belief in Providence—can surely find it in his heart to recognize the achievements of movements which he cannot in principle legitimate. It was a secular Zionist movement that brought into being a Jewish state. It was liberal Judaisms—Reform, Conservative, and Reconstructionist—that held the loyalties of substantial numbers of Jews who might otherwise have drifted altogether away from the Jewish people. There is a difference, in both Jewish law and thought, between means and ends. He may rejoice in these consequences even as he regrets the means by which they were brought about.

It might have been otherwise. The early precursors of Zionism were deeply religious Jews. Among the advocates of settlement of the land were the Vilna Gaon, R. Moses Sofer, and a number of chasidic leaders. Rabbis Yehuda Alkalai, Zvi Hirsch Kalischer, Isaac Reines, and Avraham Kook were all, in their different ways, architects of a Zionism that was itself a form of Orthodoxy. Nor did preserving the loyalty of acculturated Jews necessarily lead to Reform. In Anglo-Jewry, for example, cultural accommodation took place entirely within the boundaries of halakhah. It did likewise in Hirsch's neo-Orthodoxy. Zionism and liberalism might have evolved within the parameters of tradition and without shattering the covenant. But history is not written in terms of might-have-beens. As the sages said: what was, was. And in what actually transpired, liberal Judaism and secular Zionism played their part.

But there is a next stage. Covenantal renewal has not run its course. It has reached halfway to its destination. Until there has been, in some sense, a ratification of the *brit yi'ud*, the centrality in Jewish life of the covenant of revelation and command, the shift in Jewish consciousness we have dated to 1967 will remain unconsummated. For this to happen, there must be movement in every section of the Jewish world toward some common sense of identity and purpose. But it must surely be Orthodoxy which initiates the process. And this will mean a shift in the direction of Orthodoxy itself. How so?

Orthodoxy and the Jewish People

As Samson Raphael Hirsch noted, there is something odd about the word Orthodoxy itself. He objected to it. Judaism, he wrote, "knows of no mosaic, prophetic or rabbinic, and of no orthodox or progressive Judaism. It is either Judaism or it is not." He did not add, but we must, that Judaism knows of no Reform, Conservative, and Orthodox Jews. They are either Jews or they are not.

The phrase "Orthodox Judaism" is therefore an anomaly. For the word *orthodox* as currently used suggested a denomination, one kind of Judaism among others. Whereas Jewish Orthodoxy itself, whether defined in terms of Maimonides' thirteen principles or any of their medieval variants, established the *boundary conditions* of Judaism. A non-Orthodox Judaism would have been a contradiction in terms, for by its very non-Orthodoxy it would have parted company with Judaism. The phrase "Orthodox Judaism" at any age prior to the nineteenth century would have been tautologic. What other kind of Judaism was there? What other kind of Judaism could there be? Neither the word "Judaism" nor the word "Jew" admits qualifying adjectives.

The concept of Orthodoxy as one kind of Judaism among others has been a critical tension in the development of tradition since emancipation. In halakhah there is no such thing as a plurality of Judaisms, beyond minor local variants of custom. But in sociological terms, there was. In theory, Orthodoxy is the religion of all Jews. In practice it was the commitment of only some, and in some countries, a minority. Leaders of Orthodoxy were therefore caught in a dilemma. Were they to safeguard the religious integrity of the Jewish people as a whole? Or was their primary concern to preserve a minority within the Jewish people, those who held firm to traditional faith and practice? Tradition suggested the former. Pragmatism suggested the latter. And so the history of Orthodoxy throughout the nineteenth and twentieth centuries became a story of its progressive disengagement from collective Jewish enterprises.

In 1868 most of Hungarian Orthodoxy seceded from the general Jewish community. In 1876 Hirsch insisted that his Frankfurt community do likewise. In 1912 Agudat Yisrael was formed to mark the secession of most of Central and East European Orthodoxy from the Zionist movement. There has been increasing pressure within American Jewry for Orthodox rabbis to secede from interdenominational rabbinical groups like the Synagogue Council of America. Wherever Orthodoxy found itself in a minority, among reformers on the one hand or secularists on the other, the consensus was that they could not continue to be associated. They would be lending their names and their authority to decisions with which they could not in conscience agree. They would be helping to legitimate positions which ran directly counter to tradition.

There were those who disagreed. There was *gemeinde* Orthodoxy in Germany, "status quo" Orthodoxy in Hungary, and Mizrachi within the Zionist movement, each of which refused to sever its connections with the community as a whole. They had some distinguished representatives, but they were a minority within the Orthodox world. Faced with a general Jewish community unreceptive to its guidance, Orthodoxy turned inward and concentrated on strengthening its own ranks. In retrospect it was a successful strategy.

But that moment has now passed, or it shortly will. Orthodoxy has secured its future. It has emerged in a position of commanding strength, demographic and ideological. It has achieved the task it set for itself, or rather that was set for it by Jewish destiny. It preserved the Torah against the twin assaults of enlightenment thought and Jewish "normalization." The time has come for it to point the way to a reunification of Torah and the Jewish people. For that is the necessary next stage of covenantal renewal.

The Constituency of Jewish Law

But it is just here that we encounter a head-on conflict between the aims of "Orthodoxy" considered as a section of the Jewish world, and "Judaism" considered as the faith and way of life of all Jews. For Orthodoxy has found its strength precisely in its disengagement. No longer constrained by the need to formulate halakhah in such a way as to be livable by all Jews, no longer empowered to enforce Jewish law throughout the Jewish community, Orthodoxy was able to develop its own voluntary communities, each an elite of the most committed and intense. Halakhah itself reflected this narrowed constituency. Jewish law became, for the first time, a code not for a people as a whole but for a self-selecting group of the faithful. This was not intentional; but in many cases it was inevitable.

In the early twentieth century, R. Chaim Hirschensohn, an Orthodox rabbi who had moved to America, bemoaned the fact that halakhic authorities had not responded to the realities of an open, assimilated diaspora. In the early years of the State of Israel, Yeshayahu Leibowitz made the same complaint about halakhah there. It had not come to terms with the needs of an independent state, or a total economy, or modern technology, or military security. Orthodox Jews were able to observe *Shabbat* in Israel, he argued trenchantly, only at the cost of making other Jews their *shabbos goyim*.

But who was listening? The halakhic change they called for was revolutionary. It could hardly be endorsed by the *gedolei ha-dor*, the generation's great halakhic authorities, who had increasingly come to share R. Moses Sofer's view that any concession to modernity, even if technically permissible, opened the door to secularization. It could not be endorsed by the very people with whom Hirschensohn and Leibowitz were concerned, non-Orthodox Americans and secular Israelis. These did not seek a solution within halakhah, for they did not accept halakhah itself. So here was a solution in search of a constituency. In seeking to make halakhah applicable to everyone, Hirschensohn and Leibowitz found themselves speaking to no one. And that has been the problem of what is properly called Modern Orthodoxy ever since.

Modern Orthodoxy

Modern Orthodoxy in this narrow sense is not the Judaism espoused by Hirsch or R. Kook or R. Soloveitchik. It is not the establishment Orthodoxy of Anglo-Jewry. Nor is it what in Israel is called *dati* as opposed to *charedi*. None of these Orthodoxies proposed halakhic change or any radical revision in the way faith was conceived. The project of Modern Orthodoxy, by contrast, is to make Judaism applicable to a wider range of Jews. It recognizes that "modern consciousness" is something different from "traditional consciousness," and that as a result many Jews have become alienated from Judaism.

Modern Orthodox thinkers focus on three aspects of the rabbinic tradition. The first is that it contains considerable resources for halakhic change. The second is that, at times, it gives vivid expression to the power and dignity of human reason and interpretation. The third is a distinction between the purpose of Jewish law and its detailed enactment. When, because of changed circumstance, the law as it stands frustrates the purpose for which it was enacted, change—they argue—is halakhically mandated.

Modern Orthodoxy in this sense is a relatively recent phenomenon. Its precursors, as we noted, were R. Chaim Hirschensohn and Yeshayahu Leibowitz. Its major spokesmen have been Emanuel Rackman and Eliezer Berkovits, and more recently Shlomo Riskin and David Hartman; more radically still, Irving Greenberg. They have all been highly controversial figures. And we can now see why, and why Modern Orthodoxy did not surface a century before in the days, say, of Samson Raphael Hirsch. Modern Orthodoxy is an attempt to address the constituencies that lie *outside* halakhah, without *abandoning halakhah*.

In earlier periods such attempts had been made and subsequently forsaken. Early Reform tried to make distinctions between biblical and rabbinic law. Early Conservatism sought to stay within halakhah, liberally conceived. Early Zionism was constructed in traditional terms. One by one these attempts foundered under the pressure of radicalism. Reform cast loose from tradition in its militant conferences of the 1840s. American Conservatism did likewise under the impact of Mordecai Kaplan. The Zionist movement did so when it shifted from narrowly political to broader cultural aims.

But, as we have argued, the direction of change has since been reversed. Each of these movements has, markedly since 1967, been seeking a place within tradition. Could tradition find a place for them? Could it find a home within the categories of revelation and halakhah for the new situation of women in society? Could it enhance their position in the laws of divorce? Could Judaism confront intermarriage by a liberal interpretation of the laws of conversion? Was there a place within its values for the idea of democracy? Or for a humanistic sense of personal autonomy and dignity? Could Orthodox Jews engage in dialogue and collaborative ventures with secular and non-Orthodox Jews? These were and are the kind of questions raised by Modern Orthodoxy, and in general it found it possible to deliver affirmative answers.

Modern Orthodoxy is, in short, an attempt to locate modern consciousness within tradition. It is a symptom of an age in which "modernism" has itself become more traditional. It addresses the same issues that were once confronted by Reform, Conservative, and secular Zionist thought but stops short of their break with halakhah. Its overwhelming problem in finding an audience is that these alternatives still exist. Those who wish to give Jewish expression to feminism, liberalism, or personal autonomy can do so more freely elsewhere. Those who are attracted to Orthodoxy are so because it expresses opposite values: authority, community, and a highly defined sense of personal role.

Tradition's Many Voices

Modern Orthodoxy stands at the extreme outer boundary of tradition. It is a matter of some argument within Orthodoxy as to which side of the boundary it stands: inside or outside. It is nonetheless an important phenomenon. It is not one to which the author of this study would personally subscribe. Judaism, I believe, is far less compatible with modern consciousness than Modern Orthodoxy has suggested. Nor is halakhah as open to change as some statements within the tradition might lead one to conclude. There is a difference between the wide powers theoretically available to a Jewish court of law and the much narrower precedent of how those powers have actually been used. Nor can it be taken for granted that everything that can halakhically be permitted, *ought* halakhically to be permitted. The famous remark of Blu Greenberg, that "where there is a rabbinic will, there is a halakhic way," does not entail that where there is a halakhic way, there is a rabbinic will.

There are serious counter-arguments to many Modern Orthodox positions. Invoking the power of a rabbinical court to retroactively annul marriages, for example, on a scale never before practiced, would alleviate the position of women whose husbands refuse to grant them a divorce, but it would weaken the structure and sanctity of Jewish marriage as a whole. A more liberal policy on conversion than that practiced by many Orthodox courts in the diaspora is certainly available, and has at times been adopted by rabbinical courts in Israel. But there is a case for saying that this would be seen to be a tacit legitimation of intermarriage. One can, as David Hartman has done, write an account of Judaism in terms of anthropology rather than theology, focusing on those sources which stress human initiative and downplaying those which emphasize human dependence on and submission to the supernatural. But does this adequately represent the full meaning of such concepts as prayer, command, and Providence? There is a place within Judaism for personal autonomy. But there is also a place for the idea of obedience to law and reverence for its great interpreters.

But—and this is the crux—there is a difference between Orthodoxy as one kind of Judaism among others and Orthodoxy as the faith of the Jewish people. On this latter conception, it becomes profoundly important that the tradition speaks with as many voices as possible, and that as many positions as possible find their home within tradition. Saadia Gaon in writing his *Beliefs and Opinions*, and Maimonides in writing the *Guide of the Perplexed*, did not set out to address all Jews. They set out explicitly to speak to those whose doubts were leading them away from Judaism altogether. R. Soloveitchik, in his introductory remarks to *The Lonely Man of Faith*, declared it to be a completely personal statement, which may or may not strike an answering chord among his readers. What makes these works important is not that they represent a universal norm, but that they resolve certain cultural crises within the framework of halakhic Judaism.

I once wrote that "a sober analyst of the history of Jewish philosophy may conclude that its practitioners solved no ultimate problems; rather, they allowed certain personality types and mental frameworks to take their place in Judaism. The rationalist feels at home because of Maimonides; the antirationalist, because of Judah Halevi. R. Soloveitchik, in his philosophical writings, has answered no questions, but he has done what a great Jewish thinker should. He has given a home to the previously unhoused: to the Jew in the modern world who experiences conflict, loneliness, and the sharp unease of faith."

A similar statement could be made about Modern Orthodoxy. It has indicated certain possibilities within the tradition that had not been systematically explored before. It is possible, even probable, that Modern Orthodoxy is more significant to those outside Orthodoxy than those securely within. That explains its controversial nature and its difficulty in finding a following. It does not negate its significance. For it is Modern Orthodoxy that provides a bridge between Orthodoxy itself and Conservative and Reform Judaism and secular Zionism. Such a bridge must be found if Orthodoxy is once again to become the faith of the entire Jewish people. It must be found if there is to be a renewal of the *brit yi'ud*, the covenant of Sinai, with the Jewish people as a whole.

11

Tradition as Argument

We argued in the last chapter that if there is to be covenantal renewal, it is important that the Jewish tradition—the tradition of revelation and halakhah—speak with as many voices as possible. Behind this assertion lies a specific item of faith. That faith is one of the most distinctive features of rabbinic Judaism, and one which has fallen into disrepair in recent times.

Perhaps the best way into the subject is a profound set of remarks delivered by Alasdair MacIntyre, one of the most impressive contemporary philosophers of ethics. His book *After Virtue* (1981) is an attempt to reinstate the idea of tradition as a central category in moral thought. What is of interest here is a passage in which he describes a feature which he believes characterizes traditions in general:

> When a tradition is in good order, it is always partially consti-
> tuted by an argument about the goods the pursuit of which gives
> to that tradition its particular point and purpose.
>
> So when an institution—a university, say, or a farm or a
> hospital—is the bearer of a tradition of practice or practices, its
> common life will be partly, but in a centrally important way,

constituted by a continuous argument as to what a university is and ought to be or what good farming is or what good medicine is. Traditions, when vital, embody continuities of conflict. . . .

A living tradition then is a historically extended, socially embodied argument, and an argument precisely in part about the goods which constitute that tradition.

This characterization is extraordinarily germane to Judaism. The sages, as we noted in the Introduction, celebrated *machloket le-shem shamayim*, "argument for the sake of heaven." They epitomized it in the archetypal debates between Hillel and Shammai, about which it was said that *elu veelu divrei Elokim chayyim*, "these and these are the words of the living God." The central document or rabbinic Judaism, the Babylonian Talmud, is written in the form of sequences of argument. The argument itself and the clarification of the issues involved are often more important than the conclusions reached. Rejected opinions are considered as closely as accepted ones. Indeed, the Talmud states that the rulings of the school of Hillel became authoritative because, among other things, they studied the views of their opponents as well as their own and stated them before their own.

Argument, for the sages, was a deeply religious mode of discourse: not only argument between man and man, but even argument between man and God. The aggadic or interpretive literature of the talmudic period turns the biblical conversations between man and God—Moses' plea for the Israelites after the sin of the golden calf, for example, or Hannah's prayer for a child—into intense and dramatic confrontations which the rabbis termed *chutzpah kelapei shamaya*, "audacity toward heaven." In this respect they were continuing a biblical tradition of argument between earth and heaven—we recall Abraham's dialogue over the fate of Sodom, Job's over his tragedy, Moses' and Jeremiah's over the justice of Providence. It is a highly distinctive tone of Jewish spirituality, one that embarrassed Philo and other Jewish philosophers, but one that remained close to the Jewish heart. We hear it again in some of the elegies composed in the wake of the medieval massacres, in Solomon ibn Verga's account of the Spanish expulsion, and in the prayers of the chasidic master, R. Levi Yitzchak of Berditchev.

Reality, these arguments seem to imply, is not monolithic. There is always more than one true perspective on events. At the most basic level, there is the perspective of God and the perspective of man. Neither obliterates the other. Therefore there can be argument between them. Heaven always secures justice in the long run. But man sometimes calls for mercy, not justice; or for justice in the short run, not the long. The perspective of man has, for the sages, its own integrity and claim to attention. The rabbinic literature is, to be sure, acutely aware of the conflict between authority and argument. The angels, in these passages, attempt to silence man for his presumption. But God always allows him a hearing and often is swayed by his arguments. In argument, man reaches his full dignity before Heaven.

So too with halakhic argument. Two of the most powerful passages in the Babylonian Talmud concern the attempt to silence argument. Rabban Gamliel uses his authority as *nasi* or religious head of the community to exclude dissenting views. R. Eliezer ben Hyrcanus invokes the authority of a "heavenly voice" to overcome his opponents on a question of ritual purity. In both passages freedom of argument is affirmed. Rabban Gamliel is deposed, R. Eliezer excommunicated. The very dignity of the sage, in rabbinic Judaism, is part of the religious celebration of argument. For the sage is not a prophet. He is, said the rabbis, greater than a prophet. A prophet invokes revelation, which cannot be argued with. A sage invokes texts, interpretations, inferences, and analogies. He employs argument, therefore he can be argued with.

The process of argument, like a cubist painting, allows different perspectives to occupy the same canvas. Since reality is not monolithic, dialogue and debate are closer to its texture than systematic and reductive philosophical programs. Though the Middle Ages produced a series of great Jewish philosophers, the enterprise of philosophy never captured the Jewish imagination as much as the talmudic argument. Nor did Moses Maimonides' remarkable halakhic code, the *Mishneh Torah*, a compendium of conclusions on Jewish law with all argumentation removed, supplant the study of argument for its own sake. Indeed the entire literature of Judaism from the early rabbinic period to the threshold of modernity—halakhic, exegetical, philosophic, and mystical—is a series of commentaries on the biblical text, an ongoing and open-ended argument about the meaning of the word of God.

Diversity and Dialogue

To a remarkable degree Judaism was, is, and sees itself as, in MacIntyre's phrase, "a historically extended, socially embodied argument." It was through this argument that fierce antagonisms were channeled into a sense of common purpose. "Even a father and son or a teacher and disciple," said the sages, "who study Torah at the same gate begin by becoming enemies to one another. But they do not leave off studying until they come to love one another." The discipline of rabbinic study is precisely a matter of laboring to understand the strength of an opposing position and seeing that it too has its own integrity. It belongs within the shared tradition of texts, precedents, and canons of interpretation.

That tradition often yields more than one answer to a concrete question of how to live in a given circumstance and time according to the word of God. To be sure, not every answer is authoritative. This is implicit in the idea of halakhah. Judaism is a community of action. If, for example, there were many different ways of living out the command to rest on the seventh day, *Shabbat* would not create a *community* of rest, even though it might create a series of individualized variants of the same idea. Judaism draws the line between community and individual differently from that proposed by nineteenth-and twentieth-century liberalism. It extends communal norms into what John Stuart Mill might well have seen as the domain of private life and personal decision. That is the nature of a faith expressed in terms of halakhah, religious law.

Thus, when it came to norms of action, though there might be more than one justified inference from the sources, a halakhic *decision* is called for, arrived at by argument and consensus. A rejected opinion may be false, but it may not be. It may simply be a truth that did not find favor among the majority of the sages, or one that is not appropriate to this circumstance and time. The views of Shammai, according to one mystical tradition, though rejected as law in the present time will become law in the messianic age.

There is, nonetheless, a perceptible reluctance in the rabbinic tradition to close the argument and make a formal decision between alternative viewpoints. If a decision is not needed now, the Talmud asks: *hilkheta limeshicha?* "Will you make a ruling for the messianic age?" If there is no immediate urgency, there is no need to foreclose the discussion. So too with matters that did not affect the community of action. Questions of belief and attitudes that had no behavioral implications did not call for halakhic resolution. Neither did ethical questions of ideal temperament and disposition. Despite Maimonides' inclusion of such subjects within his halakhic code, subsequent codifiers, especially R. Joseph Karo in his *Shulchan Arukh*, omitted them.

The same is true even of the fundamentals of faith. Belief in the messianic age, ruled Maimonides, is one such fundamental; but a detailed spelling out of its implications is not. "Neither the exact sequence of these events nor their details constitute religious dogmas." Indeed the debate about the essentials of Jewish belief, which occupied thinkers for some two centuries after Maimonides had published his famous thirteen principles, took place at a philosophical rather than halakhic level. And in Jewish philosophy, unlike Jewish law, there are no decisions.

The result was to make Judaism not merely a tradition of argument, but also an unusually open-ended argument "about the goods the pursuit of which gives to that tradition its particular point and purpose." The arguments that demanded closure in the form of a halakhic ruling tended to be on immediate questions of the rules of conduct. Ultimate questions on the meaning and purpose of Jewish life were debated with equal seriousness in the literatures of *aggadah*, philosophy, biblical commentary, and Jewish ethical and mystical treatises. But there was no need to bring the argument to an end and choose between alternatives except where a view was so disruptive that it threatened the entire community of faith.

Continuities of Conflict

Held together as a people by its community of action, halakhah, and the broad framing principles of faith, traditional Jewry was thus able to find a home for an extraordinary variety of visions of what an ideal Jewish life should be. Did it include participation in work and society, or should it be devoted exclusively to the study of Torah? Should education be vocational, or purely "religious"? Were women who studied Torah to be encouraged or discouraged? Did scientific knowledge govern our interpretation of Torah, or did Torah govern our interpretation of science? Was the ideal person one who maintained an emotional balance or one who lived on the outer edge of emotional intensity? Under conditions of oppression, should one reach an accommodation with the ruling power or defy it to the point of courting martyrdom? Was the symbol of military power, the sword, a badge of honor or a mark of shame? Was the messianic age for which Jews longed an event within natural history or a supernatural break with history?

Answers on both sides are to be found in the rabbinic literature, and we are struck, in reading the debates, by the subtlety and power with which the sages kept the questions open. There are instances where we are led to feel admiration for a sage who acts against the consensus; others where we feel critical of the sage who acts within the law. There are times when an excess of piety is portrayed as foolishness. There are others when a failure to go piously beyond the law is a dereliction of ethical duty. *Vezu mishnat chassidim?* asks the Talmud Yerushalmi at one point. "You may have acted according to the teaching of the law, but is this a teaching for saints?"

Who is the ideal type within rabbinic Judaism? The sage, the saint, the zealot, the martyr, the person of simple piety, the figure of public authority, the creative intellect, the intellectual conservative, the man of learning, the woman of good deeds, the compassionate, the just? The question is impossible to answer. Each emerges as a distinctive kind of religious hero. The tradition even found it possible to portray sympathetically the relationship between R. Elisha ben Abuyah, the archetypal rebel against tradition, and his disciple R. Meir, one of the architects of the Mishnah.

This is the mark of a living tradition. It embraces diversity while preserving the structures of community. Maimonides, in the *Guide of the Perplexed*, defined this as the challenge of law and leadership. Human beings, he argued, are less like one another than the members of any other species, yet they need, even to pursue their individual aims, to form societies. The leader uses law "so that the natural variety [of human beings] should be counterbalanced by the uniformity of legislation." Halakhah creates a society, a community of action. Beyond halakhah are matters no less religiously important, but which are marked by diversity and individuality.

Beyond halakhah too are those divergent voices on the ultimate questions of how a commanding past is to be carried forward into an open future. Again MacIntyre's description is apt. A sense of tradition, he writes, "manifests itself in a grasp of those future possibilities which the past has made available to the present. Living traditions, just because they continue a not-yet-completed narrative, confront a future whose determinate and determinable character . . . derives from the past."

The arguments within nineteenth-century Orthodoxy, for example, were of just such a kind. How, given the radical change in Jewish circumstance brought about by European emancipation, was the Jewish future to be written? Did it lie, as Hirsch argued, in exemplary participation in a secular society, bringing the ethical truths of Judaism to bear on Western culture? Did it lie, as R. Kook contended, in seeing that exile was ending and a messianic process about to begin, in which Jews were summoned to leave the lands of their dispersion and come home to the promised land? Or did it lie, as R. Moses Sofer and his successors implied, in carrying on the past as exactly as possible, resisting any suggestion of the relevance of change?

These are voices within a single conversation on what is essential, and what accidental, to the Jewish vocation, and on how historical process is to be interpreted through the perspective of faith. To be sure, Hirsch and R. Kook and R. Sofer were not pluralists in the modern sense, each conceding the rightness of alternative positions. To the contrary: their views essentially exclude one another. If one is right, the others are wrong. And yet their positions remained legitimate choices within the same tradition. Adherents of one would be compelled to recognize adherents of the other as members of the same tradition and the same community of faith. That is what is meant by calling them "voices within a conversation," or more traditionally, partners in an "argument for the sake of heaven."

That is how tradition handled conflict. And the question that has become suddenly urgent is whether the current conflicts within

Jewry can be incorporated within this model of "argument for the sake of heaven." If so, there can be dialogue. If not, there can only be confrontation. The one creates community, the other destroys it. Why then has dialogue between Jews become so difficult in the twentieth century? Why is it so often replaced by mutual delegitimation? If even Reform and secular Jews have turned, in recent years, toward tradition, why has there not been a revival of rabbinic Judaism's greatest tradition: the tradition of argument, tradition *as* argument?

Tradition and "Tradition"

The short answer is that the *brit yi'ud*, the covenant of Torah, has not yet been renewed. Jewish attitudes have become more "traditional" without yet returning to tradition. The inability of Jews to communicate across their ideological divides is a measure of the extent to which Jews still stand "between two covenants." And it is here that we must examine a word we have used frequently, thus far without analysis or explanation: the word "tradition" itself.

What traditionally was "tradition?" First, it was a set of authoritative texts: the Torah, the rest of the biblical literature, the Mishnah, the Babylonian Talmud, and a range of other writings including halakhic codes, rabbinic midrash, and Jewish Bible commentaries. Together they constituted a canon, an authoritative body of literature. Its boundaries were not always precisely defined. Nonetheless the shape of the canon was relatively clear. It embodied a *Torah she-bikhtav*, a written Torah, the five Mosaic books, and a *Torah she-be'al peh*, an oral tradition, authoritatively set down in the Mishnah and Talmuds.

It was to these texts that Jews turned for guidance in the conduct and understanding of their lives. But a tradition is more than a collection of texts. It is a set of beliefs about what those texts represent and why they are authoritative. Despite the flurry of argument in the Middle Ages about what Jewish belief essentially was, there was a clear consensus, best expressed by R. Shimon ben Zemach Duran (1361–1444). Jewish belief, he argued, had three components: belief in God, revelation, and Divine justice. It was over the second of these beliefs, the nature of revelation, that argument was fiercest and schism most likely.

For rabbinic Judaism revelation meant first, that the Mosaic books were unmediated word of God; second, that they yielded a set of commandments about how to live and construct a society; third, that after Sinai, Jews were covenantally bound for all generations to keep those commands; fourth, that the covenant could not be modified or annulled by a further revelation; and fifth, that along with revelation went an authoritative tradition as to how to interpret its words and apply them to new situations: the "oral law."

There are arguments within the tradition. But there are other conflicts that transgress the boundaries of tradition. By denying the validity of the oral law, sectarian groups like the Samaritans, Sadducees, and Karaites eventually placed themselves outside the mainstream of tradition. By asserting a new revelation and covenant, so did Pauline Christianity. These groups saw themselves as heirs to the same sacred text: the Torah. But they were not heirs to the same tradition of interpretation. Argument and conversation became impossible. Schism was the inevitable result.

Jewish modernity began with another assault on revelation: that of Spinoza. This led in turn to an astonishing variety of attempts to redefine the meaning of Jewish existence. There were radicals, especially among the secular Zionists, who sought to sever all connections with the texts of the Jewish past, just as, in early Christianity, Marcion had argued that Christians must dispense with the "old Testament." For the most part, however, in modernity as in antiquity, tradition proved indispensable.

But in order to legitimate change, tradition had to be reinterpreted in revolutionary ways. For the reformers, it no longer yielded a set of commands; instead it was a collection of broad ethical truths. For the secular Zionists, it was no longer a set of religious texts; instead it was national literature, the history of a people and its relationship to a land. Such is the power of tradition over human identity that an attempt to rewrite the future almost always involves an attempt to rewrite the past. Reformers and secular Zionists were thus able—as were Sadducees, Karaites, and Christians before them—to see themselves as heirs to the same Jewish past and tradition. But it was a tradition that had become unrecognizable to those—Pharisees, rabbinites, and later Orthodox Jews—who resisted radical reinterpretation and carried on the tradition in the traditional way.

This is how traditions fragment and split apart, and how dialogue eventually becomes impossible. At a certain point one can no longer say, as the rabbis said of the positions of Hillel and Shammai, that "these and these are the words of the living God." For this presupposes that the two sides hold in common a shared idea of the meaning of the phrase the "words of the living God." When this is absent, the phrase is inapplicable. Argument no longer proceeds on the basis of shared assumptions about the authority of text and the rules of interpretation. It ceases to be "argument" in the sense understood by tradition. Instead it becomes a confrontation, to be settled by force or temporarily deflected by diplomacy.

As long as the various parties have no interest in conversation with one another, the problem is not acute. Each side is content to let history deliver its verdict, each confident that it will inherit the future. But this is a dangerous strategy. It led Christianity, for example, to assume the disappearance of Jews and Judaism; and this led to fearful animosity when both, in fact, survived. If secular and religious, Reform and Orthodox, diaspora and Israeli Jews are unable to recover the framework of argument, and are left instead with only the strategies of confrontation, other fearful consequences are not impossible. It is this more than anything else that has led thoughtful Jews on all sides to seek dialogue in recent years. But we are now in a position to see why that dialogue should prove so surprisingly difficult. For each side, while claiming to represent the same tradition, in fact embodies quite a different version of it.

Being Traditional

In what sense are Jews today "traditional"? One of the most intriguing documents of American Jewry in the 1970s was a book entitled *The Jewish Catalog*. It sold several hundred thousand copies and was succeeded by several companion volumes. It emerged from the *chavurah* movement, the Jewish equivalent of the communes that flourished in the 1960s along with the student "counter-culture." *The Jewish Catalog* seemed to signal a return to tradition. It was interested in precisely those things that most American Jews had hitherto dismissed as largely irrelevant to their lives. It was about *kashrut*, *Shabbat*, *mikveh* and Jewish learning. It was about the detailed texture of Jewish life. It was a hands-on, do-it-yourself guide to traditional Jewish living.

But as the Reform theologian Eugene Borowitz pointed out, it was not a contemporary American version of the *Shulchan Arukh*. It was not a code of Jewish law. It was, as the authors said, "a selection of materials which offer the possibility for immediate application and integration into one's personal environment." It was, as its name implied, a catalogue. And a catalogue, as Borowitz noted, "presents resources one can draw on to meet one's personal needs." A catalogue "only offers; it never presumes to tell its readers what they *must* choose." Borowitz concluded that "for all its rich Jewishness . . . *The Jewish Catalog* rejects Orthodoxy."

The Jewish Catalog represents one way in which behavior can be "traditional" without being part of a tradition. Take *kashrut* for example. Two people can be seated together at a kosher restaurant enjoying the same food but for quite different reasons. For one, *kashrut* is a series of rules about what foods may be eaten, a dietary code. For the other, kosher food is simply a feature of Jewish ethnicity. One can enjoy "traditional" cuisine once in a while, without in any way feeling that there are laws governing the act of eating. Clearly the word kosher means different things to the two people. The same systematically applies to all Jewish behavior. It may be a *mitzvah*, an act performed in human response to a Divine command, or it can be a "Jewish expression" in the same way that doing a particular kind of dance or singing a folk song can be a Greek or Russian expression.

The *Catalog*, along with Borowitz's Reform Judaism and contemporary Reconstructionism, turns tradition into a range of Jewish behaviors that have nothing to do with the idea of *halakhah* or law, but everything to do with liberal individualism. "Tradition" in this sense *excludes* nothing. Many American Jews, for example, light candles on Chanukkah, the symbol of a Jewish war against foreign worship, and at the same time buy Christmas trees. "Tradition" here has been secularized into behavior which has lost all contact with the beliefs which gave it meaning.

A similar process is at work in quite a different direction in what Jonathan Woocher in America, and Liebman and Don-Yehiyah in Israel have described as the new Jewish "civil religion." Here what is central is not the individual but the group. Religious symbols are employed to provide "sacred legitimation of the social order." The phrase "a people that dwells alone" is used to explain Israel's international isolation. The idea of covenant and collective Jewish responsibility is used to give depth to fund-raising programs. Traditional motifs are enlisted in the public rhetoric and ritual of essentially secular organizations.

The group has always been more central to mainstream Judaism than the individual, so that civil religion is in some ways closer to tradition than Borowitz's idea of Judaism as personalized choice. But it is not tradition itself. It focuses on public occasions with little or no follow-through into private life. Its function is group solidarity, not worship of a transcendental power. Its role is to endorse, not criticize, the social structure. Religious language is used with deliberate vagueness and ambiguity. Here, too, "tradition" has been domesticated and secularized out of all relationship to its past.

There is a third sense of "tradition." It is one of the undercurrents of the Conservative movement or what is sometimes called *masorti* or "traditional" Judaism. Tradition here is understood in the sense usually attributed to the political philosopher Edmund Burke and is a religious equivalent of political conservatism, defined by Roger Scruton as that outlook "which springs from a desire to conserve existing things, held to be either good in themselves or better than the likely alternatives, or at least safe, familiar, and the objects of trust and affection."

Conservative Judaism was born in 1845 when Zechariah Frankel walked out of the Reform rabbinical conference, which had just voted to abandon Hebrew as the language of prayer. Frankel's objections were not so much halakhic as sentimental and pragmatic. Judaism, he believed, could and should change, for the collective consciousness of Jews in any given age was itself a revelation of the will of God. But change should always be evolutionary rather than revolutionary. Indeed it should proceed so slowly as to seem not to take place at all. Change, he wrote, "must be grasped with such care, thought through with such discretion, created always with such awareness of the moment in time, that the goal will be reached unnoticed, that the forward progress will seem inconsequential to the average eye."

Though "traditionalism" seems to be close to tradition, there are considerable differences between them. Jaroslav Pelikan puts it thus: "Tradition is the living faith of the dead, traditionalism is the dead faith of the living." Traditionalism is always conservative whereas tradition itself is sometimes highly radical. In its early days, for example, the chasidic movement was revolutionary; so, more recently, was Gush Emunim. A traditionalist values tradition because of its age; its authority lies in its "pastness." Someone firmly within the tradition, however, values it because of its immediacy; its authority lies in its "presentness." History is a key category for the traditionalist, but not for tradition.

One of the key problems for traditionalism in general, and Conservative Judaism in particular, is knowing how and on what grounds to mandate change. Within tradition the answer is relatively straightforward: change is permitted only when it takes place according to the rules of halakhah. But conservatives have often sought to go beyond halakhic precedent and include the idea of historical evolution in accordance with the ethos of the age. And it has proved difficult to provide any criterion for distinguishing what, in the ethos of the age, should be Jewishly adopted and what resisted, and why. The confusion within the movement was evident recently when the Jewish Theological Seminary of America voted in favor of ordaining women as rabbis, some on the grounds that the change was in line with Jewish tradition, others because it was a "creative violation" of tradition.

This then is one reason why internal Jewish dialogue is so much more difficult than it seems. The word traditional creates the illusion that Reform, Conservative, and secular Jews share the same tradition as Orthodoxy. In fact, though, each of these three groups has subjected the tradition to revisionary reinterpretation. They have translated it into conceptual frameworks like personal autonomy (Reform), group solidarity (civil Judaism), and historicism

(Conservative) that have no place within tradition itself. We can imagine a hypothetical situation in which a number of villages used the same vocabulary but quite different rules of grammar. When members of two villages met, they would initially believe that they were speaking the same language. All the words they used, they would have in common. Only after a long series of mutual misunderstandings would it dawn on them that they were, in fact, speaking different languages. This is the situation within Jewry today.

Orthodoxy and Uniformity

But there is one other factor behind the demise of "argument for the sake of heaven," which has to do with developments within Orthodoxy itself. As long as tradition was coextensive with the Jewish people as a whole, it had of necessity to recognize a multitude of voices. Jews were united by halakhah; therefore they could be divided on other things. Jewish law preserved the integrity of the community. Beyond that there could be differences: of custom, culture, personal piety, and philosophical orientation. The tradition maintained a balance between uniformity and diversity.

This balance existed so long as the Jewish community was both a varied society and a halakhic society. But secularization has utterly changed the sociology of tradition. Halakhic observance, whether in Israel or the diaspora, is for the most part wholly voluntary. It is not supported by the wider cultural ambience. To the contrary, to be halakhically observant is to go against the secular tide. The Jew who is both Orthodox and involved in the secular world is regularly conscious of a deep inner conflict between the two roles. The result is that Orthodoxy is today experienced as consistent, lucid, and harmonious only in environments that exclude the secular world: in *yeshivot*, or chasidic circles, or restricted neighborhoods. These are environments that do not mirror society as a whole. To the contrary, they are composed of a voluntary self-selecting elite. They are communities of the like-minded. For the most part today, where there is a varied society, it is not a halakhic society. And where there is a halakhic society, it is not a varied society.

This leads to a shift in the balance of tradition within any given enclave of Orthodoxy, away from diversity towards uniformity. To be sure, the differences within Orthodoxy are as pronounced today as at any time in the past. Each yeshivah and each chasidic group has its own particular style. Almost every shade of political opinion in Israel has its Orthodox advocates. What is lacking is the public domain of dialogue in which the various sides meet and engage in "argument for the sake of heaven." Torah once emerged from internally diverse communities. Today it emerges from homogeneous subcommunities. And this does not encourage a serious confrontation with the views of one's opponents.

The structures of argument within the Jewish world closely mirror the structures of community. The medieval Jewish community, the *kehillah*, spanned all Jews within a given locality. It had to find religious space for diversity and argument. The *kehillah* was shaken by the divisive impact of the Shabbatean movement in the seventeenth century and by the split between *chasidim* and *mitnagdim* in the eighteenth. It eventually collapsed altogether under the impact of emancipation. In Germany, Hungary, Israel, and America, Orthodoxy began its long retreat into segregated enclaves. Orthodox Jews found themselves unable to speak a common language with other Jews and eventually even with other Orthodox Jews.

There was no overarching community to which they all belonged. As a result there was no context for a conversation that would bring different positions into dialogue. This is a potentially tragic situation, all the more so since tradition so obviously contains the resources to channel conflict into constructive argument and ultimately, consensus.

For rabbinic Judaism *is* a tradition of argument. And many of the issues that today divide Jews are precisely those to which the canonical texts yield more than one answer. How far is Judaism compatible with democracy and liberalism in a Jewish state? How far should Jewish law govern the public domain of Israeli life, even at the cost of infringing on civil liberties? Should the influence of Judaism on Israeli society be felt through the political process, or the educational system, or through personal example? Does Judaism mandate religious coercion? Is the state's religious duty to stand firm in the face of international opinion or to set an international example of the ethics of self-restraint? May Israel trade land for peace?

The same is true about Judaism in the diaspora. There are legitimate questions about the halakhic response to contemporary society. Should conversion be made easier or harder in a situation of high rates of intermarriage? Which enhancements of women's roles in Judaism reflect the concerns of the biblical and rabbinic literature, and which import values hostile to the tradition? How far, as a matter of religious duty, should Jews be engaged in the ethical concerns of their wider society? Which changes in the shifting political and moral climate are to be welcomed and which challenged and subjected to critique?

These are questions that would have traditionally created "argument for the sake of heaven." And the faith of rabbinic Judaism is that Torah lives more in the way the argument is conducted than in the conclusions reached. If it proceeds through a debate informed by text, precedent, and interpretation, it becomes part of Torah. It becomes part of the commentary each generation of Jews writes to the covenant. But if it proceeds through political pressure, mutual delegitimation, and violent confrontation, there is no real argument. There is a search for victory, not truth. The clash of opinions becomes secularized. Judaism, instead of providing the means for handling conflict, fuels the flames of conflict into conflagration. The great tradition of "argument for the sake of heaven" comes to an end.

That has happened in our time. It is a process that must be reversed.

12

To Mend the Jewish World

W$_{e}$ can now draw our long argument to a conclusion. Two alternative futures confront the Jewish people. For there are forces operating on and within it in two radically opposed directions.

The first is convergence. The predictions of the nineteenth century have proved false. Orthodoxy has not disappeared. Neither has Reform. Israel exists. The diaspora survives. What appeared to be mutually exclusive alternatives have each been realized. A new perception has come to dominate Jewish attitudes in the last two decades. The Jewish destiny is indivisible. Jews are implicated in one another's fate. The Final Solution made no distinction between Jews; neither, for the most part, does anti-Zionism. The nineteenth century was marked by its divided visions of the Jewish future. The late twentieth century has been marked by a fervent desire for a single vision and a shared future.

That vision can be simply summarized. It affirms the unity of the Jewish people across space and time. Jewish unity has ethical implications, in particular the idea that all Jews are responsible for one another. Jewish survival is a primary value and is not to be taken for granted. It is threatened militarily and politically in Israel, and socially, through assimilation, in the diaspora. Israel is a central focus of Jewish identification and concern. It supports and is supported by the diaspora, and their destinies are interlinked. Jewish tradition remains important, for it explains the uniqueness of the Jewish past and strengthens the sense of identity and community. Neither Jewishness nor Israeliness can be divorced from Judaism; nor can Judaism be divorced from a sense of peoplehood.

Such is the consensus that has emerged since 1967. We might call it "folk Judaism." And it is clear that it differs markedly from the revolutionary scenarios of nineteenth century Reform on the one hand, secular Zionism on the other. Jewish attitudes have moved far from the longing for "normalization" that dominated these two movements and forced them into a break with tradition. Just as Jewish thought has converged on Israel as its center, so it has converged on tradition as its framework.

Many of the attitudes that characterized the nineteenth century and made tradition so difficult to sustain—universalism, liberalism, humanism, acculturation, an emphasis on ethics to the exclusion of ritual, and a focus on the future to the exclusion of the past—are in decline. In their place has come a new respect for particularism, Jewish distinctiveness, textual study, ritual, and the idea of continuity with the Jewish past. This is a Copernican turn in both Reform and secular Zionist thought, and it offers the possibility for the first time of a reconciliation of these movements with Orthodoxy. Enlightenment and emancipation created a series of fateful rifts within the Jewish people. As the values of the nineteenth century come increasingly into question, those rifts begin to mend.

Conflict

Jews have, attitudinally at least, converged on tradition. But tradition, in the meanwhile, has moved further away from the majority of Jews, for two reasons, which are intrinsically connected. While secular*ism* and assimilation*ism*—the ideologies—are in eclipse, secularization and assimilation—the social processes—are still strong. This results in two phenomena. First, liberal Jewish movements like Reform are driven to provide religious legitimation for an increasingly wide range of behaviors. At its furthest extreme, as we have seen, this includes synagogues for homosexuals and a series of endorsements of intermarriage: officiating at mixed marriages, nominal rather than halakhic conversions, and conferring Jewish status on the child of a non-Jewish mother without conversion.

Secondly and for the same reason, namely that the forces of secularization and assimilation are so strong in contemporary society, Orthodoxy has been forced to define itself increasingly in opposition to the norms and ethos of the age. Its centers of strength have been in its most segregated environments—the yeshivah, the chasidic group, and the exclusively Orthodox neighborhood. The idea that there could be a synthesis, Hirschian or Kookian, between Judaism and diaspora or Israeli culture as a whole has come to seem progressively less plausible. The images that dominated Hirschian Orthodoxy and religious Zionism—unity, reconciliation, and harmony—have been displaced by the language of opposition and confontation: between Orthodox and other Jews, between Judaism and Zionism, between Torah and secular culture, and between Israel and the world.

The paradox, then, is this. The very processes that have brought about convergence have brought about conflict and made more likely the second possibility: a deep and lasting schism, whether between religious and secular Jews in Israel, or between Orthodoxy and liberal Jews in the diaspora, or between Israel and the diaspora itself. Throughout the nineteenth century, the dominant motif of Reform, Orthodoxy, and diaspora and secular Zionist thought was that it exclusively possessed the key to the Jewish future. The alternatives were unviable and would simply disappear in the course of time. Each was spared the task of coming to terms with the survival of the others.

But each has survived. Attitudes have had to be revised. There has been a turn toward Israel on the one hand, tradition on the other. And here the conflict is born. For not all Jews live in Israel, and not all Jews live by tradition. A critical asymmetry then arises. Jews in the diaspora accord centrality to Israel; but Israel cannot confer legitimacy on the diaspora without contradicting its own most fundamental assumptions. Likewise, Reform and Conservative Jews and a majority of Israelis accord centrality to the Jewish religious tradition; but Orthodoxy—tacitly acknowledged as the central bearer of tradition—cannot confer legitimacy on Reform or secularism without contradicting its most basic beliefs.

Convergence brings conflict. So long as the various strands within the Jewish world defined their future without reference to the others, Jews might simply have drifted apart. That was the situation a century ago, but not now. It is when the diaspora defines itself by reference to Israel, and when non-Orthodoxies define themselves by reference to Orthodoxy, that a clash of perceptions is inevitable and confrontation becomes increasingly likely. The most bitter arguments are those that take place within the family. For they take place between people who have conflicting expectations and are yet indissolubly linked to one another. As Jews grow existentially further apart and yet increasingly see themselves as the members of a single global family, the more the disputes between them take on the character of a family quarrel. On the one hand this is benign. It signals the current strength of the wish for Jewish unity. On the other, it is fraught with tragedy. For the dissension is real and deep and seemingly insoluble.

Schism

Nowhere is this more clearly in evidence than in the continuing controversy over "Who is a Jew?" Consider the theoretical possibilities. The Law of Return, on which the controversy is centered, might simply be abolished. But the Law recognizes a Jewish arrival in the land as an *oleh*, someone who has "returned," and not simply as an immigrant. It is central to the connection between Israel and the Jewish people as a whole. Removing the Law would remove one of the foundations on which Israel stands as the state not only of some Jews, but of the entire Jewish people. It would sever a key link between Israel and the diaspora.

Alternatively, the Law might be amended to include the insistence that a Jew is one born to a Jewish mother or who has undergone a conversion "according to halakhah." It is this proposal, advocated by many Orthodox leaders within and outside Israel, that has generated the controversy. For while it would affect perhaps no more than some half dozen cases a year, it would imply that the many thousands of conversions performed under Reform or Conservative auspices are invalid from the point of view, not only of Orthodoxy but also of Israeli law. Were it passed, the Reform and Conservative movements might choose to break their connections with Israel on the one hand, or to establish themselves as completely separate religions on the other. But this too would result in schism.

Alternatively, the Law might explicitly recognize any conversion by any Jewish religious authority in the diaspora as valid. It would then be hard to resist the de jure recognition of the Reform and Conservative movements within Israel itself. The religious divisions that fragmented German, Hungarian, and American Jewry would then be imported into Israel. The consequences are frightening to contemplate. The de facto pluralism of the diaspora is one thing; a de jure Jewish pluralism in Israel is another. It would lead, of necessity, to a direct collision between Orthodoxy and the state.

Thus, the desire not to precipitate schism holds the Law of Return in its present state of ambiguity. But the consensus is fragile. It depends on a balance of forces and restraints that cannot be guaranteed to last. The same is true about many other conflicts that lie just below the surface of contemporary Jewish life. The possibility that they might erupt into what might in effect be a civil war within the Jewish world is less remote than it seems. The previous era of Jewish autonomy within the land of Israel, initiated by the Maccabees and ended by the Roman destruction of Jerusalem, began and ended with a war of Jew against Jew: a war of zealots against Hellenizers. The parallels between the factionalization of Jewish life at the time of the Maccabean revolt of 166–164 B.C.E. and the revolt against Rome, 66–70 C.E., and the divisions now evident in the Jewish world are uncomfortably close.

There is a common pattern: a revolution against the assimilation or secularization of Jewish life by a small group of intensely religious Jews who see themselves as instruments of Providence in an apocalyptic drama. Bitter internecine conflict is not unknown in Jewish history. In *galut*, it is kept in check. Rabbinites and Karaites, *chasidim* and *mitnagdim*, enlighteners and traditionalists fought their battles, but they were minorities under a non-Jewish power. It is in Israel, where the character of a Jewish society is at stake, that conflict escalates into full-fledged war. In the struggle, the particularists always win out against the assimilated: the Maccabees against the Hellenizers, the Pharisees against the Sadducees. The zealots who initiate the conflict are a minority, but they are supported by the broadly traditional base of the population. But though the result is a religious victory, it is also a human tragedy. *Sinat chinam*, antagonism between Jew and Jew, led to the destruction of the Second Temple, said the sages. And though the records of that period are unclear, there seems to be a core of historical as well as ethical insight in that remark.

Process and Event

In the present situation, therefore, it becomes important to concentrate not only, or even primarily, on what the various groups within the Jewish world hold in common—which is less than appearances suggest—but on the resources of tradition for handling conflict. Jewish unity is less a fact than an objective. And unless it is a unity that allows for diversity, it will not occur at all.

Two hundred years after emancipation, there is still a multiplicity of answers to the question emancipation provoked: What is a Jew? But because the various sides have come closer, the controversies have become more intense. Jews are faced with a fundamental choice. Will the mood of the last two decades translate itself into convergence or schism? Much will depend on how the many arguments over policy and principle are conducted. They can become part of the "historically extended, socially embodied argument" that is Torah's application to the Jewish present and future. Or they can be distributed between groups and positions that have no mode of communication with one another.

It has been suggested that argument takes place within a tradition. Judaism did not merely contain argument. It celebrated it as a high, perhaps the highest, form of religious expression. It was in argument that the word of God became real in the life of man. It was in argument that the covenant was continued into the present and future. It was in argument that divergent viewpoints were brought into relationship with one another. It was in argument that the many voices that comprise *Knesset Yisrael*, the collective community of Israel, were orchestrated into the choral symphony called Torah.

That argument began to break down two centuries ago. With the collapse of structures of Jewish community, Jews were set free to pursue their individual or sectional destinies without reference to one another. The result was a series of divisions which are not yet mended, and which subtly and tenaciously perpetuate themselves through all talk of unity and "tradition." Potential tragedy is in sight on a number of different fronts. It can be deferred, but not forever, by diplomacy and rhetorical ambiguity. The alternative is a candid acknowledgment of what divides Jews and an attempt to locate those divisions within the framework of tradition and "argument for the sake of heaven."

How is this to be achieved? One thing is certain. It will not be achieved immediately. Divisions that took a century to create will not be healed in a matter of years. Hence our first desideratum: a sense of the importance of *process* as against *event*, slow movement toward ultimate objectives, as against a mode that has come increasingly to dominate Jewish political and religious thought: the belief that conflict will either be resolved by a single dramatic occurrence or it cannot be resolved at all.

Perhaps the single most conspicuous lacuna in Orthodox thought is its lack of a sense of historical process. This affected its relationship to the Zionist movement, and it affects today its relations with the State of Israel. Jewish thought is strong on historical contrasts. There is *galut* and *ge'ulah*, exile and redemption. There is *ha-zeman ha-zeh*, "this time," and there is, by contrast, the messianic age. But on how to move from the one to the other, it is less clear. As we have seen, this results today in two extreme positions, anti-Zionism and messianic Zionism, neither of which have close contact with political and social reality. Either the State of Israel is *not* messianic, in which case it has no religious significance, or it *is* messianic, in which case all its acts are holy. It is hard to find, in intensely religious circles in Israel today, a position which avoids these extremes.

And yet, three times every day, Jews recite an *Amidah* which sets Israel in the context of a historical process. First there is a prayer for the ingathering of exiles; then one for the restoration of "our judges"; then one for "the righteous and the pious"; then one for the rebuilding of Jerusalem; then one for the restoration of the Davidic monarchy, mark of the messianic age. Quite where the present State of Israel stands on this continuum is open to debate. Does it represent the "ingathering of exiles," or not until all Jews have made *aliyah?* Is national sovereignty the "restoration of our judges," or not until the government of Israel is religious? These questions are less important than the fact that Israel is set within an historical process, to be judged not by whether it is or is not now the "beginning of redemption" but by where it leads.

Maimonides described the messianic state in the concluding chapters of his code, the *Mishneh Torah.* It would be one in which Israel was free of "servitude to foreign powers" and at peace with her neighbors. There would be "neither famine nor war, neither jealousy nor strife. Blessings will be abundant, comforts within the reach of all." Jewish family pedigrees, which had become obscured through the course of time, would be clarified. Jews would be "free to devote themselves to the Torah and its wisdom." They would reconstruct their religious life, and through Israel, the world would come to recognize God. That defines a series of ultimate objectives. And it sets an agenda of religious debate as to whether any given policy of the state advances or impedes them. There is room here for wide-ranging argument on the economy, social justice, political and military objectives, religious freedom or religious coercion, "Who is a Jew?" legislation, and the importance of Israel's standing in the eyes of the world. But that argument concerns process. It cannot take place if the messianic age is seen as a single decisive event.

The same lack of a sense of process hinders Orthodox relations with Reform. To be sure, Orthodoxy cannot and will never recognize Reform as a legitimate expression of Judaism. But neither Jewish law nor Jewish thought mandates an all-or-nothing approach to tradition. Reform Jews have made affirmations that are significant and positive. They have chosen to identify as Jews. They have chosen to recognize the existence of God and the importance of religious expression. They have chosen, in recent decades, to emphasize Jewish peoplehood and the State of Israel. Process is important. It makes all the difference whether Reform is moving closer to, or further away from, tradition. The view that nothing the Reform movement does short of a complete return to Orthodoxy can have significance is hard to justify by any other than isolated texts. And it encourages Reform to further distance itself from the rest of the Jewish world.

It is important that Orthodoxy, in its relations with Reform, maintains the balance that the sages described as "thrusting aside with the left hand and drawing near with the right hand." The divide cannot be minimized or conjured out of existence by talk of a "pluralism" that is unavailable within the tradition. But at the same time it must be made clear what brings the two sides closer together and what drives them further apart. The recent interest of Reform in the Hebrew language, Jewish day-school education, and religious ritual are powerful moves back toward the family of faith. Reform has undergone an extraordinary *volte-face* from the attitudes expressed in the Pittsburgh Platform a century ago. These are signs of convergence. At the same time, its legitimation of homosexuality attacks one of the most basic Jewish values: the essential link between sexuality, marriage, and the family. And its policy on conversions and patrilineal Jewish status may yet completely divide the Jewish world. Here, as forcefully as it can, Orthodoxy must say to Reform, *lo zu ha-derekh*, this is not the way.

One passage in the writings of Maimonides has always been controversial, precisely because it describes the role of process in Jewish history and law. It took forty years in the wilderness, he argues in the *Guide of the Perplexed*, before the Israelites could cast off the mentality of slaves and acquire the courage needed to inherit the land. Human nature changes slowly. And God never intervenes to change it miraculously. The Torah did not immediately legislate an ideal society. It made concessions to a people used to idolatry. It adopted the path of gradual education toward a series of ideals. Even Divine legislation must reckon with human realities. Maimonides implies that the process to perfection is slow and beset with obstacles. The legislator must maintain a constant dialectic between ultimate aims and present human possibilities. There is no such thing in history as a sudden redemptive event that changes human nature, and no such thing either as a predetermined messianic process. Halakhah aims at creating an ideal society, but it must always be workable within a real society.

That perspective is a voice within Orthodoxy that needs to be sounded forcibly and often. It would lead to a renewal of religious Zionism. It would give direction, too, to the relationship between Orthodoxy and Reform. It is the single most compelling reason for moderation rather than extremism as a religious ideal.

Recovering the Argument

The second desideratum, we have suggested, is that tradition finds a home for many voices and that many voices find their home in tradition. We have argued that Reform and Conservative Judaism in the diaspora and secularism in Israel are not yet tradition even if they have become "traditional." But at least some of their concerns can be stated within tradition. It is important that they are. For every cultural crisis that is expressed within the framework of revelation and halakhah becomes part of the "argument for the sake of heaven." And every one that is not, becomes instead the scene of a divisive confrontation.

Examining the literature of Judaism, we are struck by how many incompatible positions it gives expression to. The Torah is the source of all knowledge; yet one learns astronomy from the Greeks, honoring of parents from the Romans, manners from the Persians, and one makes a blessing over "sages of the nations of the world." Men are pious when they trust in miracles; but they are pious when they do not rely on miracles. Converts are dangerous to Israel; but Israel went into exile only to acquire converts. The messianic age will be supernatural; but it will be natural, marked only by an end of Jewish subjection to foreign powers. Each of these views finds its place within the tradition. And one could multiply examples almost without limit.

The question is: How is this phenomenon to be interpreted? Does it mean that there is no one right answer to any question of Jewish values? Or that to the contrary, there is, and dissenting sources must be ignored? Or that, in R. Soloveitchik's imagery, to be a Jew is to be torn by ceaseless conflict? We would argue that it means none of these things. Judaism is best understood not as a set of correct positions but as a set of axes of tension: between universalism and particularism, action and passivity, freedom and constraint, individual and community, equality and hierarchy, past and future, timelessness and responsiveness to time. It strives to maintain a balance between these opposing values. But there is, as Maimonides so clearly saw in his ethical writings, no universal point of equilibrium that can be prescribed in advance. It depends on the person, place, and time.

This structure begins to fall apart when opposing forces and values are no longer linked in a single argument. For example: we noted in an earlier chapter that, according to Josephus, Pharisees, Sadducees, and Essenes were divided in their view of history. For the Sadducees, history was made by man; for the Essenes it was determined by God. The Pharisees—precursors of the rabbinic sages—argued that it was a complex interplay between both.

Zionism presents a fascinating parallel two thousand years later. The secularists took the Sadducean view. History is made by man. Orthodoxy in the 1860s, in the writings of Alkalai and Kalischer, had originally taken the Pharisaic position. Redemption is brought by God but initiated by man. But under pressure to distance itself from the secular Zionists of the 1890s and 1900s, it was increasingly driven into an Essene stance. History is made only by God. Therefore any human attempt to build a State of Israel would be heresy. Orthodoxy was driven into an extreme position, not fully representative of tradition, by the opposite extremism of the secularists. The religious argument over Zionism suffered a blow from which it has never fully recovered.

Or again: consider the argument over the role of women in Judaism. The Reform and Conservative movements have argued that there should no inequalities in the religious life. There should be mixed seating in the synagogue. Women should be rabbis and cantors. These provisions clearly breach halakhah. A number of Orthodox authorities meanwhile have argued that women's prayer groups, even when conducted within the parameters of halakhah, should nonetheless be forbidden, on the grounds that they import

Reform and secular values into the sanctuary of prayer. Two extreme positions are thus distributed between noncommunicating groups, and argument comes to an end.

In fact, however, the tradition was more complex. Undeniably the priesthood, paradigm of public prayer, was a male preserve. Yet there is evidence of deep concern for the feelings of women. The biblical narrative presents Eli the priest in an unfavorable light for misunderstanding and mocking the prayer of Hannah. The Talmud records that a peace sacrifice was once brought into the women's court so that women could lay their hands on it and feel involved, *kedei la'asot nachat ru'ach le-nashim*, "in order to satisfy women's feelings." That there is a pragmatic and religious duty not to let women feel excluded lies behind two important twentieth-century responsa by the distinguished halakhist, R. Yechiel Weinberg. Yet such is the sociology of halakhah that when one extreme position is adopted by nonhalakhic groups, halakhic rulings tend to move to the opposite extreme in an understandable concern to create a protective fence around Orthodoxy. When this happens, the *balance* of halakhah is disturbed.

It is important, then, that alternative positions be stated within the parameters of tradition. Not every position can be. Neither halakhah nor the principles of faith are open-endedly flexible. The fact nonetheless remains that, in general, the larger the question about Jewish identity and purpose in a given age, the more rich in alternatives the tradition is. Once the alternatives are stated within tradition, they belong to a single conversation. They provide a home inside tradition for Jews who would otherwise be driven outside. They provide a bridge between Orthodoxy and Jewish secularism and liberalism. They give balance to the halakhic and ideological argument. They allow it to embrace more than one pole in the continuum of Jewish values. For the faith of halakhic Judaism was that tradition provided a framework, not for a section of the Jewish people, but for *knesset Yisrael* in its entirety and diversity.

The conventions of "argument for the sake of heaven" have broken down within the Orthodox world. Scenes of angry confrontation between disciples of rival chasidic leaders and yeshivah heads, along with mutual accusations of error and heresy, have punctuated the media in recent years. They are, in a double sense, a *hillul ha-Shem*. They are a "desecration" of Torah, bringing it into disrepute. More profoundly, they are a "secularization" of Torah, a recourse to power, politics, and sensationalism in place of the protocols of argument and mutual respect.

The renewal of the Judaism of argument is, in one important sense, the renewal of Torah in our time. For Torah, being covenantal, faces in two directions. On the one hand, as revelation, it is the voice of God speaking to the people of Israel. On the other, as interpretation, it is the voice of the people of Israel addressing itself to God. The more inclusive Torah is of the Jewish people, the wider the tensions it resolves and the greater the range of the arguments it embraces, the closer it approaches its covenantal ideal. That is the monumental faith the rabbis expressed when they said that "the Torah was only given to make peace in the world."

From Orthodoxy to Judaism

I have not argued any particular case on any of the questions at the forefront of contemporary Jewish debate. I have argued something different and hopefully deeper. As the Jewish world split apart under the impact of social and intellectual change in the nineteenth century, Orthodoxy began to be seen by its opponents as a kind of denomination, one version of Judaism among many. In principle, Orthodox thinkers resisted the idea. They were bound to do so, for Judaism does not admit of denominations. Yet under pressure of circumstance they increasingly began to act as if it were so. Orthodoxy became a segment of the Jewish people, an embattled minority, defending its own integrity and sectional interests. A mutual alienation gathered momentum between Orthodoxy and what was, in America and Israel, a majority of the Jewish community. At the time, surely there was no alternative. Both communities were in headlong flight from tradition.

The situation is changing. In recent years Orthodoxy has emerged as a force of power and great ideological strength. But it has not yet shed the attitudes, appropriate a century ago, of sectional thinking. In many quarters confrontation still comes more naturally than reconciliation. The search for authority overrides the etiquette of argument. Yet the covenant was addressed to the Jewish people as a whole. And the Jewish people as a whole cannot be identified with the views of any particular group. It lives in the conversation between the various groups. The importance of that conversation transcends any particular statement made within it. It was the faith of rabbinic Judaism that argument for the sake of heaven eventuates in truth, even if one cannot predict in advance what that truth will be. That faith needs reinstatement.

Jewish mystics used to preface their performance of a religious act with a dedication, *le-shem yichud*: "For the sake of the unification of the Holy One, blessed be He with His Divine Presence." Their acts "mended" a "broken" world. A similar dedication is needed now: "For the sake of the unification of the Jewish people with Torah." A religious act should seek to mend a divided Jewish people. No one strand within tradition can do so. Only the tradition as a whole has that power. But we believe it *does* have that power.

If Orthodox Jews are to mend the Jewish world, they must rise beyond sectional thinking to a position where they can recognize alternatives within the tradition. Some will formulate new alternatives within tradition. The tradition of argument calls for respect for positions with which one does not agree. It leads one to admire stances one does not seek to imitate. These are values powerfully implicit in the rabbinic texts. And not accidentally. For rabbinic Judaism emerged from the ruins of one disastrous division within the Jewish world. We face another. What mended divisions then has the power to do so now. For whether the future translates into convergence or schism depends less on the chimera of Jewish unity than on how conflict is handled.

There is no sudden, decisive, and miraculous event that will renew the covenant of purpose and reunite Jews with Judaism, just as there is none that will overnight bring all Jews to Israel. But there is a process, slow, arduous, and fraught with risk though it is. In this process, many kinds of Jew have many different parts to play: some by being living examples of religious intensity, others by being courageous advocates of religious reconciliation, some by rejecting secular culture, others by imaginatively appropriating it, some by building yeshivot, others by building society, some by their courage in war, others by their advocacy of peace. Tradition speaks with many voices and is enacted in many kinds of lives. It lives precisely in the extended argument over what it is to be a Jew. To see this is already to have begun the transition from Torah as the faith of some Jews to Torah as the constitution of the whole Jewish people.

PART V
EPILOGUE

13

A Family Portrait: Jews Tomorrow

We began our analysis with a portrait of an Anglo-Jewish family. It is time to return to them now, sitting around the *seder* table. How have the Cohens, David, Miriam, and their children, been affected by the long search for Jewish identity whose history we have charted in the intervening chapters?

On the face of it, Anglo-Jewry has been an island of tranquility, far removed from the storms that raged through other centers of Ashkenazi Jewish life. Unlike nineteenth-century Germany and Hungary it had no major Reform presence. By the turn of the century there were still only three Reform synagogues in Britain, and until the Second World War 90 percent of Anglo-Jews were affiliated with Orthodox congregations. There was no sudden collapse of tradition such as occurred in the major cities of Eastern Europe under the impact of Enlightenment. There were no violent confrontations between secularists and traditionalists. The divisions that American Jewry inherited from Germany, and that Eastern Europe brought to Eretz Yisrael, largely passed it by.

English society was tolerant, traditional, and respectful of religion, if not deeply religious. Anglo-Jews acquired these attitudes. They were traditional but neither intellectual nor ideological. They

233

subscribed to a religious establishment that was Orthodox but at the same time broadly inclusive of a wide range of commitments. If we were to ask, hypothetically, how European Jewry might have developed without the undercurrents of anti-Semitism that gave rise to Reform and secular Zionism, Anglo-Jewry might be one such model.

Even so, that picture is slowly changing. David and Miriam's children have had to make choices they themselves were spared. The culture in which Ruth and Richard, Pinchas, Susan, and Avi have grown up is less traditional, more individualistic than it was in their parents' day. They cannot assume as easily as did a previous generation that Jewish and secular values are essentially in harmony. What Judaism has to say about sexual ethics, or the significance of the family, or the role of women is not the same as the message projected by the media and lived out by their contemporaries. The values preached in the synagogue are not the values of the world outside.

Nor do the children of our imagined family carry with them their parents' memories of *bubba* and *zeida* who could hardly speak English, of hard times struggling to make a living, and of the long, slow social journey to suburbia. They have no memory of the Holocaust years or of the tense times that surrounded the birth of Israel. The anxieties and euphoria of the Six Day War played no part in their lives: the eldest, Ruth, was only a year old at the time. They have no consciousness of being outsiders to British society. As Jews, they may be members of a religious and ethnic minority; but so too are the Moslems, Sikhs, and Hindus, the Indians, Pakistanis, and West Indians around them. There are times when they feel highly aware of their Jewishness—when Israel is being criticized in the media, for example, or when Ruth was approached by Christian missionaries while at college. But for the most part they feel socially secure and at ease.

But for just that reason, while Jewishness was something their parents took for granted, for them it is a matter of a series of conscious choices. Why should they go to synagogue? Why refrain from eating certain foods? Why not go for a drive on *Shabbat*? Why should they feel bound in some special way to the State of Israel? Why should they mix with Jews? Why should they marry a Jew?

They are fully part of a society that sees such behavior as eccentric at best, at worst, clannish and exclusive. They have had to think through their positions more deliberately than did their parents. Their options are wider and their sentimental attachments to Jewishness are less deep.

The Inward Turn

Which is not to say that their Judaism is more superficial. To the contrary, we saw how Ruth, Pinchas, and Avi have chosen to let Judaism play a larger part in their lives than it did for their parents. For Ruth it has meant membership in a more strictly Orthodox community. For Pinchas, the *baal teshuvah*, it has meant a complete change of life-style, a kind of spiritual rebirth. For Avi it has meant leaving England for a lonely settlement in the Judean hills. Each of them has decided that being and remaining Jewish is important to him or her. But each is aware of how fragile that fact has become in a highly secularized and socially integrated diaspora.

They do not want constantly to be making difficult choices. They want their Jewishness to be a complete identity, not a role or an occasional allegiance. What habit and memory gave to their parents, they now seek and find in community: a sense of being securely and unselfconsciously Jewish. They want their children's attachment to tradition to be beyond risk. Their parents, children of immigrants, sought to make themselves at home in English society. They, at home in English society, have reversed the process. They sense that a certain *distance* is essential to Jewish identity and continuity. Avi has found it in Israel, Pinchas in his yeshivah completely disengaged from the outside world. Ruth has found it in a strict discipline of halakhah and a community life strong enough to protect her and her husband-to-be from being influenced by the wider society in which they both still participate.

By now we recognize these choices. Avi has adopted the religious Zionism of R. Avraham Kook. Ruth, a product of an Orthodox seminary and an English university, embodies the *Torah im derekh eretz* of Samson Raphael Hirsch. Pinchas has become a *chasid*; but in choosing to turn away from the modern world he has aligned himself with the position of R. Moses Sofer. These alternatives were born in the nineteenth century in Central and Eastern Europe. Each was a sharply defined reaction to the breakdown of tradition. Anglo-Jewry at that time was less intense and more conservative. Its Orthodoxy did not have to define itself in conscious opposition to Reform or secularism. There were no Anglo-Jewish equivalents of Hirsch, R. Kook, or R. Sofer. Its Judaism was sedate, establishment, and "catholic." But by the late twentieth century these choices have come to Anglo-Jewry too.

Yet Avi, Ruth, and Pinchas are products of their time, not of the nineteenth century. In their lives we can trace the developments that have made *Torah im derekh eretz* and religious Zionism today quite different from what they were in Hirsch and R. Kook's day. Ruth, though she has had an advanced Jewish and secular education, does not use the phrase *Torah im derekh eretz*. She does not speak of "synthesis." She does not seek to be a conspicuous example to her non-Jewish neighbors. She has not read Hirsch's *Nineteen Letters*, though if she had, she would probably find it wildly optimistic. It is enough for her that she and her husband lead a Jewish life and bring up Jewishly committed children.

She is not inspired by the thought of a creative synthesis of Shakespeare and Isaiah or even Wittgenstein and Soloveitchik. Her secular involvements are one thing, her Judaism another, and she needs no elaborate theories to unite or divide them. She lives naturally in two cultures. One represents *where* she is, the other represents *who* she is. She, and more especially her husband, a mathematics lecturer at a London college, would probably recognize Charles Liebman and Samuel Heilman's description of their identity as "compartmentalized." Compartmentalization is what happens to Hirschian Judaism in a more pessimistic age than the early nineteenth century.

Avi, too, and his friends in Gush Emunim are less optimistic than was R. Avraham Kook about the relationship between religious and secular Jews in Israel, and between Jews and Arabs. They still see religious and messianic significance in the state. But they do not understand this in terms of harmony. On the contrary, they see it in terms of conflict, primarily with the neighboring Arab states, but also with international and sometimes domestic Israeli opinion. The images that live most powerfully in their imagination are biblical ones of Joshua and David's conquest of the land, and of the battle against Amalek, symbol of a world hostile to Jews. Where R. Avraham Kook saw the Jewish revival in Israel in terms of its literature and culture, they see it in terms of its geographical boundaries and military strength. To be sure, Avi is not militaristic by choice or temperament. He would like nothing better than to live at peace with the Palestinians in the nearby villages. But by the time Avi came to Israel the prospect was already remote, and the *intifada* has made it, for the moment, impossible.

In short, their Judaism is more inward and embattled than Hirsch's and R. Kook's. It is less universalist, less concerned with ethical mission and example, and more concerned with the brute fact of survival. Like Pinchas, they have chosen their particular ways of stepping back from the wider world. And in the lives Ruth, Avi, and Pinchas have chosen we can see why phrases like "modern" or "centrist" Orthodoxy no longer inspire. The word "modern" contains not only a description but also an evaluation. It suggests that what is modern is good, better than what is old. It implies that the future will be better than the past. That word does not fit the way they see the world. For them what is modern is for the most part negative. It suggests a secular society bent on personal success and private gratification. It suggests an economy and technology that threaten the environment. It evokes images of a world of rising intolerance and racial and religious conflict. For Ruth, Avi, and Pinchas, Judaism inspires precisely because it is *not* modern. It is not old-fashioned either. It is an antidote to modernity, a way of creating an alternative society. And if that means a measure of withdrawal from their secular contemporaries, so be it.

The word "centrist" also holds no appeal. What are they supposed to be centrist between? Between religion and secularism? Orthodoxy and Reform? Israel and the diaspora? Jew and Arab? There is no middle ground here, and they do not understand anyone who thinks there is. Ruth, Avi, and Pinchas do not see themselves as fanatics, though they know their parents think they are. Maimonides understood the "middle way" less as a static center than as a point of equilibrium between opposing forces. An earlier generation of Anglo-Jews found that they could maintain an

equilibrium between Jewish identity and English integration by a
relatively easygoing Judaism. They went to synagogue, kept *kashrut*
at home, and celebrated *Shabbat* and the festivals. That undemanding balance is less readily available today. As Maimonides himself
noted, there could be societies so uncongenial to Jewish values that,
merely to preserve Jewish identity, one had to segregate oneself.
That is how Ruth, Avi, and Pinchas read their environment. To
maintain their own personal equilibrium they have moved dramat-
ically to what their parents call the right-wing. That, for them, is
were the center lies.

They have made tough-minded choices. They have decided to
put Judaism first among their priorities and have constructed their
lives around that fact. They are, we have to say, a minority within
the Jewish world, but they are characteristic of a new generation of
Orthodox Jews, the first generation in two centuries to be more
Orthodox than its parents. The sociological evidence suggests that
they will be a growing force in future decades. Each of them is
likely to have a significantly larger family than their less religious
Jewish contemporaries. Their children will be many times less
likely to intermarry. Divorce will not be unknown in their respective worlds, but they will nonetheless be more secure in their
marriages and families than they would otherwise have been. The
open society has made them more religious precisely because they
recognize that in it, only the most intense commitments survive.
Ruth, Avi, and Pinchas will be among the Jewish survivors.

Complications

But so too will be the other children, Richard and Susan and
those many others, a clear majority of their generation, who have
drifted away from rather than closer to Judaism as traditionally
understood. That is the paradox and the source of potential
conflict.

Richard, the rebel of the family, is hostile to Jews, Judaism, and
Israel. He has already dropped out. It is quite likely that he will
marry out. But it is possible that he will continue, perhaps even
aggressively, to think of himself as a Jew. For one thing, his very

hostility sets him apart from his non-Jewish friends who, whatever they think of Judaism, do not consider it something to get agitated about. For another, his decision to live completely among non-Jews will remind him daily of his Jewishness no less than Pinchas's decision to spend his life in a yeshivah. He may well identify the inevitable tensions between himself and his non-Jewish colleagues as anti-Semitism. This feeling may intensify if, for whatever reason, his marriage to—let us say—a non-Jewish girl with an Anglo-Catholic background, fails to work out.

Richard, ten years from now, may find himself reassessing his Jewishness. It is unlikely that he will become religious like his two brothers and one of his sisters. It is even less likely that he will go back to the way of life of his parents. But he may find a whole range of Jewish writers and intellectuals with whom he can identify. He may begin to feel a sense of kinship with Spinoza, Marx, Trotsky, Freud, Levi-Strauss, Einstein, Arnold Schoenberg, and with their struggles to find new languages of expression and new modes of personal, artistic, or social organization. He may be drawn to Kafka or Gustav Mahler. He may recognize himself as one of the characters in Frederic Raphael's portraits of Oxbridge life. He may be drawn to George Steiner's vision of the Jew as outsider to all cultures and nationalisms. Almost certainly he will be deeply gripped by the literature of the Holocaust. In short, Richard may well discover what is by now already a tradition of its own: that rebellion is itself a mode of Jewish identity.

What of Susan? Alone among the children of our imagined family she has not made firm choices. Judaism does not play a large part in her life. For her it lies somewhere between a bothersome duty and a leisure activity and its impact on her time, except on major holidays, is minimal. Jewishness, on the other hand, is important to her. She enjoys the company of Jewish friends, with whom she feels at home. But what they have in common has to do with where they live, the kind of clothes they wear, the kind of music they like, and the kind of life-style they expect to have. It includes a sympathy for Israel and a commitment to fundraising causes, but beyond that there is little Jewish to her Jewishness.

Susan is a problem for religious thinkers and leaders. For whatever views they hold about Judaism, they find it difficult to have a conversation with someone who approves of it vaguely but believes it simply to be irrelevant to most of life's choices and pleasures. Yet studies like those of Goldscheider and Steven M. Cohen of American Jewry, together with such evidence as we have of Anglo-Jewry, suggest that Susan represents the majority of contemporary Jews. To use Cohen's categories, she is neither "observant" nor "activist" but is "affiliated." She is likely, in due course, to belong to a synagogue, observe the major festivals, and light candles on Friday evenings.

Thus far, from the point of view of Orthodoxy, Anglo-Jewry's striking characteristic is that figures like Susan have stayed within its ranks. This has resulted in an establishment Orthodoxy criticized by religious purists for its bland, undemanding, and inclusive character. This criticism is, we believe, wide of the mark. It comes from a way of thinking that had its genesis elsewhere, in communities like those of Central and Eastern Europe, where Jewish identities were radicalized into sharply defined oppositions. To be a Jew of any kind was to have made a clear and firm decision that, in effect, cut one off from any further contact with Jews of other kinds. To force such a choice on Susan would not answer to any real feeling she has. It would divide the community, which neither Susan nor most other Jews want. It would probably result in her severing her ties with Orthodoxy; and judging by the assembled evidence of the American sociological studies, she would then be likely to practice her Judaism less rather than more.

But Susan may not stay within Orthodoxy. Let us trace her future through an imaginary scenario. At one of her social groups she meets, likes, and falls in love with a Jewish boy, Michael. He comes from a Reform community, but that does not seem important to either of them. Each is willing to make adjustments. They agree that the marriage will take place in her parents' synagogue. It turns out, however, that Michael's mother was converted to Judaism by a Reform rabbi. Susan's rabbi tells Michael that, halakhically, he is not a Jew. He is willing to conduct the marriage, but only on condition that Michael undergoes a halakhic conversion.

Michael is bewildered and furious. No one has ever cast doubt on his Jewish status before. As far as he is concerned, he was born, raised, and has always seen himself as a Jew. He goes to synagogue more often than Susan. His knowledge of Judaism is better than hers. He is not willing to undergo the conversion, for that would imply that his whole previous life has been built on error. Susan agrees. She does not want to see Michael hurt. She does not want their wedding delayed. She does not want it to be overshadowed by controversy. She knows that she cannot altogether avoid it, because whichever way she chooses, someone will be offended. But she wants to marry Michael. And that means, right now, having the wedding in his synagogue, not hers. After a fierce family row, Susan's parents eventually agree.

The wedding takes place. Ruth, Avi, and Pinchas are not at the ceremony, though they come to the reception afterwards. Susan and Michael become members of a Reform community. Susan finds it strange at first, but eventually gets used to it. She likes the idea of sitting next to her husband in the synagogue, but she finds the service a little too Anglicized for her taste. They have children. The years pass. Some of their children meet and want to marry non-Jews. Their rabbi suggests that they convert to Judaism. They agree, and he supervises their instruction and conversion. Michael and Susan both know that some of their grandchildren will not be considered halakhically Jewish. But they feel, as did Michael's father many years earlier, that it is better that they be Jewish in Reform terms than not Jewish at all. Besides which, they have few Orthodox friends, and those they do have also come to terms with the situation. As for Ruth, Avi, and Pinchas, Susan hardly sees them at all except at family *simchas*. And on those occasions they avoid talking about Judaism.

Family Ties

Let us come back from the future to the present. How do five such different people as our imagined children come to have anything in common at all? The answer is, of course, that they are brothers and sisters, members of a single family. They grew up together. They have memories in common. If one of them was in trouble, the others would feel a duty to help. If one became famous, the others would feel pride. They are bound by ties of kinship and loyalty. That is what it means to be part of a family.

And that, above all, is what it means to be a Jew. Jewish history begins in choice of a family, the Divine election of Abraham, Isaac, Jacob, and their children. "I have known him," says God about Abraham, "so that he will command his children and his household after him, and they will keep the way of God, doing charity and justice." The choice of Abraham was the election of a family. Judaism is difficult to define in conventional categories. It is not simply a religious faith, for a secular Jew is still a Jew. It is not simply a nationality, a state, a country or a land, for the Jew who lives outside Israel is still a Jew. It is not a race or a mode of ethnicity, for there are Jews of many races and colors and backgrounds and cultures. Judaism embraces these things, but it is something other than and prior to them all. To be a Jew is to be a member of a family. Perhaps Michael Wyschogrod put it best:

> The collectivity that stands before God is thus the people of Israel as the seed of Abraham, Isaac and Jacob. It is not an artificial collectivity, constituted as an interest group or a group sharing common ideas. Interests and ideas change. We drift in and out of artificial groups. . . . But a family does not change. We may like or dislike our relatives. We may seek their company or avoid it. But we cannot sever the bond that binds us to our blood relatives. A wife or a husband can be divorced. But a child or a parent cannot, and that is the kind of bond that connects the Jewish people with God.

Historically and theologically, though, it is not that simple. What kept the Jewish people as a family in the long centuries between the destruction of the Second Temple and the threshold of modernity was a series of shared beliefs and the unifying bond of Jewish law. Islam called Jews "the people of the book." George Steiner has spoken of "our homeland, the text." How far a family extends is a matter of convention rather than biology. The conventions of the Jewish family were defined by Torah. They were clarified in the rabbinic literature in the sages' famous statement that "all Israel is responsible for one another." Jews were a family because a book, the Torah, said so.

And experience matched that definition. Throughout the long Christian and Islamic Middle Ages, Jews not only kept themselves, but were treated by others, as a people apart. We can hear both theology and deep personal feeling in the following ruling of Maimonides about the Jewish duty of charity: "All Jews and those attached to them are like brothers, as it is said, 'You are sons to the Lord your God.' And if a brother will not show mercy to his brother, then who will have mercy on him? And to whom can the poor of Israel look for help? To those other nations who hate and persecute them? They can look for help only to their brethren."

That was a high point in the sense of family. But it began to collapse under the impact of emancipation. Reform and Orthodox Jews in Germany, for example, began to feel they had more in common with their fellow Germans than with one another. And when the *Ostjuden*, Jews from Eastern Europe, began to enter Germany, they were looked on more as strangers than as brothers. Some of the more radical secularists in Israel, for their part, argued that their real kinship was with their Arab neighbors rather than with Jews in the diaspora. They saw themselves as Hebrews, or Canaanites, or at least as Israelis, not Jews.

The history of modern Jewry could, in a real sense, be told in terms of the shifting fate of the idea of Jews as a family. Reform and secular Zionism in their different ways were an assault on the idea that all Jews everywhere constituted a single family. And yet, despite this, racial anti-Semitism throughout Europe and angry tensions between Jews and Arabs in the years before the state made Jews aware that to non-Jews at least, even if not to themselves, they were still a people apart. And as the Holocaust and anti-Zionism have begun to alter Jewish perceptions, Jews have come to see themselves once again as a family. The passage we quoted from Michael Wyschogrod about Judaism as a family dates from the mid-1980s. It could not have been written much earlier. It is part of the new post-1967 consciousness. Its central feature is an image of Jews throughout the world bound by ties of kinship and loyalty. Their destinies are interlinked even against their will. They are a family.

Or rather, they would like to be. For the picture we have drawn of David and Miriam's children lets us see in microcosm how that family is breaking up. Twenty years from now, will the generation of *their* children, first cousins to one another, feel themselves linked to one another in any substantial way? Already the five children have grown apart. Avi in Israel has severed his ties. He believes that the *golah* has no future. Pinchas has entered a world of his own, a chasidic yeshivah which rejects the way of life of the rest of the family. Ruth is almost certain not to let her children play with Susan's, for fear of compromising their Orthodoxy. Richard, in rejecting Judaism, has turned his back on the others. And Susan is married to a man her sister and two brothers do not believe to be Jewish.

Families have broken up before. A fair proportion of the Jewish literature over the last hundred years has been devoted to the theme. We recall *Fiddler on the Roof* and its many variants. But the present situation is different. The older literature was about the collapse of tradition, the generational gap of acculturation, and about the remorseless march of assimilation. Jews were on the way out. The pain was that of farewell. That is not true in our family. Our prediction is that in twenty years from now, all five children will still define and think of themselves as Jewish—but in extraordinarily different ways, some within the rabbinic tradition, others outside. They will all see themselves as in some way part of the Jewish family. But paradoxically, it will be Judaism more than anything else which divides them.

Nonsolutions

What then will keep them together? What can be done *now* to prevent their drifting apart? Some lines of thought are well-meant but simply fail to address the reality. Perhaps—it will be said— Richard should never have been allowed to go to a non-Jewish school. Perhaps Susan should never have been allowed to have Reform friends. Ruth, Avi, and Pinchas, in their different ways, have decided just that for their own children. But Richard and Susan, though they are fictional characters, represent a great many real ones. In both Anglo- and American Jewry, increasing numbers of children go to Jewish day schools. But in both communities an increasing number of children are receiving no Jewish education at all. In both communities, the Reform presence is growing. So too is the percentage of Jews who go to a university, where they meet and mix with Jews of all shades. Segregation is a solution for some. It is not a solution for the Richards and Susans who exist in growing numbers.

There is an alternative way of seeing the situation. It has been implicit in a certain kind of Orthodox thought since the nineteenth century. It comes to the fore more in informal conversation than public theology. But it is this. The situation has to be accepted that Richard and Susan will be lost to the family. This, so the argument goes, is not new. There were many Jews before who assimilated and intermarried. They effectively disappeared from Jewish history. It happened in the early nineteenth century among the acculturated Jews who thronged the salons of Rachel Varnhagen and Henriette Herz. It happened in fifteenth-century Spain. It happened in first-century Rome. Judaism is sustained by the *she'erit ha-peletah*, the faithful few, the surviving minority. The rest disappear.

There is, on this view, a Darwinian law operative in Jewish history. Only the fittest survive. In an open society, only those who are willing to make sacrifices—and they *are* sacrifices—to have Jewish children, send them to Jewish schools and then to yeshivot and seminaries, to fulfill to the fullest the demands of a life lived according to halakhah and to separate themselves whenever necessary from the rest of society: only they have a Jewish future. Who is a Jew? Not one who has Jewish grandparents, but one who is certain of having Jewish grandchildren. As for the rest, what can anyone do? Judaism today is for the most part lived out in free societies. Coercion is impossible, persuasion ineffective. There will be Jews who will not make those sacrifices. And whether in one generation or two or three, assimilation will eventually take its toll. The overwhelming likelihood is that somewhere along the line their children's children will cease to have any meaningful contact with Judaism. They will disappear. In the meanwhile, Orthodoxy must concentrate on its own strongholds among the most intensely committed. They at least will hand the tradition on across the generations.

There is much to be said for this line of thought. In three of its variants, this is exactly what Ruth, Avi, and Pinchas have chosen. But let us be clear what it is and what it is not. It is a prescription for individuals and communities. It is not a prescription for the Jewish people as a whole. There is a clear distinction between *individual* Jewish futures, and the *collective* Jewish destiny. And when thought is transferred from one domain to the other, what is highly responsible in one context becomes highly irresponsible in another.

This distinction has been central to the argument throughout the book. I believe that Ruth, Avi, and Pinchas are right. We believe that the evidence of acculturated diaspora communities in prewar Europe and present-day America suggests that—even at the level of survival strategy, let alone at the level of religious conviction— substantive accommodation to secular culture and its ethos makes no sense. It results in high rates of intermarriage, low birthrates, and incoherent identities. It imports into Judaism values that are incompatible with its own deepest assumptions. The same is true, though it is less immediately threatening to Jewish continuity, of a highly secularized interpretation of Israeli society. The same is beginning to be true—and this was the point of our family portrait—even of "establishment" Orthodoxy in traditional communities like Anglo-Jewry.

We believe with Maimonides—and here we refer to the whole thrust of his writings, not just to isolated texts—that Jewish life consists in striking a series of balances, a "middle way," between conflicting values: universalism and particularism, Jewish study and secular study, the community and the individual, law and liberty, defense and the pursuit of peace, Jewish law and the values that underlie the law. But we do not believe that what is the "middle way" in one community and one generation is necessarily so somewhere else or at another time. A synthesis that was available a century ago may not be available today. A mode of social integration that secured Jewish continuity a generation ago may not do so today. Ruth, Avi, and Pinchas have decided that their lives must be Jewishly more intense if their commitment is to be securely passed on to their children. Their "middle way" is, to use an unfortunate but inevitable label, to the "right" of what it was for their parents. We believe that their judgment is correct.

It answers the personal question of how they should lead their lives. But as to the question of how leadership is to be exercised to keep Jews as members of a single family, it is not an answer at all. The Richards and Susans may not be written out of the Jewish fold. Darwinism is no basis on which to conceive the collective Jewish future, for three reasons.

Against Jewish Darwinism

Firstly it is morally unacceptable. After the *shoah* we may not make that kind of distinction between Jews. The hatred which sought the destruction of all Jews can only be "redeemed" through a love which seeks the inclusion of all Jews. The "authentic Jew who faces up to his singled-out Jewish condition," to use Emil Fackenheim's phrase, recognizes the irrevocable bonds that bind him to a people in its awesome totality across time and space. There is, in post-Holocaust time, no morally acceptable scenario that focuses on the selective survival of one group of Jews while abdicating responsibility for the others. That applies to selective survivalism of any kind, whether it be an Orthodox version that sees Reform and secular Jews as destined for oblivion, or an Israeli version that sees the diaspora as doomed.

Secondly it is sociologically blind. Richard and Susan and their many counterparts are not about to disappear. The central thrust of our argument is that they will continue to identify as Jews, though in ways increasingly estranged from Orthodoxy. That has been the recurring paradox of modern Jewish identities. In the most unpredictable ways, assimilated, alienated, and even deeply self-hating Jews have seen themselves as Jews and have sought to give Jewish expression to that fact. They have reinterpreted Jewishness and Judaism, reconceived the Jewish past, constructed alternative canons of antecedents, and thus created and placed themselves within an astounding variety of Jewish "traditions." There is no easy parallel here with the Jews in the past who sought a way out

from membership in the Jewish people by intermarriage or conversion or willful and deliberate assimilation. To imagine that Orthodoxy alone will be the sole claimant to the Jewish future is to
misread the whole thrust of Jewish modernity.

Thirdly it is theologically offensive. The Book of Genesis tells
the prehistory of the covenantal people. There is Abraham, one of
whose children, Isaac, continues the covenant, and one of whom,
Ishmael, does not. There is Isaac, one of whose children, Jacob,
carries on the promise, and one of whom, Esau, does not. The pain
of these separations, Ishmael from Abraham, Esau from Isaac,
are among the most affecting in the entire Jewish literature. But
with Jacob, history enters a new phase. To be sure, there is still
conflict between brothers. Jacob's other children seek to kill Joseph
and eventually sell him into slavery. There is conflict between
father and child: Jacob favors Joseph and at the end of his life
effectively disowns Reuben, Shimon, and Levi. But these conflicts between human beings are set against an implicit Divine
judgment that becomes explicit as Genesis moves into Exodus.
From now on there is to be no selection. All of Jacob's children are
chosen. None of them is to go the way of Ishmael and Esau. None
of them will be unchosen. From here on, there will be no dramas
of selection and rejection. All of Jacob's offspring, the children of
Israel, are children of the covenant. The people Israel embraces all
Jews.

Let us put the point more strongly. For at a certain point in
history, a dissenting voice was heard. Not all Jews, it was said,
were worthy to inherit the Jewish future. Not every child of Jewish
parents was, by that fact alone, a child of the covenant. The author
of this idea was emphatic in insisting that only some Jews would
spiritually survive as the true Israel. As he put it, "Not all who are
descended from Israel are Israel. Nor because they are his descendants are they all Abraham's children. . . . It is not the natural
children who are God's children, but it is the children of the
promise who are regarded as Abraham's offspring." The language is
slightly strange, but the point is clear. There will be selective
survival. Israel is a subcommunity of believers, not a total family
bound by birth. The author of these words was Paul, architect of

early Christianity. The idea of selective survival has no place in Judaism.

Against it we must argue that there is no coherent or acceptable thought about the Jewish future that does not place at its center the idea of *knesset Yisrael*, the indivisible collectivity of all Jews, righteous and rebellious, committed and indifferent, learned and ignorant, affirming and assimilated. R. Joseph Soloveitchik put the point simply: "A Jew who has lost his faith in *Knesset Yisrael*, even though he may personally sanctify and purify himself by being strict in his observance of the precepts and by assuming prohibitions upon himself—such a Jew is incorrigible and is totally unfit to join in the Day of Atonement which encompasses the whole of *knesset Yisrael* in all its components and all its generations."

Judaism's Public Domain

But it is just this dimension that is missing from the lives of Ruth, Avi, and Pinchas. Why should it be otherwise? They have their own lives to lead. They have acted to secure their own and their eventual families' future. Why should it concern them that they are drifting apart? Richard and Susan are free agents in a free society. If they choose to move, slowly or rapidly, away from tradition, whose concern is it but their own? Is any one of our five children his brother's or sister's keeper?

That question was first uttered by the biblical Cain. And it is a measure of how far we have drifted from the Jewish sense of collective responsibility that, asked at any time before the nineteenth century it would have invited the answer Yes, whereas today it almost certainly invites the answer No. One of the greatest of all Jewish values is dying. Not dead, for Jews still feel deeply involved in the political and economic fate of other Jews. But to feel involved in their spiritual fate breaches the great liberal axiom of John Stuart Mill, that private morality is a private concern.

John Kenneth Galbraith, in *The Affluent Society*, coined the phrase "private opulence and public squalor." That, in spiritual terms, is what has happened to religion in a secular age. It is not that Judaism has waned. To the contrary. Ruth in her strict community, Pinchas in his yeshivah, and Avi in his Judean outpost live private lives of great Jewish richness and intensity. But there is nothing to link them, or even their leaders and mentors, to the collective enterprise of the Jewish people. The very idea of such a thing sounds either mystical or abstract, a subject for sermons but one devoid of empirical content. What has vanished in the process is Judaism's public domain. The substantive reality of *Knesset Yisrael* has disappeared.

What remains is a highly secularized equivalent: fund-raising for Israel or activism on behalf of politically threatened Jewish communities; in a phrase, "civil Judaism." Were this a stable state, we might lament the secularization of Jewish peoplehood, but rest content that this at least had survived. But it is not a stable state. For in Judaism, religion and peoplehood are deeply intertwined. Most of the major conflicts that have surfaced in world Jewry in the last decade have been over matters of religion. And when Judaism loses its great traditions of the public domain—the ideas of halakhah as the constitution of a people, of collective *religious* responsibility, and of argument for the sake of heaven—it loses its ability *religiously* to handle those conflicts. Even the most religious handle them in secular ways: by street fights and demonstrations, burning bus shelters, media-inspired events, and political pressure and manipulation. Thus is Torah shamed.

So our question returns: what can be done now to prevent the Jewish family drifting apart? Religious coercion is impossible. In the diaspora it cannot be done. In Israel it ought not to be done. It was one of the great halakhists of the early twentieth century, R. Meir Simcha of Dvinsk, who following a suggestion of Maimonides, pointed out that coercion in Jewish law presupposes an underlying assent, on the part of the person affected, to the processes of Jewish law. That assent cannot be taken for granted in a secular society. As R. Avraham Karelitz, the *Chazon Ish*, pointed out, the concept of "rebellion" against tradition is inapplicable in the modern age. And as R. Nachum Rabinovitch and R. Aharon Lichtenstein have reminded us, human freedom is an essential value of the Jewish tradition itself. The very idea of covenant presupposes free assent. Coercion is no way to bring Jews within the ambit of tradition.

Dialogue with Dissent

What is left are education and persuasion. And this immediately suggests the kinds of Jews there would have to be in a given society to keep the dialogue open with Richard and Susan. There would have to be Jews who could lead Richard to see his rebellion in a Jewish context. There are voices within the tradition with which Richard could identify. Many of the most powerful prophetic passages in the Torah are critiques of the ruling powers in the name of social justice. Some of the most masterful voices in the rabbinic literature are those raised in defense of freedom of argument against authoritarianism, of human dignity against the idea of religion as passivity. In more recent times, the most sustained critique of Israel's military and political policy since 1967 has come from the Orthodox thinker, Yeshayahu Leibowitz. The work of David Hartman has been a continuing attempt to engage Judaism with the concerns of a secular humanism.

The point we have striven to make is that it is irrelevant whether these views are "correct" or normative or whether we ourselves subscribe to them. It was the vision of R. Avraham Kook that ultimately all such voices would enter into the great collective argument which is the Jewish people in dialogue with its past and future. This, for R. Kook, was what Torah was: the continuing engagement of a people with the covenant. Even atheism and Marxism, he argued, contained within them important critiques of a Judaism which had become routinized and "religionized." They were destructive only if they led away from tradition. Brought back inside tradition, they would renew it from within.

There are models of dissent within tradition. The great East European secular Zionists were often saturated with traditional values. Several of them, as we noted, were alumni of the great Volozhyn yeshivah. The secularist scholar Gershom Scholem tried to trace an entire revolutionary tradition through the literature of Jewish mysticism. Richard's discontent could find Jewish expression if there were someone to connect him with tradition.

It is a large "if." The present American Jewish community, for example, is one of the most highly educated in history. Some 90 percent of young American Jews attend college. Yet it is probably one of the least Jewishly educated of all time. Some half will have had no significant Jewish education at all. The concern of Jewish communities since Second Temple times, that there be universal Jewish literacy, has evaporated in the past century. Instead secular education has seemed a sufficient end in itself. The result is that Richard and the many secularists like him who find no inspiration in institutionalized Jewish life can only drift away. They are not merely Jewishly alienated. They are Jewishly ignorant. Richard could be a force for a revitalization of the tradition of Jewish social criticism if there were someone, or some literature, that mapped his views onto the total landscape of the Jewish imagination. Judaism has paid a heavy price for the alienation of its intellectuals since emancipation.

Extending the Argument

There would have to be Jews, too, who would enter into the dialogue with Susan. Most urgently there must be some who will engage in conversation with Michael's Reform rabbi and his colleagues, to establish a common standard for conversions and divorces to be performed under halakhic auspices. It cannot be in the long-term interests of the Jewish community as a whole that the problems of individuals be solved nonhalakhically at the cost of creating larger problems in the future. For they or their children will be regarded either as non-Jews or as *mamzerim*, illegitimate, by the majority of Jews throughout the world. That argument must be pursued courteously but relentlessly, for the very integrity of Jewish peoplehood is at stake.

There must be others who investigate ways, within *halakhah*, that will allow Susan to find greater personal meaning in the Jewish tradition: alternative services perhaps, or women's groups, or residential retreats, or *chavurot*, learning fellowships. There must be others again who explore ways of extending the life of Torah beyond the confines of synagogue, school, and home. For Samson Raphael Hirsch's idea of synthesis has suffered a stunningly premature and ironic defeat. As Jews become more integrated and prominent in society, so the possibilities expand for Hirsch's ideal of Jewish life as a model to others of the ethical enterprise.

But it is precisely now that the idea has become problematic. What is it to serve God through urban planning, the development of industries, the writing of novels, or the development of political programs? One of the goals of the halakhic system, according to Maimonides, is *tikkun olam*, a term which includes the building of an economic, social, cultural, and environmental order. The perfection of society is a precondition of the perfection of the soul, he wrote; therefore it is a religious duty. But what is the perfection of society, in terms that are both contemporarily relevant and faithful to the Jewish sources? The exploration of this issue has never been more urgent, in Israel above all, but also in the diaspora.

In short, while Ruth, Avi, and Pinchas have turned inward, there must be others, no less committed to tradition, who turn outward if Richard and Susan are to find a continuing place in Judaism. And here we must reiterate another of our central contentions: Orthodoxy is not a denomination. It is not simply one version of Judaism among many; it is Judaism *tout court*. The corollary is that there is no one single type of Orthodoxy. It embraces as many types of temperament, cultural style, and intellectual orientation as there are Jews. Halakhah and the framing principles of Jewish faith preserve community while admitting diversity. The greater the diversity within Orthodoxy, the more it approximates to its ideal state, the religion of the Jewish people as a whole.

From History to Destiny

Above all there must be a determined attempt by Jewish leaders and thinkers of all kinds, to rise above the rhetoric of Jewish unity and reinstate the Judaic tradition of argument. The language of Jewish unity is seductive and misleading. It is, by turns, ambiguous and mystical. It can coexist with the unqualified pursuit of sectional self-interest which makes the divisions within the Jewish world progressively more intractable.

We believe that "argument for the sake of heaven" is a more

cogent model than "Jewish unity." Those who wish to enter that argument must recognize that there are preconditions. Argument proceeds through text and interpretation. It presupposes a certain depth of Jewish education. We believe that it is through Jewish education alone that Reform and secularist no less than Orthodox Jews can engage in dialogue with the Jewish tradition and thus with the entire Jewish people. It is the only common language we have.

But "argument for the sake of heaven" has its own ethic. It involves a respect for the integrity of opposing positions. It means exposing one's own positions to critical scrutiny. It leads to a sense of the pull of conflicting values. It is Judaism's great public domain of debate. It is the vehicle through which tradition handled conflict. And it is the way in which rabbinic Judaism, after the destruction of the Second Temple, healed the wounds of a nation lacerated by internal strife and kept them as a single people throughout eighteen centuries of dispersion.

Which brings us back to our five children. Tonight at least, along with Jews throughout the world, they are part of a single family. For they are telling the same story of how a people once enslaved emerged into freedom and made their way through an uncharted desert to a covenantal destination at Sinai. They are telling it not as history, but as *their* story: the origins of a people they affirm as their own.

For this is the miracle: that after all the exiles and exoduses, the pogroms and persecutions, after the unprecedented assault on the people of the covenant in the twentieth century, Jews still wish to make that story their own. They feel participants in a common history. The *shoah* and the State of Israel, however interpreted, have led to a renewal of the *brit goral*, the covenant of fate.

It is our faith that a sense of shared fate is always succeeded by a covenant of common purpose, as Sinai succeeded the exodus from Egypt. But the sages who added the section of the "four children" to the Haggadah made a telling point. Judaism must be made meaningful to many kinds of children: to the wicked no less than the wise, to the child without questions or interest no less than the child of single-minded intensity. Each member of the family, however different, must find the tradition accessible. That is the challenge before the contemporary expounders of tradition.

Each child will interpret the story differently. But that is their argument, as it is ours. So long as they continue to tell the story and make it their own, they will remain in conversation with one another. The past two centuries have witnessed another momentous Jewish exodus: from the enclosed walls of tradition into the open society. But that exodus has no shared story. Jews agreed on what they were leaving, but could not agree on where they were going. Some moved far from Torah; others stayed within. As a result, the Jewish family came precariously close to disintegration.

How then is it to stay together? The people of the book were a people because of the book. In Torah, they read their lives. Each new mode of Jewish living, if it stayed within Torah, became a new commentary to the covenantal text. Jews were different: they lived in different countries, had different customs, spoke different languages, and took part in different cultures. But because they shared a tradition, they could engage in conversation. Because they had texts in common, they could enter the collective argument. Because they kept halakhah, their acts created a cross-cultural community. We see no alternative basis of Jewish peoplehood. The Jewish family is as strong as its shared religious heritage. The renewal of Torah in the life of Jews is the only route to the renewal of the Jewish people.

The literature on modern Jewry, especially in America, is vast and varied. The following suggestions are not intended as an exhaustive bibliography, but they should allow the reader to explore the arguments further. The works selected are confined to those in English and are arranged by chapters.

1: A Family Portrait: Jews Today

The portraits in this chapter are fictitious and do not represent any particular ideology or institution. The following, though, may flesh out some of the portraits. An American equivalent of Ruth might be found in the "modern Orthodox" congregation studied in Samuel C. Heilman, *Synagogue Life: A Study in Symbolic Interaction* (Chicago: University of Chicago Press, 1976), a brilliant sociological analysis. Heilman's *People of the Book: Drama, Fellowship and Religion* (Chicago: University of Chicago Press, 1983) uses the same techniques to study traditional learning circles.

Richard's complex relationship with Judaism and Jewishness is illuminated by Sander Gilman, *Jewish Self-Hatred: Anti-Semitism and the Hidden Language of the Jew* (Baltimore: Johns Hopkins University Press, 1986).

On Pinchas, see Janet Aviad, *Return to Judaism* (Chicago: University of Chicago Press, 1983), a sociological study of *ba'alei teshuvah*. A personal account is to be found in Mayer Schiller, *The Road Back* (Jerusalem: Feldheim, 1981). Another is given in Michael Graubart Levin, *Journey to Tradition: The Odyssey of a Born-Again Jew* (Hoboken: Ktav, 1986). For those contemplating the journey back to tradition, Adin Steinsaltz's *Teshuvah: A Guide for the Newly Observant Jew* (New York: Free Press, 1987) is an invaluable introduction.

Little is available on Susan's "nominal Orthodoxy." Background reading on Anglo-Jewry is provided in V. D. Lipman, *Social History of the Jews in England 1850–1950* (London: Watts, 1954); Aubrey Newman, *The United Synagogue 1870–1970* (London: Routledge and Kegan Paul, 1976); *A Century of Anglo-Jewish Life, 1870–1970*, edited by S. S. Levin, (London: United Synagogue, undated); Todd M. Endleman, "The Englishness of Jewish Modernity in England," in *Toward Modernity: The European Jewish Model*, edited by Jacob Katz (New Brunswick: Transaction Books, 1987) 225–246; and Eugene C. Black, *The Social Politics of Anglo-Jewry 1880–1920* (Oxford: Basil Blackwell, 1988). Also of interest is the survey of attitudes among contemporary French Jews in Dominique Schnapper, *Jewish Identities in France: An Analysis of Contemporary French Jewry* (Chicago: University of Chicago Press, 1983).

Secular equivalents of Avi's "negation of the disapora" are to be found in A. B. Yehoshua, *Between Right and Right* (New York: Doubleday, 1981) and Hillel Halkin, *Letters to an American Jewish Friend* (Philadelphia: Jewish Publication Society, 1977). Modern Jewish thought on the subjects of exile and redemption is elegantly surveyed in Arnold Eisen, *Galut: Modern Jewish Reflection on Homelessness and Homecoming* (Bloomington: Indiana University Press, 1986). The best reader on Zionism is Arthur Hertzberg's anthology, *The Zionist Idea* (New York: Atheneum, 1981).

2: A Religion or a Nation?

The best introduction to the themes of this chapter are three books by Jacob Katz: *Tradition and Crisis* (New York: Free Press, 1961); *Out of the Ghetto* (Cambridge: Harvard University Press, 1973); and *Jewish Emancipation and Self-Emancipation* (Philadelphia: Jewish Publication Society, 1986). A superb anthology of sources is provided by *The Jew in the Modern World: A Documentary History*, edited by Paul Mendes-Flohr and Jehuda Reinharz (Oxford: Oxford University Press, 1980). See also Michael A. Meyer, *The Origins of the Modern Jew* (Detroit: Wayne State University Press, 1967) and David Rudavsky, *Modern Jewish Religious Movements* (New York: Behrman House, 1979).

Moses Mendelssohn's *Jerusalem* is available in a new translation by Allan Arkush (Boston: Brandeis University Press, 1983). The best history of the Reform movement is Michael A. Meyer's recent *Response to Modernity: A History of the Reform Movement in Judaism* (Oxford: Oxford University Press, 1988). A documentary history of early Reform is available in W. Gunther Plaut, *The Rise of Reform Judaism: A Sourcebook of Its European Origins* (New York: World Union for Progressive Judaism, 1963). Interesting material is also contained in Gil Graff, *Separation of Church and State: Dina de-Malkhuta Dina in Jewish Law, 1750–1848* (University: University of Alabama Press, 1985).

Moses Hess's *Rome and Jerusalem* is available in translations by Meyer Waxman (New York: Bloch, 1943) and Maurice J. Bloom (New York: Philosophical Library, 1958). A recent study is Shlomo Avineri, *Moses Hess: Prophet of Communism and Zionism* (New York: New York University Press, 1985). The transition between classical and modern conceptions of Zion is studied in a collection of essays, *The Land of Israel: Jewish Perspectives*, edited by Lawrence A. Hoffman (Notre Dame: University of Notre Dame Press, 1986). The best brief introduction to the history of anti-Semitism is *History and Hate*, edited by David Berger (Philadelphia: Jewish Publication Society, 1986).

3: Traditional Alternatives

Not enough has been written on the history of Orthodoxy in the last two hundred years. For accounts of the German experience, see

Hermann Schwab, *The History of Orthodox Jewry in Germany* (London: Mitre Press, 1950), and Robert Liberle's account of Hirsch's Frankfurt, *Religious Conflict in Social Context* (Westport: Greenwood Press, 1985). On Hirsch, see also Noah Rosenbloom, *Tradition in an Age of Reform* (Philadelphia: Jewish Publication Society of America, 1976). On Hirsch's influence, see I. Grunfeld, *Three Generations* (London: Jewish Post, 1958).

Hirsch's own writings are best studied in *The Nineteen Letters on Judaism*, translated by Bernard Drachman (New York: Feldheim, 1960); Judaism Eternal, translated by I. Grunfeld (London: Soncino Press, 1959), and *Horeb*, translated by I. Grunfeld (London: Soncino Press, 1962). Hirsch's Torah commentary is available in a five-volume translation by Isaac Levy (Gateshead: Judaica Press, 1982) and a one-volume anthology translated by Gertrude Hirschler (New York: Judaica Press, 1986).

An anthology of the writings of R. Kook is available in English: *Abraham Isaac Kook*, translated by Ben Zion Bokser (London: SPCK, 1979).

There are some excellent brief surveys of the subject under review. See, for example, the essays by Jacob Katz and Eliezer Goldman in *Studies in Contemporary Jewry II*, edited by Peter Medding (Bloomington: Indiana University Press, 1986); Samuel Heilman's outstanding essay, "The Many Faces of Orthodoxy," in *Modern Judaism* 2:1 (February 1982) and 2:2 (May 1982); Charles Liebman's "Religion and the Chaos of Modernity," in *Take Judaism, for Example*, edited by Jacob Neusner (Chicago: University of Chicago Press, 1983, 147–164), and his "Orthodox Judaism" in *The Encyclopaedia of Religion*, edited by Mircea Eliade (New York: Macmillan, 1987); and Moshe Samet's "The Beginnings of Orthodoxy," *Modern Judaism* 8:3 (October 1988, 249–270). Aspects of modern Orthodoxy are explored in Zvi Kurzweil's *The Modern Impulse of Traditional Judaism* (Hoboken: Ktav, 1985).

4: Contemporary Affirmations

Among the major sociological studies of contemporary Jewry that inform this and the next chapter, see Steven M. Cohen,

American Modernity and Jewish Identity, (London: Tavistock, 1983); *American Assimilation or Jewish Revival?* (Bloomington: Indiana University Press, *1988); Calvin Goldscheider, Jewish Continuity and Change* (Bloomington: Indiana University Press, 1986); Calvin Goldscheider and Alan Zuckerman, *The Transformation of the Jews* (Chicago: University of Chicago Press, 1984); Sidney Goldstein and Calvin Goldscheider, *Jewish Americans: Three Generations in a Jewish Community* (Maryland: University Press of America, 1985); Charles Liebman, *The Ambivalent American Jew* (Philadelphia: Jewish Publication Society of America, 1973); *Aspects of the Religious Behaviour of American Jews* (New York: Ktav, 1984); Stephen Sharot, *Judaism: A Sociology* (London: David and Charles, 1976); Charles Silberman, *A Certain People: American Jews and Their Lives Today* (New York: Summit, 1985).

5: The State of Survival

On intermarriage, see Egon Mayer's highly readable study, *Love and Tradition: Marriage between Jews and Christians* (New York: Schocken, 1987). Jewish birthrates in the modern period are analyzed in *Modern Jewish Fertility*, edited by Paul Ritterband (Leiden: Brill, 1981). On the Jewish family generally, see Samuel Heilman, "The Jewish Family Today: An Overview," in *Tradition and Transition*, edited by Jonathan Sacks (London: Jews' College, 1986, 179–208).

One study of *aliyah* is Chaim Waxman, "American Aliyah: Dream and Reality," in *Morasha* 2:3 (Winter-Spring 1987, 1–8). Moshe Shokeid's study of *yordim* is entitled *Children of Circumstances: Israeli Emigrants in New York* (Ithaca: Cornell University Press, 1988). Important studies of the same phenomenon are contained in *Contemporary Jewry*, volume 7, edited by Arnold Dashevsky (New Brunswick: Transaction Books, 1986).

6: What Is a Jew?

Jean-Paul Sartre's study of anti-Semitism and the nature of Jewishness is *Anti-Semite and Jew* (New York: Schocken, 1965).

Emil Fackenheim's recent thought is best encountered in his *The Jewish Return into History* (New York: Schocken, 1978) and *To Mend the World* (New York: Schocken, 1983). An anthology of his writings is presented in *The Jewish Thought of Emil Fackenheim: A Reader*, edited by Michael Morgan (Detroit: Wayne State University Press, 1987).

On the Holocaust and modern Jewish identities, see Amos Oz, *In the Land of Israel* (London: Flamingo, 1983), Charles Liebman and Eliezer Don-Yehiyah, *Civil Religion in Israel* (Berkeley: University of California Press, 1983), and Jacob Neusner's three volumes of essays, *Stranger at Home* (Chicago: University of Chicago Press, 1981), *The Jewish War against the Jews* (New York: Ktav, 1984), and *Israel in America* (Boston: Beacon Press, 1985).

On Jewishness and Judaism see Nathan Glazer, *American Judaism* (Chicago: University of Chicago Press, 1972) and Will Herberg, *Protestant, Catholic, Jew* (New York: Anchor, 1960). A critique of "transformationist" Jewish sociology is contained in Charles Liebman's "The Debate on American Jewish Life," in *Studies in Contemporary Jewry IV*, edited by Jonathan Frankel (Oxford: Oxford University Press, 1988, 175–184).

Rabbi J. B. Soloveitchik's essay, "The Lonely Man of Faith," appeared in *Tradition* 7:2 (Summer 1965, 5–67). Reuven Bulka's analysis of the possible future Orthodox-Reform schism is contained in his *The Coming Cataclysm* (Oakville: Mosaic Press, 1984). Irving Greenberg's essay on the same themes is *Will There Be One Jewish People by the Year 2000?* (New York: National Jewish Resource Center, 1985). Lawrence Schiffman's study of the issue in the context of the Jewish-Christian schism is to be found in his *Who Was a Jew?* (Hoboken: Ktav, 1985).

7: The Reemergence of Orthodoxy

The best collection of materials on the subject of this chapter is *Dimensions of Orthodox Judaism*, edited by Reuven Bulka (New York: Ktav, 1983). An interesting if unscholarly collection of materials on the collapse of Orthodoxy prior to the Second World War is contained in Bernard Maza, *With Fury Poured Out* (Hoboken: Ktav, 1986). Oscar Fasman's reminiscences are taken from his "After Fifty Years, an Optimist," *American Jewish History* 59:2 (December 1979). The whole issue is devoted to a study of Orthodox Judaism in America.

Charles Liebman's landmark essay on "Orthodoxy in American Jewish Life" is reprinted in Bulka's anthology, 33–105. The rise of yeshivot in America is studied in William Helmreich, *The World of the Yeshiva* (New York: Free Press, 1982). Daniel Elazar's remarks on the demography of Orthodoxy are found in his "Who is a Jew and How?" (*Jerusalem Newsletter*, 24 September, 1986). Orthodoxy in contemporary Israel is studied in Charles Liebman and Eliezer Don-Yehiyah, *Religion and Politics in Israel* (Bloomington: Indiana University Press, 1984). The Israeli soldiers' reflections on the Six Day War were published as *The Seventh Day* (London: Penguin, 1971). Amnon Rubinstein's critique of the influence of the new religious nationalism is contained in his *The Zionist Dream Revisited* (New York: Schocken, 1984); Yehoshafat Harkabi adds remarks in a similar vein in his *Israel's Fateful Decisions* (London: Tauris, 1988).

The urban sociology of Orthodoxy is studied in Menachem Friedman's "Charedim Confront the Modern City," *Studies in Contemporary Jewry II*, 74–96. Peter Berger's remarks on childhood and the family are scattered throughout his many writings, but in particular see Brigitte and Peter Berger, *The War over the Family* (London: Penguin, 1983). Bruno Bettelheim's study of kibbutz families is *The Children of the Dream* (London: Paladin, 1971). On rethinking modernity, see Peter Berger, *Facing up to Modernity*, (London: Penguin, 1979); Peter Berger, Brigitte Berger and Hansfried Kellner, *The Homeless Mind*, (London: Penguin, 1974); and Robert Bellah and others, *Habits of the Heart* (London: Hutchinson, 1988).

8: Assimilationism and Assimilation

The quotation from Jacob Neusner comes from his *American In Israel*, 125. See the articles of Leonard Fein, Moshe Adler, David Singer, and Neusner under the heading "If Orthodoxy is the

Answer, What is the Question?" *Moment* 9:3 (September 1978, 28–44). Eugene Borowitz's restatement of Reform attitudes is set out in his "The Autonomous Jewish Self," *Modern Judaism* 4:1 (February 1984, 39–56). Jonathan Woocher's study of the "civil religion" of American Jews is in *Sacred Survival* (Bloomington: Indiana University Press, 1986). Norman Mirsky's remarks are taken from his "Nathan Glazer's American Judaism After 30 Years: A Reform Opinion," *American Jewish History* 77:2 (December 1987, 232–246). Michael Walzer's analysis of group membership can be found in his *Spheres of Justice* (Oxford: Basil Blackwell, 1983, 31–63).

9: The Radicalization of Orthodoxy

The key document here is the symposium devoted to "The State of Orthodoxy," in *Tradition* 20:1 (Spring 1982). The remarks of Lord Jakobovits are taken from his *New Priorities on the Orthodox Agenda* (London: Office of the Chief Rabbi, 1989). R. Soloveitchik's account of the relations between Jewish and secular thought can be found in his *Halakhic Man*, translated by Lawrence Kaplan (Philadelphia: Jewish Publication Society of America, 1983), and *The Halakhic Mind* (New York: Free Press, 1986). An interesting collection of sources which includes an essay by R. Soloveitchik, "Kodesh and Chol," as well as the address by Norman Lamm quoted in the text, has been published by Yeshiva University as the *Torah U'Mada Reader* (undated).

Charles Liebman's remarks on compartmentalization are taken from his essay "Orthodox Judaism Today," in *Dimensions of Orthodox Judaism*, 106–120. The debate about vacations was set out in David Singer's "Is Club Med Kosher? Reflections on Synthesis and Compartmentalization," and Shalom Carmy's rejoinder, "Synthesis and the Unification of Human Existence," *Tradition* 21:4 (Fall 1985, 27–51). Michael Walzer's analysis of free time is contained in his *Spheres of Justice*, 184–196.

The debate about religious Zionism can be followed through the various issues of the journal *Morasha*. The religious anti-Zionist argument is set out in I. Domb, *The Transformation* (London: Hamadfis, 1958) and Emil Marmorstein, *Heaven at Bay* (Oxford:

Oxford University Press, 1969). Messianic politics in contemporary Israel are studied in Menachem Kellner, "Messianic Postures in Israel Today," *Modern Judaism* 6:2 (May 1986, 197–210); Ehud Luz, "The Moral Price of Sovereignty," *Modern Judaism* 7:1 (February 1987, 51–98); Chaim Waxman, "Messianism, Zionism and the State of Israel," *Modern Judaism* 7:2 (May 1987, 175–192); Shubert Spero, "Does Traditional Jewish Messianism Imply Inevitability?" *Modern Judaism* 8:3 (October 1988, 271–287); Uriel Tal, "Contemporary Hermeneutics and Self-Views on the Relationship between State and Land," in *The Land of Israel: Jewish Perspectives*, 316–338.

10: Between Two Covenants

Irving Greenberg's analysis of the state of the covenant is contained in three papers published by the National Jewish Resource Center in New York: *On the Third Era in Jewish History* (1980), *The Third Great Cycle in Jewish History* (1981), and *Voluntary Covenant* (1982). Versions of "Modern Orthodoxy" in the sense used in this chapter are set out in Emanuel Rackman, *One Man's Judaism* (Tel Aviv: Greenfield, undated); Eliezer Berkovits, *Crisis and Faith* (New York: Sanhedrin Press, 1976); and *Not in Heaven* (New York: Ktav, 1983); David Hartman, *A Living Covenant*, (New York: Free Press, 1985).

11: Tradition as Argument

Alasdair MacIntyre's study of morality and tradition is contained in *After Virtue* (London: Duckworth, 1981). The quotation is from pp. 206–207. The argument is continued in his *Whose Justice? Which Rationality?* (London: Duckworth, 1988). Also on this subject see Edward Shils, *Tradition* (London: Faber and Faber, 1981) and Jaroslav Pelikan. *The Vindication of Tradition* (New Haven: Yale University Press, 1984).

Two classic studies of the interplay, in Jewish tradition, between revelation and interpretation are Gershom Scholem, "Revelation and Tradition as Religious Categories in Judaism," in his *The Messianic Idea in Judaism* (New York: Schocken, 1971, 282–303); and Simon Rawidowicz, "On Interpretation," in his *Studies in Jewish Thought* (Philadelphia: Jewish Publication Society of America, 1974, 45–80).

The *Jewish Catalog* was published in Philadelphia by the Jewish Publication Society of America in 1973. Eugene Borowitz's remarks on it are contained in his *Choices in Jewish Modern Thought* (New York: Behrman House, 1983, 244). Attempts to state a Conservative position on halakhah are set out in Joel Roth, *The Halakhic Process: A Systemic Analysis* (New York: Jewish Theological Seminary, 1986) and Elliot Dorff and Arthur Rosett, *A Living Tree* (Albany: State University of New York Press, 1988).

13: A Family Portrait: Jews Tomorrow

The quotation from Michael Wyschogrod is taken from his article "A Theology of Jewish Unity," *L'Eylah* 21 (Spring 1986, 26–30). His book *The Body of Faith* (Minneapolis: Seabury Press, 1983) is highly relevant to the theme of the chapter. The quotation from R. Soloveitchik is taken from his *On Repentance*, translated by Pinchas Peli (Jerusalem: Oroth, 1980, 137).

INDEX

267